Running by Feeling

2-23-03

Peah

Thank you for your
support

Aloha

Brian

Running by Feeling

A Year on the Racing Comeback Trail

Brian L. Clarke

Competitive Running Press, Inc.
Honolulu

Copyright © 1999 by Brian L. Clarke.
Published by Competitive Running Press, Inc..

This publication is designed to provide accurate and authoritative
information in regard to the subject matter covered. It is sold with
the understanding that neither the publisher nor author are engaged
in rendering coaching or training advice or other professional
training services via this book. If fitness training advice or other
expert assistance is required, the services of a competent
professional trainer should be sought.

Library of Congress Cataloging in Publication Data:

Clarke, Brian L., 1944-
    Running by Feeling: A Year on the Racing Comeback Trail /
    by Brian L. Clarke.

    ISBN 0-966-3595-9-3
    Library of Congress Catalog Card Number: 98-92952

Respectfully dedicated to
Bill Bowerman,
My track coach at the University of Oregon,
Whose wisdom inspired many of the ideas in this book.

Foreward

Somewhere, there may be a runner so perfectly attuned to his body that he may ignore this book.

The rest of us could still be looking for the path between useless laxity and compulsive overtraining. Brian Clarke has--there is no other word--persevered to define for us this optimum zone.

Brian was close to running a sub-four-minute mile in 1966 when a training injury ended his collegiate track career. Since then, during thirty years of coaching and road running, he's wondered how to prevent such injuries so we might achieve our racing goals.

This book is his answer. Employing scales that quantify our running labor, he measures precisely how it *feels* to train too easily, too hard, or just right. But he does far more. He details a year of his own training at age 50, which required unsparing honesty because, as he writes, "Half the battle is to recognize when our training is being adversely affected by a lack of psychological balance."

It is a battle he loses again and again. He adds "confidence building" speed work to an already loaded schedule and there goes a calf. In the euphoria after a good race, he "sneaks" in rapid intervals on a recovery day and blows a hamstring. Yet all the while this goal-obsessed, hyper-competitive, relentlessly analytical searcher is drawing us into kinship with his quest.

Brian searches so earnestly that I found myself calling out to him to heed his own advice, to listen to his body and heal himself. Does he? Does this driven soul succeed in attending to reality's beeping heart monitor? You'll see. And in the seeing, you cannot help but be improved.

Kenny Moore
1968-72 Olympic Marathoner
Senior Writer, Sports Illustrated.

Contents

List of Figures

Acknowledgments

This book would not have been written without the support of three special people: Gar Williams whose encouragement and galvanizing influence started me on the path to writing the book in 1993. Phil Damon who opened me to the possibility that I could be the hero of my own story. And my wife, Nancy Heck, who gave me the time and space to write. Thanks also to the many runners who have read this book and suggested changes.

A Chronology of 1994-'95 Races

My running story is intended to add human interest to what might have been a dry exposition of training principles. Since I sometimes double back on the same events, however, the following chronology of races may assist you to find your bearings among the various anecdotes.

Waikiki Pro-Bowl 5-K
February 5, 1994
Johnny Faerber All-Men's 10-K
March 13, 1994
Norman Tamanaha Memorial 15-K
April 10, 1994
Lanikai Bike Path 8-K
June 5, 1994
Hard Rock Cafe 10-K
June 19, 1994
One-Hour Run on the Track
July 9, 1994
Hawaiian Style 8-K
August 21, 1994
Pearl Harbor Bike Path 10-K
January 8, 1995
RRCA 20-K Championship
February 12, 1995
Johnny Faerber All-Men's 10-K
March 12, 1995

Introduction

I once asked Joan Benoit's training advisor, Bob Sevene, whether he ever taught his athletes how to run by feeling. "No, I don't think it's possible," he said. "Running by feeling is an intuitive skill; runners either have it or they don't. A coach can't teach that kind of knowledge."

I had to respect Sevene's point of view. He was giving a running clinic in conjunction with the 1980 Honolulu Marathon when I met him. And although I didn't realize who Joan Benoit was at the time, she would soon become the women's marathon world record holder, as well as the 1984 women's Olympic marathon champion. Sevene and Benoit obviously knew their business.

Nonetheless, for the next dozen years Sevene's answer would challenge me to break new ground in my own professional life. With my background in education, I already viewed the coaching process as partly teaching. In fact, in 1980 I had started a school for recreational runners who wanted to improve their training and racing.

And although I agreed with Sevene that the training process is largely intuitive, I was nonetheless committed to teaching my students how to run by feeling.

My Purpose in Writing: This book is about making training decisions, especially those that lead to injury-free running and improved racing performances.

Good runners are smart people. They know how they are responding to their training because they can focus on pertinent physical manifestations of the training process. Moreover, they know how to use these feelings and sensations within the context of a cogent and systematic training theory.

My training theory is the product of my running and coaching experience, including what I've learned from my own coaches--among them former University of Oregon track coach, Bill Bowerman, who coached me to a 4:06 mile in 1965. Bowerman trained his runners by a gradual process of progressive adaptation. I use a similar system to prepare my athletes, prescribing hard and easy workouts within recurring training cycles to build five racing abilities.

As they train, my runners also learn to focus on their inner experience of the training process. At the experiential level, training consists of workout effort, pace exertion, running energy and capacity for exertion. These are not new ideas; the best runners and coaches have been using them for years. Together they form the basis of the hard-easy training system and the fundamental tenets of a useful theory of progressive adaptation.

This book uses these ideas to answer the question: What does adaptive training *feel* like? By approaching training in this way, I've avoided the pitfalls of discussions that focus exclusively on how elite runners train. To some extent that's common knowledge. The Bob Sevenes and Joan Benoits are usually willing to share their workouts with other people. Often missing in their workout descriptions, however, are discussions of the underlying sensations upon which crucial training decisions were made.

Since the running literature only alludes to these feelings in general terms, I've attempted to delineate as precisely as possible the range of relevant feelings and sensations. In the process, I have described a system of adaptive training--one which transcends specific training schedules and describes the fundamental adaptive experience so any serious endurance athlete can understand it.

The Inner Game as Story: Endurance training is fundamentally an inner game. It takes place in a mental context and it cannot exist outside of a runner's life story. Furthermore, our training and racing stories give meaning to the activity of running, while also providing a context for personal growth.

This book illustrates these principles by describing the training process from the perspective of my racing comeback in 1994. Of course, most runners would prefer to learn about running from their own experience. Nonetheless, this book can assist you by enabling you to see the training process from the perspective of an experienced coach and runner.

For in attempting to solve my own running problems, I've shared some useful insights into our common concerns. In addition to my story, you will find a synopsis at the end of each chapter that defines key concepts and answers practical "how to" questions about the training process. Together, the synopses and my comeback story provide a vehicle for learning the tenets of the hard-easy system.

For example, my runners and I measure workout energy on the following scale: sluggish, tired, lazy, ready, and eager. Hard workouts cause our energy to fluctuate in cycles, typically between ready-to-run-hard and tired. Since I planned to train hard in 1994, I would have to coordinate my hard and easy workouts with these changes in my energy, otherwise I wouldn't improve.

In other words, if I wanted to become a faster runner, I would have to run by feeling. And while I don't claim to be a faultless practitioner of this technique, I do understand the basic principles and I was able to apply them with some success.

The Mental Side of Training and Racing: My few racing successes notwithstanding, my story also demonstrates that training is not a simple matter of running textbook-perfect workouts. In fact, in the game of running, our training and racing results are determined by our way of thinking.

As a competitive runner--often caught up in my ambition--the difference between disciplined training and obsessive overtraining wasn't always clear. Nor was it easy to keep my psychological balance in the face of competitive pressures. Thus, at times, I've had to deal with myself as the antithesis of who I wanted to be as a runner, a coach, and a leader in the running community.

Though, by national standards, I am not an elite athlete, I am a serious recreational racer and a student of the competitive game. As such, I wish my training decisions always turned out for the best. In fact, at various times I've overtrained and injured myself in pursuit of winning races. At first, I didn't think I could describe my mistakes without damaging the credibility of my training system. Eventually, however, I realized my mistakes weren't a reflection of the principles I teach and advocate, but of my own human foibles.

Thus, my story also illustrates how personality can affect training and racing. In this regard, Bob Sevene may have been correct. It is difficult to make effective training decisions because they presume thoughtful self control and constant sensitivity to the inner experience of running.

And while it may be difficult for some readers to apply my story to their particular circumstances, I've found that most recreational runners--even elite athletes--eventually make many of the mistakes I write about from my own experience.

This Book in Perspective: I have written this book from my experience as a twenty year-old on the track team at the University of Oregon, as a professional fitness trainer, and as a competitive age-group runner. The anecdotes I share illustrate the principles inherent in the decisions I made at the time.

There is nothing new in running but the perspectives creative thinkers bring to it. In the future, exercise physiologists may fine-tune the training process, but I believe the major discoveries have been made already by the great innovators such as Bill Bowerman. From my own perspective, I never knew how simple running was until I realized how complex it was.

As you consider the complexity of the training process, I encourage you to also consider the utility of my ideas. The runners and triathletes in my training programs have discovered these ideas to be useful tools for thinking about endurance training.

Part I
Workout Effort and Running Energy

I was burned out on competitive running when I quit in 1986. I had immersed myself in the training process for seven years, writing a book on the subject, teaching seminars, and directing training programs for recreational runners and triathletes. I would continue directing training programs, but in 1986 I needed a break from my personal training and racing.

I still thought of myself as one of the best runners in Hawaii, but in my early forties I was getting too old to compete with guys in their twenties. I had trained hard since 1979, yet I'd slipped from placing in the top ten to the top twenty-five in major Hawaii road races. I was still near the top of my age group, but age group running had never motivated me. Besides, there were other things I wanted to do with my life than continue seeking vain glory in the already well established pecking order of local running.

Furthermore, I was tired of being wiped out and injured by my training. Sometimes I would come in from a long run feeling so weary from exertion that all I could do was take a nap. I was often stuck in martyrdom: nobody understood the suffering I endured for the sake of winning races. I had chronic bursitis at the base of my left achilles tendon that hobbled me whenever I got up and tried to walk. I had recently exacerbated the injury to the point where I couldn't train at all, and I didn't want to mark time until it healed enough to begin again.

Moreover, I was feeling guilty about the impact intense running had had on my marriage. My wife, Nancy Heck, was a non-runner, who during the early years of our marriage had been marvelously supportive and enthusiastic about my training and racing. We were married in 1979, the same year I'd begun my current comeback, and since then she had seen a side of me that hadn't come with the territory of our courtship. My training often left me feeling non-communicative and irritable, and by the mid-eighties it was a sore point in our relationship.

In short, there was nothing in 1986 that could have motivated me to continue with competitive training and racing.

During the next eight years, I coached a range of athletes with a variety of reasons for wanting to join my fourteen-week training programs. My groups typically consisted of forty people meeting three times a week in city parks to do a workout. Most of them were there because they needed group support and a formal program.

Athletes in my programs were recreational racers who enjoyed swimming, biking and running, and for the most part they simply wanted to stay in shape with moderate training. The Honolulu Marathon, the Tinman Triathlon, and the 10-K races on our spring calendar gave them a racing focus, but they weren't necessarily driven by ambition to do well at all cost in these events.

Yet there were some in every group who were ambitious about their training and racing. Sometimes it even seemed their identity was tied up with hard work and competitive success. Coming from the "hard work" school of running myself, I could empathize with their plight, which at times could be as self-destructive as mine had been. As a professional fitness trainer, I was constantly developing ways to measure and promote injury-free training and improved performance. I knew that overtraining could ruin competitive performance, but I was inept when it came to teaching the most ambitious runners to find the adaptive optimum between too little and too much training.

Sometimes I wondered whether this inability on my part was a reflection of something I had failed to learn myself. Thinking back on my career in running, I usually assumed I'd been good at it. Perhaps I should have made a distinction between my considerable physical talent and my debatable ability to train myself. In fact, I still had a lot to learn as a runner, which partially explains why--eight years after I'd decided to take an extended break from running--I suddenly began to train again.

I could overlook the suffering I had endured in the eighties so I was now open to another round of hard training. Even Nancy seemed amenable to the new project, realizing how important it was for me to make a comeback at this point in my life. I was writing another book on endurance training and I needed to immerse myself in the training process. I was also entering a new age division--fifty to fifty-four--and I yearned to pit myself against the best.

Perhaps most important, my father had recently passed away from a heart problem--the symptoms of which I had inherited--so I was also feeling vulnerable to an untimely death. In late 1993, I'd discovered I could deal with my heart arrhythmias by increasing my mileage. Thus, if I were going to make a competitive comeback, the circumstances could not have been more auspicious.

Five weeks after I started training, I ran a race that set the tone for most of the races I would run during the following year. I think of it as a "preliminary skirmish" because I wouldn't run my first race as a fifty year-old for another month.

Yet the Pro-Bowl 5-K put me in touch with the part of running I hated most: being forced by competitive circumstances to run an all-out effort for which I was neither mentally nor physically prepared.

Chapter One
A Preliminary Skirmish

I've always been a natural runner--tall, lanky and blessed with speed and power. In my high school and college years, I specialized in the mile and half-mile, but I was also interested in longer events. My friends at the time were mostly pure distance runners, but I was an anomaly, with my ability to run short and fast, as well as long and slow.

As versatile as I was, however, there were limits to my running ability. For instance, in the early eighties I decided I was physically and temperamentally unsuited to run the marathon. My racing ability seemed to peter out after ninety minutes, which limited my effectiveness to races in the fifteen-mile range. I enjoyed racing half-marathons (13.1 miles), but I was most competitive at much shorter distances, such as five kilometers (3.1 miles).

Thus, when I started training again in January, 1994, I knew my bread and butter racing distances would be short and fast. And when the group of athletes I was training at the time decided to run the Waikiki Pro-Bowl 5-K in early February, I decided the Wednesday before the race to do it, too--as much to impress them as to assess my competitive ability. I had been training for exactly four weeks, so I didn't expect to set the world on fire, but I thought I could perform well enough in a 5-K to be competitive against the best runners in my training program.

Candas "Candy" Smiley was the one person from the group whom I most wanted to beat. Candy had once been the best woman runner in Hawaii. Now, in her mid-thirties, she was in her third year of a racing comeback after several years of maternity leave. Though not as strong as she once was, Candy was still an expert racer--well versed in the psychological aspects of the game. Blond, brassy and irrepressible, she could egg her competition into outlandish statements of their competitive intentions, while never revealing her own. She exuded confidence, but, under close scrutiny, her eyes sometimes revealed a layer of well-concealed anxiety.

I had known Candy since the early eighties, having coached and advised her during her years of elite racing. I knew how tough she could be in spite of inner fears. Candy had never been shy about seeking training advice from diverse sources, choosing the people and ideas that made the most sense to her. But thinking about training wasn't her forte. True to her extroverted nature, she was most effective reacting viscerally to her competition, sometimes driving them to distraction during races with mocking remarks about their running form, the difficulty of a coming hill or their heavy breathing. There was no doubt in my mind that Candy relished the prospect of racing me in the Pro-Bowl 5-K.

As her coach and, recently, one of her training partners, I knew exactly where Candy was competitively. I knew she could give me a good race, but I also knew I could use my natural speed to out kick her if we were together at the finish of a 5-K. I was less certain, however, of where I stood in relation to some of the younger guys in our 10-K training. On Monday before the race, I decided to test myself against two of them during our last hard workout. We were scheduled to run on a grassy quarter-mile loop around the perimeter of Thomas Square--a tranquil city park with a huge fountain at its center and several magnificent banyan trees scattered about for shade.

There were twenty runners under my tutelage that afternoon, and I divided them into ability groups of five runners, each to do--what we called--"ladder" intervals, building and descending from one to four laps around the park.[1] On the four-lap intervals, one person in each group was designated as the "rabbit," whose task was to surge ahead after the first half lap, then resume the original pace so the others could catch up during the rest of the interval. Given our competitive nature, the guys in my group gave no quarter during the workout, surging powerfully and pursuing diligently. On the last interval, one of the younger runners and I raced the last furlong, breathing at the end like horses in the Kentucky Derby.

This workout gave me a good idea of what the guys could do, and I was confident I could stay with them in the 5-K. I'd noticed, however, that Candy had run the workout from the rear of our group, declining when it'd been her turn to take the lead and claiming a lack of energy

---

[1] I'll refer to "interval" training a lot in the following pages, but I don't really explain the concept in detail until part two. I assume that most of my readers understand that intervals are a form of training that alternates relatively high and low levels of exertion so a runner can practice race pace running interspersed with intervals of recovery jogging.

whenever she'd failed to catch the front runners. Candy was wily. If she said she was tired, I had no cause to doubt her, but I wouldn't have put it past her to hang back on purpose, knowing she had a more important race to run on Saturday.

As I glanced back at her, cruising to the finish forty yards behind me, I realized the insanity of my behavior during the workout. I may have increased my confidence vis a vis the young male runners, but I may have also over extended myself vis a vis Candy. That thought would be a source of major concern as my energy deserted me the following day and for the rest of the week.

Racing All-Out: I was still feeling flat an hour before the Pro-Bowl 5-K. I was excited to be racing again for the first time in eight years. But during my jogging warm-up prior to the race I could tell I hadn't recovered sufficiently from the interval workout the previous Monday, and I was anxious about my competitive prospects. The young guys--my competitors from the training program--looked equally concerned, but Candy acted gay and carefree as we warmed up before the race.

Knowing my energy was limited, I didn't want to run harder than necessary to beat Candy, so my plan was to stay right behind her from the get-go. As we lined up at the start, I positioned myself at Candy's shoulder, which revealed my strategy and caused her to immediately sound off in a loud voice to the effect that *she* knew what I was up to, *using* her to set the pace so I could *try* to out kick her at the finish. Of course, her harangue attracted the attention of everyone in our vicinity, embarrassing me to the point to extreme chagrin, as she knew it would.

I stood my ground, however, and when the gun went off I tucked in behind Candy and held on for dear life. I knew immediately that this was going to be a tough race because, in projecting myself ahead to the finish, I could tell intuitively I was at my maximum sustainable pace for the distance. This was the first race I'd ever run with a heart rate monitor, and after a minute or two it occurred to me to check my heart rate. Glancing down, I saw 178 beats per minute (bpm), but looking closer, I was surprised to see my stop watch wasn't running. In my discombobulation over Candy's outburst, I had pressed the wrong button at the start. To start the watch now, I would've had to reach over to my left wrist and press a button on the side of the monitor. But I wasn't able to do it without disrupting my concentration. And at that moment, I needed all my concentration to keep from falling behind Candy.

We were running on the bike path that encircles Kapiolani Park--the broad expanse of green and open space between Diamond Head and Waikiki. On the back stretch of the park, we ran through a ribbon of trees separating the cliffs of Diamond Head on our left from the wide open playing fields on our right. In the early going, I could feel myself gliding by other runners, but I kept my eyes on Candy's calves several yards ahead.

Candy is a beautiful runner, smooth and powerful, and I let her flowing stride mesmerize me as we approached the sharp right turn onto Kalakaua Avenue. She was running with two of the guys from our group, both of whom were confident enough to lead the way at that point. My breathing was audible, but still under control at the first mile. Nonetheless, my concern was growing because Candy and the others were beginning to pull away, and I couldn't summon the temerity to maintain contact.

The course had been designed to finish at the Honolulu Marathon finish line, and passing there we had a 1.76-mile lap of the park to go. A minute later, I pulled even with Carl Elsworth, the top sixty year-old in the race and a former associate of mine in the Mid-Pacific Road Runners Club. As I passed Carl, he glanced over at me--the new kid on the block. I forged ahead, barely acknowledging him, embarrassed by my heavy breathing, but intent on maintaining the flimsiest of contact with Candy and the others. I was also trying not to kick myself emotionally for having trained so hard the previous Monday.

Not only was I still running as fast as I could for the distance, I was also becoming aware again of what I hated most about the racing game: the extreme discomfort of near maximum exertion, compounded by the despair of not being able to respond to a competitive challenge. My heart rate had been in the 180 bpm range early in the race, but it climbed close to 190 bpm by the time we headed up the back stretch of the park again--a mile from the finish. Candy and the others continued to hold a twenty meter lead on me, and for the fourth time in the last several minutes I conceded victory to them.

I could already hear Candy crowing to the group at Monday's workout, describing in detail how she had beat me in the BIG race. Yet I wasn't willing to pay the price to close the gap. I was hurting so much from the intensity of the effort that even the anguish I anticipated in facing Candy and the group on Monday was insignificant motivation to run harder. Dead in the water, I could only hope my cohorts would fade in the last mile. But as we made the final turn onto Kalakaua Avenue--a thousand meters from home--I saw the younger guys surge away from Candy, and I realized they weren't coming back in this race.

Now the only question was whether Candy would fade. I had gained a few meters on her during the last quarter mile, and I knew I hadn't accelerated. I concentrated on my spot on the road ahead and projected myself to the finish, now a half-mile away. I glanced quickly at my heart rate monitor--193 bpm--well into my maximum exertion range, as if I needed confirmation. I was hyperventilating and in extreme discomfort, but I was holding my pace, even if I couldn't increase it. And when I looked up I took heart, because Candy was clearly coming back to me.

She would tell me later how she'd tried to lose me with a sustained surge during the second mile. Now, at last, she was fading, and still hanging on to my own pace, I was able to close the gap between us. At the tennis courts two hundred meters from the finish, I finally caught her. She took a quick look at me, withered momentarily, but with a sort expletive, issued her assessment of my very heavy breathing. To no avail, however, because I was going by her, personally unperturbed that I was clearly working harder than she.

Assessment Time: It had taken an all-out effort on my part to beat Candy. And though I'd probably worked harder than necessary--given the energy-sapping workout of the previous Monday--I was immensely relieved to have come in first. There had been a lot of trash talking between us in the past ten days, all in the spirit of fun, but with a note of seriousness nonetheless.

The first thing others in the group wanted to know when they finished was who had won--not between me and the guys, but between me and Candy. Even though I was the one who had just returned to running, it seemed to me that somehow I'd had the most to lose from the showdown. She was a female and I was a male, as well as her coach. I was also on record as having said I could beat her. Ultimately, she had only laughed and said, "We shall see." It had been a perfect set up and I hadn't seen it coming.

Nonetheless, I would take my victory over Candy for what it was: an all-out effort under adverse circumstances. To my credit, when the race began I'd known from the outset that a faster pace would've been downright foolhardy. My only hope had been to run as evenly as possible, and in fact, my three mile-splits had been exactly even. Thus I probably ended up running as fast as I could for the race as a whole. It was Candy who'd over-extended herself during the second mile, and she who'd had to slow down at the finish.

Perhaps she'd believed my pre-race propaganda: that I was fast enough to beat her at the finish. In that case, maybe she'd had no choice, psychologically, but to break away in the middle. And I'd be the first to admit her strategy had almost worked. I'd been close to giving up, but not quite.

Though I was coming back to running after a long lay-off, I could still hark back to lessons learned years before. In this case, I'd learned early in my career that I could always count on winning against someone of my ability who went out too fast.

This Skirmish in Perspective: Having placed fourth in the 45-49 age division, I was out of the money for recognition during the awards ceremony after the race. But I was relieved when my name wasn't called because I wasn't ready to reveal myself as "in the game" at that point of my comeback. I'd managed to place enough pressure on myself during the last week. If my name were mentioned in the newspapers, I'd have that much more to live up to the next time I raced.

Other than beating Candy, I'd wanted see how I stacked up against the fifty year-olds in the race. I compared my 19:12 time with their results and saw I would have placed second, but well behind the first place finisher. I was encouraged to be "in the money," which was where I wanted to be as a first objective. But my main objective--one I was toying with but to which I still hadn't committed--was to win my new age division in a major race before the end of the summer. And I had a long way to go to accomplish that.

At this point, I simply wanted to enjoy my training and racing. I had to admit, however, that racing Candy hadn't been fun. I hadn't been prepared to run all-out, but I'd done so anyway, paying too high a price in the process. It would take a while to forget the agony of that effort and the specter of doom I'd felt, racing with my energy so low.

In fact, this race would establish a negative mental context for all the races I would run during the following year. I couldn't foresee this at the time, however, as I continued toying with my training, running hard when the spirit moved me, and waiting for my desire and my ambition to coalesce.

Chapter One Synopsis:

- **The Main Issue:** What is an all-out effort? What happens when I am forced by competitive circumstances to run an all-out race for which I am neither mentally nor physically prepared?

- **Concept:** An "all-out effort" is a race or workout in which you run as fast as you can for the distance as a whole. You have run all-out at that point when fatigue forces you to run slower than your average pace for the whole distance.

- **Theoretical Tenet:** Every race or workout requires that you exert an effort. Some efforts can be deeply satisfying, while others can be extremely disagreeable. Whether positive or negative, your attitude about an effort can have long term psychological repercussions on your running.

- **Principle:** To avoid the negative consequences of extreme exertion, you have to be mentally prepared and physically ready to exert the effort. Practically speaking, you've got to feel energetic enough to *want* to run all-out.

- **Questions and Answers:**

    1) What can I do if I'm physically and mentally unprepared for an all-out racing effort?

        Obviously, the solution to this problem is to prepare ahead of time. However, if your energy is low on race day, the best you can do is hang back until it develops. If it doesn't develop, you've got to pace yourself as evenly as possible to conserve your energy for the race as a whole.

        Racing is a game of mental toughness. If the object is to win a race, then the first rule is never give up. Of course, you've got to be clear what "winning" means. And you've got to be realistic about your chances. Still, as long as there is hope, you should maintain the pace in spite of adversity.

2)   How should I train the week before a race to be able to race effectively?

You've got to conserve your energy the week before a race because effective racing requires a lot more energy than ordinary training. Moderate workouts are okay early in the week, with easy and very easy efforts during the last few days. (See chapter three for definitions of these terms.)

3)   How can I avoid becoming mentally scarred by an all-out racing effort, with repercussions which could affect my performances in workouts and races even months later?

This book is partly an inquiry into this problem. As you read ahead, you'll understand that the problem has more to do with a lack of running energy than all-out running *per se*.

Chapter Two
The Commitment to Hard Training

For the first time in eight years, I was giving myself permission to take on the discipline of competitive training. The years of relative inactivity had left me feeling mentally soft and indolent, and though I was excited about starting again, I was used to running only 35-minute jogs at odd hours, and rarely more than three times a week. It would be tough giving up that freedom for the constant discipline of a hard-easy schedule.

I could be faithful to a training schedule, but I had no drive in early 1994 to train hard on my own. I'd been absent from local racing for so long that most of the names and times of fifty year-olds appearing in newspaper race results meant nothing to me. I was low on ambition, which was just as well because I was deeply concerned about becoming obsessed with training and racing, as I had been years before. I needed a middle way to break into hard training, and my first inclination was to train with the runners in my 10-K training program.

In 1994 my 10-K program consisted of mostly experienced runners, and they preferred that I run with them rather than coach from my motorcycle. I also realized it would be a lot easier and more enjoyable for me to train with them instead of by myself.

An Early Challenge: The training was designed to prepare beginner and intermediate runners for a series of races in the January to April time frame. The final race was the Norman Tamanaha Memorial 15-K in April, but most of the women runners wanted to peak for the Straub All-Women's 10-K in early March, and the men were aiming for the Johnny Faerber All-Men's 10-K on the same course the following weekend.

As the training built toward these March 10-Ks, I decided to run the 1994 Johnny Faerber 10-K and test myself against some of the better runners in our group. In the club atmosphere of a training program, it's easy to develop friendly rivalries, and there's no question I wanted to beat my male cohorts in the Faerber 10-K. I'd already run a 5-K against them in early February, losing to two of the better runners. My keenest rivalry, however, was still with Candy Smiley--the fastest marathoner in our program.

Still egging one another on, Candy and I devised a way to race in two different 10-K events--the winner being the person with the fastest time. I had eked out a narrow victory over Candy in the Pro-Bowl 5-K in February, but I suspected the longer 10-K distance would favor her base of stamina over my inherent speed. Moreover, she got to establish the time to beat in our contest, which would place the pressure on me to perform. Nonetheless, I was glad to have an incentive to run the Faerber 10-K. Having been out of racing for so long I needed group support to jump in, and Candy's challenge made it easier for me to make the plunge.

There was another factor adding to my incentive to run the Faerber 10-K. I would have just celebrated my fiftieth birthday, and I harbored a secret ambition to win my new age division--even though I had no idea who would enter or how I would stack up against them. Of course, not knowing the competition added to the anxiety I was already feeling about racing Candy and the younger guys in our small group of racers. It was the sort of mental anguish that could have only signaled high expectations and inadequate preparation.

In the weeks before the race, I talked a lot about my chances with a jogging partner in the slowest group. I had it all thought out in my favor, reckoning I'd do well against Candy and the others based on our recent training results. Of course, all I had to do was perform. But a week before my race, Candy stuck it to me by running 40:12 in the Straub 10-K. Afterward, she told me the course was very tough and hilly, and she'd give me credit if I could run it under forty minutes. In other words, I not only had to beat her time, I had to beat the course as well. She was working on my mind, and her strategy was effective because I soon began thinking negatively.

It was indeed a hilly course and for that reason I'd never liked it, feeling that its constant ups and downs were a hinderance to someone with long legs like mine. I had run a time trial on the course a week before, taking it easy on the first half, but working hard enough on the second 5-K to finish in forty-three minutes. It had been only a hard workout, but after Candy's race, I couldn't see where I'd be able to chop the three minutes necessary to beat her time. The week before my race, I bought a new pair of racing shoes, hoping to lift my spirits, but I wasn't feeling good about my ability. I'd been tired during my runs since the time trial, and I didn't relish the prospect of attacking the hilly 10-K course again.

On the morning of the Faerber 10-K I led a stretching routine for my runners, but I decided to warm up on my own. As I started jogging, I immediately developed a painful side ache. I shouldn't have eaten salad dressing the night before, but it was too late to do anything about that. Nonetheless, I couldn't stop my mind from screaming at me for my choice of foods.

I had less than thirty minutes to get rid of the stitch before the race started, but I was afraid I didn't have enough time. In desperation, I tried everything I knew to make it go away, but no matter how slowly I jogged or how hard I massaged, it persisted up to the last moment.

The Faerber Disaster: The starting line was packed with glaring male runners as I squeezed into the second row. I stood there for a minute--feeling like a party crasher--before I realized I still had a few minutes to slip away and continue playing with my achy gut.

Kalakaua Avenue, where the race would begin, was divided by a grassy medial strip, with a row of ironwood trees forming a natural barrier between the mountain and ocean sides of the street. I had the ocean side to myself as I tried to jog the stitch away. When I returned to the starting line, I positioned myself on the grass where I could be at ease near the front and where I wouldn't get caught up in the initial charge. A moment later, the cannon blew and I took off at a quick tempo, relaxed enough to barely feel the stitch.

We were running on the flat through Kapiolani Park, heading along the coast toward the front of Diamond Head--the famous promontory in the background of most pictures of Waikiki. As the throng of runners left the green and open spaces of the park, one of my former athletes, Howard Wiig--the only fifty year-old I was aware of in the race--called out from behind me. "Say, isn't that Brian Clarke?" he said. "I hear he's a pretty good runner." At that moment, with the stitch weighing heavily on my mind, I felt too serious for light rejoinder. Besides, there was a note of sarcasm in Howard's voice that was probably intended to rile me, so I remained aloof. Receiving no response, he repeated himself in a louder voice. At one level, I scoffed at Howard's challenge. He ran almost every race in town and he was just good enough to win the 50-54 age division when the "big boys," as he called them, didn't show up. I knew Howard's best would be about forty-two minutes for the 10-

K, and, considering myself to be one of the big boys, I planned to keep him were he was--behind me. Yet I was also anxious about my competitive circumstances. Howard was race-seasoned and clearly confident enough to issue me a verbal challenge. The only way I knew to respond was to look down and run.

Several minutes later, as we headed up the steep hill to the Diamond Head lighthouse, I looked up and was shocked to see that Howard was running ten yards ahead of me, and steadily pulling away. During the next half mile I gradually tried to respond, but the side stitch got progressively worse, and by the end of the second mile I was in deep trouble. Soon Howard was so far ahead I had no sense of being in the race with him. Shortly after the mid-point, knowing I couldn't beat Candy's time and knowing this wasn't my race, I gave up and resolved simply to finish with minimal discomfort.

I'd raced before with side stitches, but rarely with one so painful. There had to have been something about my preparation that caused it. Using salad dressing the night before had been the immediate cause, but too much talking about the race ahead of time had contributed to my uptight emotional state. After the race, I was too embarrassed about my performance to stay around for the awards ceremony so I persuaded Candy to take a jog with me around Diamond Head. I didn't know it at the time, but I had come in third among the fifty year-olds, and a distant second to Howard Wiig.

I was surprised to have finished third. I would have stayed to receive my award had I known, but I wouldn't have felt right about it. My time of 43:20 put me several minutes behind Candy's performance, and even twenty seconds behind the practice time I'd run two weeks earlier. And though I could have done better in the race, I'd been much too cavalier about my training to expect it. I simply hadn't done my homework. It was one thing to avoid obsessing about the sport. It was quite another to expect to win without having built a base of quality workouts.

Ostensibly, I was running three hard workouts per week with the runners in my 10-K training. Actually, I'd never run two hard workouts in a row. Sometimes I ran with my fastest runners, who gave me a hard workout. More often, I ran with the middle or slowest groups, usually because I wanted extra time to recover from the hard workouts. I'd been relieved to let Candy and the others train, while I took it easy coaching the slower runners.

My performance in the Faerber 10-K was a wake-up call. If I wanted to walk my talk in future races, I would have to train a lot harder. I was beginning to itch for a training schedule of my own, but I was still reluctant to do more on my hard days than I'd scheduled for the group. Nonetheless, I was ready to raise the ante on my off-days.

Raising the Training Ante: In mid-March, I decided to create a new workout to run in lieu of some of my easy thirty-five minute runs from home. I began going to Kapiolani Park twice a week to run ten quarter-mile intervals on a grassy course. Even though it was an interval workout, it was also supposed to be an easy recovery run between harder workouts with my athletes in the 10-K training.

I was adding the recovery intervals as much for the pleasure of running in the park as I was to get an edge on my competition, including Candy. I knew I could do a lot better against her than I'd shown in the Faerber 10-K, so I'd challenged her to race the Tamanaha Memorial 15-K in April 1994. We were tied at one win apiece after her excellent performance in the Straub 10-K and my narrow victory over her in the earlier Pro-Bowl 5-K. And I intended my new interval workout to be my ace in the hole for our rubber match in April.

As I began this interval regimen, I still hadn't decided to start serious training on my own. I only wanted to supplement the running I was doing three days a week in the 10-K program. Nonetheless, the addition of an off-day interval regimen was the first sign I'd shown of independent training. My ambition was growing and I was looking forward to an opportunity to redeem myself in the Tamanaha 15-K.

Another Practice Race: I had run the Norman Tamanaha Memorial 15-K many times. It was one of the most competitive events in Hawaii on a classic out-and-back course developed by Norman Tamanaha during the late fifties. Tamanaha had placed fifth in the 1952 Boston Marathon and he was one of the founders of the Mid-Pacific Road Runners Club. He had also been my high school track and cross country coach so I felt a special affinity to the man and the race.

I'd had only a few weeks to train, but I'd made them count. By race day in early-April, I was feeling stronger and more confident than I'd been for the Johnny Faerber 10-K. The course would take us around Kapiolani Park, over the hill fronting Diamond Head, and into the posh and shaded residential area of Kahala. There were long flat sections where I could relax and use my stride to my advantage. And at the turn-around, I could size up the competition with four miles to go.

At the start, however, I forgot about the competition and settled into a quick relaxed pace. The first half went well, with no recurrence of the stitch that had bothered me in the previous race. As I approached the turn-around, I watched the runners ahead of me for early signs of weakness. I was feeling very aggressive, and when I saw Howard Wiig coming back I pointed straight at him as he passed--as if to say I was coming up to catch him. Candy was a short distance behind me at the turn-around, and I glared at her as she passed, but Candy wouldn't be intimidated.

As we headed back through Kahala six miles into the race, Candy came abreast and asked me how I felt. "Great!" I said, perhaps too quickly. I was tiring, but looking at Howard several hundred yards ahead, I could see by a characteristic turning of his head that he was tiring too. Candy, on the other hand, was clearly picking up steam, and in the next two miles she left me in her dust. I might have been able to stay with her, but doing so would have taken much more effort than I was willing to give. With the memory of the extreme discomfort I'd experienced during the Pro-Bowl 5-K still weighing heavily on my mind, I was determined to follow through with a pre-race promise to myself: to have fun with the race, and to avoid an all-out effort.

Meanwhile, as I charged up the back slope of Diamond Head, I could see my pace was fast enough to catch Howard before the finish. At the entrance to Kapiolani Park, with a thousand yards to go, I had him in my sights twenty yards ahead. I was in no hurry to close the gap. I had coached Howard for ten years and I could tell he was running at his limit. When I finally pulled even with him at the tennis courts, I took a long side-ways look at him, waiting for a response. With two hundred meters to go, this was his moment to sprint--if he had one in him. But he didn't, so I easily moved ahead to finish third in our age division. Afterward, Howard remarked to my wife that this had been the first time he had finished out of the money since he'd turned fifty, several years ago. The young "whipper-snappers" were coming up to get him.

I was pleased with beating Howard. But I'd never doubted my ability to do so--if not in this race, then the next. I was also satisfied with not falling apart physically or psychologically as I had during the Faerber 10-K. I could still do better, but I wasn't particularly motivated to do so. Even losing the rubber match to Candy wasn't a major concern.

The age-group medals were not yet handed out for the Tamanaha 15-K, and my competitive goals were still undecided. The front runners in my age group were my real competitors, but I didn't even know who they were. My competitive attitude was about to shift dramatically, however, as I finally became aware of two other runners in my division.

A Change in Attitude: In my previous two races, my age-group position had been overshadowed by the way I'd felt about my performances. I had been so upset after the Faerber 10-K in March, for instance, I couldn't even recall who came in first in my age division.

The Tamanaha 15-K, however, was the first race in which I didn't feel like a pretender. I had done my homework and I had taken my first competitive step by beating Howard Wiig for recognition in our age group. Now as I approached the stage at the Waikiki Bandstand, I would get to see who two of the top guys were.

Before the race, I had visualized the awards ceremony. Knowing that most runners come forward dressed in running duds, I'd decided to dress in street clothes. I chose a black T-shirt, a black belt and charcoal gray pants--subtle, but a "Darth Vader" uniform nonetheless. I also wore my black F.B.I. cap, knowing it would add to the intimidating aura I wanted to create. Intimidation made no sense in local running circles because, ostensibly, in the land of Aloha nobody takes competition that seriously. I couldn't help myself.

By the time my name was called to receive my third-place medal, these details were far from my mind. I recall them now only because I'm looking at the photograph taken of me on stage with the other age-group winners. They are dressed in white and they stand together, shoulders touching, shaking hands with one another, easy smiles on their faces. I stand sneering at the camera six inches away from the second place finisher. If it weren't for the medallion hanging on a ribbon around my neck, one would wonder why I was in the picture with the other medal winners.

The first and second place finishers may have wondered, too. They shook hands, but seemed to overlook shaking mine. Of course, it was up to me in placing third to shake their hands, and for that reason I'm certain they didn't intend to slight me. They were simply congratulating one another without a thought of how their gesture might affect me.

Yet from having often been the best runner in my day, I expected--on an emotional level--to be treated deferentially. Thus, being overlooked raised my ire, and I kept the photo of that moment in my office as a reminder of my intention to let neither beat me again.

Commitment in Perspective: My prior reluctance to get into tougher training changed markedly after the Tamanaha 15-K. Pride is a foolish vice, but in competitive running it can be a source of motivation. The problem with using pride as my motivation was the psychological shadow it would cast on my training and racing.

Competitive running is a public game, and comments I received from diverse observers of the local scene indicated many people paid attention to race results. Deep down, I cared what they thought, especially in relation to my professional status as a coach. I wanted to show I could be a good runner, as well as teach and coach it. In this sense, I *had* to do well, as if the extra pressure I placed on myself could compensate for something less than honorable about my motivation.

Ordinarily, I didn't care what people thought about me. No matter what the project, I was usually satisfied knowing I had done the best I could. Thus, whether people thought I was a pretender because I came in, say, fourth in my age division with a "slow" time should have been immaterial. With my current comeback, however, I had specific expectations of myself and I was caught up in meeting them, including winning my age division in a major Hawaii road race.

Moreover, I simply wouldn't be satisfied unless I had given it my best shot. I took courage from knowing I could train much harder than I had thus far. And with my ambition now supplying the driving force, I could finally apply myself to the discipline of hard training.

Chapter Two Synopsis:

- **The Main Issues:** Why do I seem to blow some races psychologically? What is hard training? What does it take to motivate myself to undertake the discipline of difficult training and racing?

- **Concepts:**

    1)   Hard training is the discipline of mixing hard and easy workouts into a weekly training regimen.

2)   Ambition is the driving force that motivates goal oriented activity. There can be many sources of ambition, each adding its unique motivating force.

- **Theoretical Tenets:**

1)   In order to develop your potential as a runner, you've got to train hard, meaning a minimum of one, or a maximum of three hard workouts a week.
2)   It's difficult to enter into or sustain hard training without being in touch with your ambition.
3)   You have to be psychologically ready and willing to commit yourself to the discipline of hard training.

- **Relationship:** The more involved you are with your ambition, the more willing you'll be to raise the training ante.

- **Questions and Answers:**

1)   Why do I seem to blow some races psychologically?

Whenever you are insufficiently prepared to meet your expectations for a race, you'll have to mentally rationalize the discrepancy. Despite a lot of self-talk to the contrary, you'll know you are not prepared. This knowledge will show up as prerace anxiety, negative thinking, and the tendency to create an excuse for not performing at your best: a cold or an injury, a side stitch, or other ailment.

There are only two ways to solve this problem: lower your prerace expectations or prepare yourself to meet them. In the game of competitive distance running, adequate preparation may mean hard training.

2)   What is hard training?

Hard training is the discipline of mixing hard and easy workouts into a weekly training regimen. The purpose of hard training is to build your ability for competitive racing.

(See chapter three for details on how to set up hard workouts.)

3)   How can I develop the motivation to train hard?

      You've got to develop a competitive goal. This may mean knowing who you want to race against and beat. Or it may mean challenging yourself to achieve a certain performance goal.

      Since distance running can require tremendous effort, it will help to nurture your ambition, meaning the various factors motivating you to perform. You may also need to find people to support you with your training and racing goals--a training partner, a coach or a group to train with and challenge you.

4)   How can I deal with the feeling of *having* to train hard?

      How to deal with compulsive training is one of the themes of this book. Half the battle is to recognize when you are being compulsive. In other words, know yourself.

Chapter Three
Measuring Workout Effort

My central focus as I began training on my own in April 1994 was to improve my 10-K racing performances. In this regard, I was no different from many of the beginners I was coaching. Whether plodders or elite athletes, we all wanted to become faster racers. I was different in one respect, however. Having once been in excellent condition, I knew I couldn't reach my potential without training hard.

In fact, the process of adapting to a series of hard workouts was the foundation of my training system. Hard workouts were stressful, and adaptation was the body's way of adjusting to that mental and physiological stress. As my runners and I adapted, we'd be able to run farther or faster with no additional effort. In short, our capacity for training and racing would expand. Thus, if we wanted to improve we had to adapt, and much of what I taught my runners had to do with apportioning their workout effort so they could stress themselves optimally, without severe breakdown.

When I first started running in the early 1960s, I couldn't have summarized the training process in this way. But I knew there was a connection between difficult training and becoming a faster runner. My goal at the time was to run a four-minute mile, and my hero was the Australian, Herb Elliot, who had been the recent world record holder in the mile. I had read Elliot's book, *The Golden Mile,* with its descriptions of his workouts on sand dunes and in the weight room. For a while, I emulated Elliot by lifting weights and running in sand. But, ultimately, I was most impressed with the New Zealanders, Peter Snell-- the world record holder in the mile at the time--and his coach, Arthur Lydiard.

While I was an underclassman at the University of Hawaii, Lydiard and his small band of runners occasionally swept through Hawaii on their way to track meets on the mainland U.S.A. Their custom was to stop over in Honolulu for an exhibition meet, with our local runners getting blown away by Snell in the half-mile and Murray Halberg in the two-mile. Afterward, while a group of six or eight Hawaii runners sat attentively under the kiawe tree at the west end of the Punahou High School track, Lydiard would give a short talk on his training system.

Lydiard insisted that the New Zealanders' success was based on what he called "marathon training." I had read Lydiard's book, *Run to the Top*,[2] in which he described a staple 100-mile training week, with workouts ranging from ten to twenty miles a day. In the text, the daily mileage came with cryptic references to effort, such as "1/2 effort" or "3/4 effort." Most amazing to me was a mid-week 18-miler at a "1/4 effort." I wondered what Lydiard meant by effort. Was it the effort necessary to hold the pace from moment to moment, or to run the workout as a whole? I had never run eighteen miles, but I reckoned it would take a huge effort to run that far, especially if the workout were sandwiched between others averaging fourteen miles a day.

The previous summer, I had tried running twelve miles a day, and I soon became exhausted. In fact, by the third day of my new regimen I was so tired I could barely finish the run. And since I was feeling even worse on the fourth day, I decided to run three miles instead of twelve. This easy day enabled me to start again with twelve miles the following day, but, again, by the fourth day I was so tired I had to do another three-mile, easy run to recover. These forced recovery days notwithstanding, I continued trying to maintain successive twelve-mile workouts, and I soon came down with a severe cold that kept me in bed for a week.

Since that schedule obviously wasn't working, I began repeating a cycle of two 12-mile days, followed by a shorter recovery-day. I was still tired at the end of the second 12-mile run, but at least the easy 3-miles the next day enabled me to carry on without illness. Nonetheless, I wondered how the New Zealanders were able to sustain an average of fourteen miles a day during their marathon training.

In 1963, while Lydiard was giving a clinic in Honolulu, I asked him what he meant by a "quarter-effort" (18-mile run). I can't remember his exact answer, except that he referred me back to the "Tables of Effort" in his book. The tables tied running effort to the pace of an athlete's best performance for a certain distance. For instance, a runner who could do a full-effort ten miles at six minutes per mile could run a half-effort ten miles at six minutes and thirty seconds per mile. In other

---

[2] *Run to the Top,* by Arthur Lydiard and Garth Gilmore, copyright 1962, 2nd edition 1967 by Minerva Limited, Auckland, New Zealand.

words, a quarter-effort referred to a relatively slow pace.

Lydiard had a strong influence on me and my running mentor, Harold "Ky" Cole, who was the best runner in Hawaii during the early sixties. Ky was the first local runner to do a twenty mile training run-- the symbol for us of Lydiard's system. Ky told me how fast he had run his 20-miler, and since I was challenging him for the top spot in local running, I went out to beat his time for the distance. I didn't realize it then, but this all-out, competitive approach to marathon training defeated its purpose, which was to build a base of mileage at a *slow* pace. Naturally, I was dog tired when I finished my twenty-mile run and not at all interested in doing them on a regular basis.

Not withstanding these forays into "marathon training," my staple training regimen at the University of Hawaii consisted mostly of intervals. From January to June and from Sunday to Thursday, I ran intervals every time I did a workout. These were intense workouts, including eight one-mile intervals on Sunday, twenty quarter-mile intervals on Tuesday and Thursday, and twenty-five 220-yard intervals on Wednesday. I took a day off before a track meet on Saturday and another day-off on Monday to recovery from the mile intervals on Sunday. My ability improved on this schedule, but it wasn't marathon training.

The last time I saw the New Zealanders, Peter Snell took me aside and angrily accused me of wasting my talent with intervals. If I wanted to improve, he said, I had to build a base of one-hundred mile training weeks, before I started intervals. I was taken aback by Snell's vehemence. I believed in Lydiard's system, but I didn't understand it and, furthermore, I wasn't willing to pay as high a price as the New Zealanders. Few people in this country were, which was probably why we hadn't caught up with their performances in the early sixties.

Nonetheless, I *was* improving, and since my times were coming down, I was satisfied to dabble in long runs during my off season, rather than throw myself into marathon training. Besides, I had recently decided to transfer from UH to the University of Oregon. For better or worse, I was about to come under the tutelage of Oregon track coach, Bill Bowerman.

Training Effort at Oregon: I consider myself fortunate to have been on the track team at Oregon. I raced the mile and the half-mile during the 1965 track season, and that year our team won both the

Pacific Athletic Conference Championship and the NCAA Track and Field Championship. I wasn't the best runner on the team, but I came away from my years at Oregon with an excellent grounding in Bowerman's hard/easy training system.

The Oregon coach was an innovator, as ready to learn from others as he was to develop his own ideas. Many people know the story about how he used his wife's waffle iron to invent waffle soles for Nike running shoes, but few remember that Bowerman went to New Zealand in the early sixties to visit Arthur Lydiard, whose runners had been winning Olympic medals and breaking world records. When I got to Oregon in 1964, I recognized Lydiard's influence on the Oregon training system.

I was struck immediately by Bowerman's references to running effort. Each Sunday, he wrote individual training schedules for each of his runners and posted them in our lockers on Monday afternoon. I was scheduled to run two workouts a day. On Mondays, for example, I ran an easy-effort, four-mile jog in the morning and the afternoon. In Bowerman's system, "easy" referred to the effort of the workout as a whole. In this case, I knew my four-mile jogs were supposed to be much easier than the "hard" fifteen-mile workout he wanted me to run on Sundays. In Bowerman's system, the difference between hard and easy was couched in terms of both pace and mileage.

Bowerman was a successful coach, and I believe this was partly because he realized the importance of scheduling easy workouts for his runners. In the Oregon system, hard workouts were always followed by shorter, slower ones that gave a runner time to recover his energy and reduce inflammation. Yet as far as I know, Bowerman never bothered to explain the meaning of effort to his runners. Nor did he explain the way we were supposed to feel in response to training effort. Bowerman assumed that our feelings of energy, inflammation and fatigue would fluctuate as we followed his hard-easy schedule.

He also assumed that runners who followed his schedules would improve without injury, illness or exhaustion. Unfortunately, this was not always true. In my own case, I had a good year of running as a junior under Bowerman, but my senior year ended prematurely with an injury. Though I took full responsibility for injuring myself, I noticed my experience was similar to that of other runners on the track team. Some had deviated from their schedule and injured themselves, while others had followed it to a tee and still became injured.

Endurance training is a complex activity, and no two runners are physically or psychologically alike. Furthermore, there was always leeway within Bowerman's schedules for a runner to train ineffectively, however unwittingly. Years later, as I began my coaching career, I vowed to provide more than a schedule for my runners. I intended to teach them how to run by feeling, so they could avoid or at least mitigate the pitfalls of personal ambition.

My Early Coaching Experience: There were thousands of people in Hawaii who wanted to run a marathon in 1979, but there were only a few experienced runners and even fewer coaches. Having recently quit high school coaching, and being inspired by the sudden boom in marathon running, I decided to devote some years to coaching adult distance runners.

My goal was to establish a clinic for people who had already run a marathon and who wanted to run the next one faster. In 1980 I asked the Honolulu Marathon Association (HMA) to support me financially while I developed a new training program. The president of the HMA, Willie Williamson, must have seen the need for my program because the HMA awarded me a three-year grant to train recreational marathoners.

The *HMA's Advanced Running Program* soon attracted a group of fifty athletes, most of whom were preparing for their second Honolulu Marathon. I organized two workouts a week for the group, in addition to leading an in-class seminar for them on the training process. In the seminar, we asked the question: what does the adaptive process feel like? We all wanted to become better runners, and we thought that understanding the experience of adaptation was the key to faster races.

At the time, I was working with a wide range of athletic talent, from "joggers" who did a marathon in seven-hours, to "racers" who could do it under three. Since each runner had a unique capacity for exertion, an optimum, adaptive training pace for one was often inappropriate for another.

Knowing their ability, I could generally get them in the ball park by prescribing a workout pace and mileage. But since I couldn't be with everyone on every run, I decided that teaching my runners how to measure training effort should be a major objective of my marathon training program.

Workout Effort and Pace Exertion: In the early years, my student runners and I developed two effort scales. The first measured the exertion necessary to generate a running pace. Although we measured pace itself in minutes per mile, the driving force was exertion, which in my opinion was the more fundamental aspect of the training process.

I started by dividing exertion into five components (heart rate, breathing, power, tempo, and intensity) and combining them to form six levels of exertion[3]. For example, I described steady state as a quick, relaxed and comfortable tempo, at approximately seventy-five percent of maximum heart rate, with deep slow breathing and a "huff" during conversation.

With this as our understanding, I could tell my runners to run for, say, eighty minutes at steady state exertion. In following my instructions, the fastest might cover ten miles, while the slowest might cover only six. Though their training pace and mileage would be different, their experience of the workout from the perspective of its relative difficulty would be about the same. But exactly how difficult would the workout be?

The Pace Exertion Scale

Mild: Very slow, soothing jog. Normal breathing at 50-59% of maximum heart rate (MHR).

Light: Slow tempo, holding back the pace. Conversational breathing. Very comfortable. 60-69% MHR.

Steady State: Quick, relaxed tempo. Deep-slow, inaudible breathing. 70-79% MHR.

Threshold: Rapid, pressing tempo. Audible, controlled breathing, with tolerable discomfort. 80-89% MHR.

Ragged Edge: Fast, forced tempo, heavy, noisy breathing. Uncomfortable. 90-94% MHR.

Maximum: Very fast, straining tempo, labored/hyper breathing, very uncomfortable. 95-100% MHR.

Whenever we met as a group, my runners were supposed to run hard workouts, but they sometimes interpreted this to mean a hard pace. Most novices, for example, understood that light exertion meant slow

---

[3] For a detailed list of the components of exertion, see page 83.

running while ragged edge exertion meant fast running, but they often failed to make the distinction between pace exertion and workout effort. They thought, for example, that light exertion--because it felt slow and easy--made the *overall* effort of a workout easy, too.

But a ninety-minute workout, even at light exertion, was not an easy workout for most of my novice runners. The ninety-minute duration made the workout at least moderate, if not hard, because the longer they ran, the harder their workout would become. This was clear to me, but it wasn't always clear to my novice runners.

The Workout Effort Scale

Very Easy: Very short and very slow. Hardly a warm-up.

Easy: Short and slow. Requires twelve hours for recovery.

Moderate: Neither hard nor easy. Almost to the point of fatigue. Requires 24 hours for recovery.

Hard: Long and slow, or short and fast. A moderately fatiguing workout, requiring 48 to 60 hours for recovery.

Very Hard: Very fatiguing. Requires 72 or more hours for recovery. High risk of injury.

All-Out: Couldn't have run faster for the distance or farther without slowing down. A week or more recovery time needed.

Thus, the workout effort scale was a useful innovation because it measured the effort of a race or workout as a *whole*. I derived this scale from my experience under Bowerman, who used the same terms to tell his runners how hard to run their workouts.

By using the pace exertion and workout effort scales, I could accurately delimit the effort of a workout for my athletes. This was a boon especially for my novice runners because they often didn't have a clue how hard they should run.

What is a Hard Workout? My personal experience of training in early 1994 was similar to my novice runners, because I didn't know how much running I could do and still remain within the bounds of injury-free, adaptive training.

I wanted to do hard workouts, but I didn't even remember how they felt because I hadn't trained hard in eight years. I had to relearn the technique of training hard, and like the beginners in my training programs I was enjoying the process immensely.

I had just turned fifty and I was beginning another competitive campaign, but not as the younger man of limited experience I'd been in the early eighties. My years of coaching since then had taught me that every runner has an adaptive limit beyond which additional workout effort doesn't result in improved ability, but rather injury, illness and exhaustion. This time, I was committed to staying within my adaptive limits because, ultimately, doing so was the only way I could reach my goals.

My training goal in April 1994 was to develop a regimen of workouts that were hard enough to stimulate improvement but easy enough to continue for several months without getting injured. Although I wasn't sure in early 1994 whether I could still do hard workouts on a regular basis without injuring myself, I was certain that *very* hard workouts would be much too difficult. Thus, every time I finished a major workout, I asked myself: was it moderate, hard or very hard?

Of course, other things being equal, an eighty-minute workout at steady state would be harder than a forty-minute workout at the same level of exertion. But at what point during an eighty minute run might the workout become "hard"? My personal reference point was my experience of fatigue (see Figure 3.1).

A hard workout--whether long and slow, or short and fast--would leave me slightly fatigued at the finish. Not wiped out, not blown away, but knowing I could've done more--even if I were satisfied not to have done more. A hard workout would also leave me confident of my ability to repeat the workout a week later. Not cowering in fear, not overcome by the thought of how burdensome or painful it would be, or how exhausted it would make me feel between workouts.

Thus, as I forged my way into hard training, it was my experience of fatigue--not of exertion *per se*--that determined how hard a workout was. By definition, a "hard" workout was moderately fatiguing, while a very hard workout was a killer.

Establishing Hard Workout Standards: Many runners have performance standards for their hard workouts, i.e., they think of a hard workout as a certain number of miles at a certain pace. Of course, in the months ahead I would strive to know exactly what I could do in a hard workout, too. But sometimes I simply wouldn't know.

Every time I would begin running a new workout, for instance, I'd often have to repeat it four or five times, playing with its duration and my level of exertion to find an optimum level of effort for the whole workout. Sometimes I'd have to make a workout longer, yet just as often I'd have to make it shorter. But in early 1994, after eight years of doing nothing but easy workouts, I was stepping gingerly into hard training.

Figure 3.1:   Hard Workouts and Fatigue.[4]

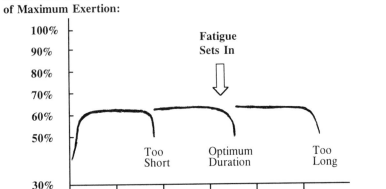

Any workout can be too short, too long, or just long enough for injury free adaptation and improved performance. In this hypothetical example, exertion remains at 65% of maximum heart rate. But if you are aiming for a "hard" workout, then (by definition) you should stop running as fatigue sets in. Running longer makes the workout too hard, and running shorter makes it too easy. Figure 3.2 on page 36 illustrates another perspective on this idea.

------

[4] This discussion of hard workouts assumes that you are feeling *ready* to run a hard workout, i.e., that you have sufficient energy to complete the planned workout without undue fatigue.

I was a lot older than I had been the last time I trained hard. Emotionally, I wanted to do the same workouts I had done then, but intellectually I knew I couldn't do them and still remain within the bounds of hard training. Some middle-aged runners would try to do what they did when they were younger, and they'd end up training *very* hard instead of hard. I was clear, however, that I wanted to train hard, not very hard. Thus, I had to establish new performance standards, including a standard for measuring the impact of my efforts on fatigue.

Hard workouts cause fatigue--a lack of running energy, inflammation, stiff and heavy leg muscles, difficulty maintaining running form, flagging concentration and an inability to sustain a fast pace. It would be okay to feel some fatigue because of a hard workout, as long as subsequent training efforts didn't keep my running energy at a constant low. In the next chapter, I will describe the way my runners and I measure our workout energy: sluggish, tired, lazy, ready, eager. Here I'm concerned about the specific relationship between hard workouts and fatigue.

In my training programs as well as my personal training, I have only one rule: always allow at least forty-eight hours to recover between hard workouts. During those recovery periods, I can do easy workouts, and sometimes moderate workouts, but never hard workouts. If I try to cheat on the 48-hour rule by sneaking in another hard workout, I can count on drastically increasing my risk of injury and exhaustion. A classic case of this in my experience was the 12-mile per day regimen I described on page 27.

In trying to imitate the New Zealand brand of marathon training in the early 1960s, I had attacked my schedule of 12-mile runs as if each one were a hard workout. Of course, I survived for a couple days, but by the third or fourth day I was dead on my feet. At the time, my solution to this problem was to take an easy run after two consecutive hard workouts. But I soon discovered I could only do two of these cycles before having to take a weekend off, while I lazed around at the beach and took long naps.

If I had wanted to run twelve or more miles a day as the New Zealanders were doing, I would have had to run much slower. Naturally, the quicker I ran any given workout, the sooner fatigue would set in (see Figure 3.2). But I wasn't thinking about fatigue in those days. I was totally focused on my performance, and unwilling to run a pace that seemed too slow for the 25 kilometer race I was about to run.

My training schedule at the time had been a potential disaster, but I was fortunate on two counts. Being young and resilient in the early 1960s, I survived the training regimen and I even did well in the race. And since I was soon to come under Bowerman's tutelage at Oregon, I would learn the discipline of hard and easy training. For as brutal as some of my hard workouts were at Oregon, I was almost always recovered for them because I was willing to follow Bowerman's schedule of short, slow runs between hard days.

Thus, the recovery time between hard workouts is an integral part of the performance standards for hard training. And with my new regimen in 1994, I wanted to establish and maintain standard performances with standard recovery periods because as long as I felt ready to run hard, I could count on being able to repeat a hard workout with roughly the same experience of fatigue and approximately the same necessary recovery period.

Figure 3.2: The Degree of Exertion
Determines the Onset of Fatigue.

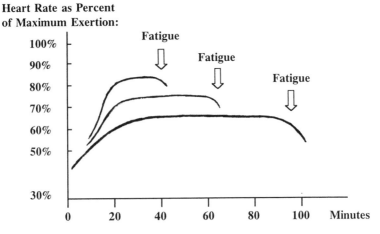

This graph shows heart rate curves for three hypothetical hard workouts, each ending at the onset of
fatigue. Other things being equal, the higher the level
of exertion during a run, the sooner the onset of
fatigue.

With so many variables to consider, hard training sometimes

seemed to be a complex process. But basically I was either training too hard, just right, or not hard enough. And though the basic rules of training were easy to understand and accept, it was in their application that breakdowns were sure to occur.

Hard Workouts in Perspective: In the past, most of my training breakdowns had occurred because I refused to recognize my adaptive limits. I couldn't accept my inability to overcome fatigue with will power.

The crucial distinction here is between being *willfully* driven to succeed, regardless of the costs involved, as opposed to being in *control* of my ambition to the extent that I could balance it with a realistic sense of my adaptive limits.

With my current racing comeback, I not only knew from the outset that there were limits to the effort I could exert in training, but I was also much clearer about how to define those limits. Nonetheless, I had been clear enough about my limits before, and I'd still overtrained. For instance, I could vividly recall the incident that had driven me out of training and racing in 1986.

I'd gone out to do an interval workout on the grass in Kapiolani Park. It was a holiday afternoon and there were hundreds of picnickers scattered about on my quarter-mile straightaway. I was coming back to doing quarters after a layoff, but I was feeling good so I blitzed them, showing off my ability to people who were probably unaware of my presence or unable to appreciate what they were seeing. The irony of this situation was not lost on me, because that evening the bursa of my left achilles tendon became severely swollen and inflamed.

I tried to train on the injury for several weeks, but I finally decided the cause was hopeless. I backed off on hard training and eventually I gave it up completely. It took me years to get over the physical and mental trauma of that injury, and at the outset of my current comeback, I was determined to remain injury-free. On the surface, this seemed to be a simple matter. On a personal level, the issue was whether I could learn to face myself.

For instance, I would have to face up to being the same person I had been when I last competed in 1986. I had the same penchant for jumping into a training regimen with too much effort. I still wanted to compare my performances unfavorably with those when I was younger and stronger. And although I had tremendous discipline, I had the same tendency to misdirect it, becoming obsessed with winning to the point where I'd be incapable of controlling my impulse to overtrain.

In April 1994, however, these were not conscious considerations. From my perspective in the moment, my current comeback offered me an entirely new set of circumstances, not another opportunity either to fall into old traps or master myself.

I hadn't realized yet that my future success in running would depend as much on self knowledge as on technical know-how, and that to be a winner, I'd have to work on myself as much as my training.

Chapter Three Synopsis:

- **The Main Issues:** What is a hard workout? How can I establish a regimen of hard workouts without becoming injured or exhausted?

- **Concepts:** (Note: "effort" is a generic term encompassing two major constructs: pace exertion and workout effort, each of which is made up of several concepts. A "concept" is a unit of mental awareness, which is made up of several essential ideas.)

  1) Exertion is the effort necessary to generate a running pace. Exertion consists of your heart rate, breathing, power, tempo, and intensity, each of which can be measured on a six-level scale (see the components of exertion on page 83.) These components meld into six levels of perceived exertion, which you can measure as mild, light, steady state, threshold, ragged edge, and maximum.

  2) Workout effort is the cumulative impact of all the exertion moments of a run. You can measure workout effort as very easy, easy, moderate, hard, very hard, and all-out. Workouts are relatively hard or easy in relation to the amount of fatigue they cause, including the time necessary to recover from that fatigue and the risk of injury incurred by it.

  3) A "hard workout" is a difficult workout. It can be either long and slow, or short and fast. It is hard enough to leave you moderately fatigued at the finish, and it requires 48 to 60 hours for recovery.

  4) Fatigue is a short term contraction of your capacity for exertion. It is associated with having some, little, or no

running energy, as well as increased inflammation, muscle
stiffness, heavy legs, difficulty maintaining your running
form, flagging concentration and an inability to sustain a fast
pace.

5) Exhaustion is a long term, noticeable change in your capacity
that decreases racing ability. When you are exhausted, you
must exert more effort to achieve the same racing results
because you have less energy.

6) Performance standards are statements about satisfactory
training or racing performance. For example, in my system,
the standard recovery period for a hard workout is a minimum
of forty-eight to sixty hours.

7) Overtraining is the activity of adding too much effort to a
workout or a regimen of workouts.

8) Breakdown is the body's inevitable response to overtraining.
Breakdown shows up as injury, illness or exhaustion.

■ **Theoretical Tenets:**

1) Hard workouts are the basis of the hard-easy training system.
The goal of the system is to develop a training regimen that
is hard enough to stimulate improvement but easy enough to
continue for a training period of several months without
injury, illness or exhaustion.

2) You are either training too hard, too easy or just hard enough
to improve without breaking down.

■ **Relationships:**

1) Other things being equal, the higher your level of exertion and
the longer the duration of a run, the harder your overall
workout effort becomes.

2) Other things being equal, the longer the duration of a workout, the lower your level of exertion must be to avoid injury
and illness, and to stay within the bounds of adaptive training.

■ **Questions and Answers:**

1) How do I know when I've run a hard workout?

    You should know the difference between moderate and hard, and between hard and very hard. With regard to fatigue, for example, a moderate workout takes you to the point of fatigue, but not into it, while a hard workout is moderately fatiguing and a very hard workout is a killer.

    The harder a workout, the longer you'll need to recover before you can do another hard workout. A hard workout requires 48 to 60 hours to restore your energy and reduce inflammation, while a moderate workout requires 24 hours and a very hard workout requires 72 hours or more. (See chapter four to learn how to measure your recoveries.)

2) How can I set performance standards for a hard workout when I have no recent experience running it? Suppose, for instance, I want to run a hard workout consisting of half-mile intervals. How many intervals should I run and at what level of exertion to end up having run a hard workout?

    The only way you can develop accurate performance standards is to repeat the workout and learn from your experience. The fun of training is playing with the duration and intensity of your exertion until you find an optimum level of workout effort. Ultimately, a hard workout will consist of the number of intervals you can run at your racing tempo and still recover within sixty hours.

3) How can I establish a regimen of hard workouts without becoming injured or exhausted?

    You must learn to balance your tendency to overtrain with a realistic sense of your adaptive limits. At the most fundamental level, you must be absolutely committed to training within your adaptive limits. The next several chapters will begin to explore this idea.

Chapter Four
Measuring Running Energy

Training with a group of fellow athletes for the previous three months had tempered my usual aggressiveness. Thus, I was concerned about self-destructing once I began training on my own. I'd often injured myself in the eighties, and I was apprehensive about overtraining as I jumped back into the competitive game.

My primary goal was to race effectively as soon as possible, so I had to do some high quality workouts. But my new schedule had to be flexible enough to accommodate whatever time I needed to recover from them. In other words, it would have to allow for the likely possibility that I'd slip off the path of moderation.

I thought about running three hard workouts per week, but I didn't think I was ready to train hard that frequently without becoming sick or injured. I decided, therefore, to run two hard workouts instead of three, and to keep my weekly mileage down to fifty so I could keep my pace exertion up as high as possible. Obviously, when it came to racing, I wasn't into delayed gratification.

My two hard workouts would consist of an interval session on Sunday and a long run on Thursday. This schedule gave me three days to recover between Thursday and Sunday, and four days between Sunday and the ensuing Thursday (see Figure 4.1).

Figure 4.1: A Weekly Schedule With Two Hard Workouts.

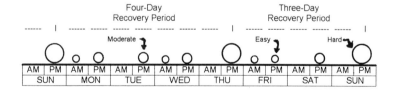

The circles are rough indications of the relative amounts of effort exerted during a workout. The largest circles are hard workouts, with three and four-

day recovery periods between them. These recovery periods were long enough for me to be assured of regular and adequate recovery, while also accommodating several easy or moderate workouts between the hard ones.

With the addition of several loosely scheduled recovery runs from my home, plus a moderate hill workout on Mondays and Wednesdays with my triathletes, and some easy-to-moderate interval workouts (to be described below), I maintained this schedule from mid-April until the end of August, 1994. I planned to run three races in that four-month period, and winning my age division in the Hard Rock 10-K was my first major objective.[5]

Playing With Recovery: I wanted to build a base of tempo running for the Hard Rock 10-K so, in addition to my hard interval workout on the track, I planned to do a workout of ten quarter-mile intervals on the grass in Kapiolani Park. This was the same workout I'd been running since mid-March and it filled out my new schedule on Tuesday, Friday and Saturday afternoons.

I had done a similar tempo regimen while training for the 1984, Diet Pepsi 10-K. I was injured at the time so I ran an easy workout of ten quick quarters every day because that was all the injury allowed me to do. They weren't hard workouts, nor were they fast, but they provided a constant tempo stimulus. And when the injury went away, I returned to hard training and ended up performing well in the race. I wasn't injured in April 1994, but I decided to reduce my risk of injury by focusing on my running energy, and adjusting my pace accordingly.

Unfortunately, the hard workouts I had added recently were causing wide swings in energy from day to day, and, since I was now running during my recovery periods, I was having to adjust to levels of running energy I wasn't used to. After all, until recently, I had been running only three easy jogs from home each week and I experienced mostly ample energy on those runs because I had so much time to recover from them. But now I couldn't tell if I had "some" energy or "little" energy, as I had defined these terms for myself and my runners years before.

---

[5] In part two, I'll discuss the specifics of my training for the Hard Rock 10-K in the context of how to build racing ability. In this chapter, my concern is how to achieve regular and adequate recovery during hard training.

This was a humbling experience because I'd assumed that anyone could measure their running energy by sitting in a chair and thinking about it, rather than getting out on a run and learning how to *feel* it. Nonetheless, as I compared the way I felt from workout to workout, and as I tracked my running energy in my diary, I soon began to identify changes in the way I felt from workout to workout, as well as changes within the workouts themselves.

Measuring Running Energy

No Energy. Legs feel stiff and sore. Constant concentration needed to sustain even a very slow pace.

Little Energy. Legs feel heavy, dull and achy, but a slow pace feels okay.

Some Energy. Legs still feel somewhat logy, but a quick pace feels okay for a little while.

Ample Energy. Legs feel sufficiently loose and robust for a long run or a rapid tempo.

Abundant Energy. Legs feel sufficiently strong and powerful for a race. A fast pace feels great.

Of course, knowing how much energy I had and adjusting my pace to avoid injuries were two different tasks. My first inclination would have been simply to force myself to train at race pace, no matter how I felt. After all, how could I race fast if I didn't train fast? This argument seemed logical, but it could become a major pitfall, especially if I became distracted by my workout performances.

Since I wanted to be free to focus entirely on my running energy during a workout, I timed each quarter-mile interval, but I didn't look at my watch until I got home and recalled my times from the watch's memory. In tracking these times, I discovered that whenever I ran strictly according to the way I felt, my pace on the intervals varied accordingly. For instance, I ran about 7:30 per mile when I had little energy, and I ran about 6:40 per mile when I had some energy. These times were slower than the 6:25 I would average during my next race, but sometimes the heaviness and dullness of my legs stood in such opposition to my running that I felt it best to take it easy.

Clearly, I could have run a lot faster, but by holding myself back, my pace felt *right*. To run slower would have been too easy, and to run faster would have been distinctly dissonant. In my experience, it was this feeling of dissonance--caused by too much speed and too little energy--that led to injury. As long as I could remain focused on the middle path of right effort, I had a chance of staying injury-free.

On my intervals in the park, right effort often resulted in something between a trot and an easy canter. I didn't care. All I wanted was to take my effort up a notch from light to steady, to get airborne instead of merely gliding, and to experience my tempo as quick instead of slow. I was training faster than I would have on my other recovery runs through the hills from my home. And that's all I was interested in.

Measuring Energy Patterns: While I expected my hard workouts to propel me into another realm of racing ability, I never considered my easy interval workouts to be useless when it came to building my ability. The question was whether I could do the intervals and still recover my energy in time for my next hard workout. I was sure of one thing: I would have to hold myself in check, otherwise my schedule would fall apart.

With a new schedule, I could never anticipate exactly how my energy would fluctuate from workout to workout. Nonetheless, having run thousands of workouts in my career, I was intimately familiar with the basic energy cycle (see Figure 4.2). Every time I did a workout, my sensation of energy would move through six distinct phases, starting with the moment I began the run and ending the moment I began the next run. As long as I knew which phase was about to eclipse the other, I could anticipate the ebb and flow of running energy and regulate my workout effort accordingly.

For instance, my energy at the start of an interval workout in the park was usually low because I wasn't recovered from my previous hard workout. I often felt terrible during the first few minutes of the run, with little or no energy, and the harder my initial effort the worse I could expect to feel. I'd discovered long ago that it was better to run as slowly as possible during this transitional phase, than to "hammer" from the get-go.

If I waited patiently, I would eventually begin to warm up, my energy would expand and my pace would quicken, with seemingly no added effort on my part. At that point--ten or twelve minutes into the run--I was ready for my first interval, which--with my energy still relatively low--was only a little faster than the warm-up jog had been. Thereafter, however, I could expect my pace to quicken from interval to interval as I continued warming up and I began feeling looser, stronger and more energetic.

The more recovered I was from my last hard workout, the more energy I would have during the interval workout as a whole. Furthermore, my energy would develop in unique and predictable patterns, each of which was characteristic of a different level of recovery. I called these patterns of energy sluggish, tired, lazy, ready, and eager because each term described my experience of energy as it developed during the whole workout.

Thus, "workout energy" was the *pattern* of running energy that developed during a workout, and, within twenty minutes of starting a run, it told me exactly what to expect of my running energy during the rest of the workout (see "Patterns of Workout Energy" on page 46).

Figure 4.2: A Basic Workout Energy Pattern. (Feeling Ready-to-Run-Hard)

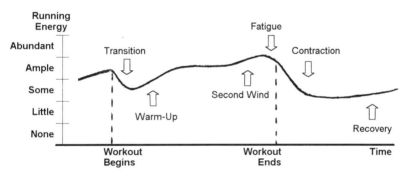

The energy cycle begins with the first steps of a workout and ends with full recovery from it, or the start of the next workout. You can experience this cycle in six phases: a transition from resting to running, a warm-up, an occasional extra spurt of energy, a period of fatigue (if the run were long enough), a contraction of energy after the workout, and a period of energy restoration between workouts. The arrows indicate the metabolic forces that affect running energy during the cycle.

Note: The pattern in this figure is characteristic of the "ready-to-run-hard" level. The other four levels

of workout energy have their own characteristic patterns, as described below.

Along with inflammation, workout energy set the limits within
which I would be able to train. Thus, I had to be willing to adjust the
intensity and duration of a workout in the training moment, otherwise I
could overtrain and injure myself. When I was sluggish, for instance,
I usually cut the number of intervals from ten to eight, running them at
light exertion so I could feel at least satisfied with a very easy workout,
rather than burdened by a harder one.

Patterns of Workout Energy

Sluggish: Having no energy, with none developing
during a run, no matter how long or slowly you jog.
Tired: Starting with little or no energy, but with some
energy developing at the end of a short run.
Lazy: Starting with little energy, but with some to ample
energy developing after a long warm-up.
Ready (to run hard): Incomplete recovery. Starting
with some energy, ample energy develops quickly after
a short warm-up, and this energy is sufficient to perform
at a quality level.
Eager (to race):   Complete recovery.   Starting with
ample energy, abundant energy develops quickly, along
with an aggressive attitude. Outstanding performances
are possible.

On the other hand, when I felt lazy, I could expect ample energy to
develop near the end of my ten intervals. At that point I might be
approaching race pace and feeling like carrying on for a few more
intervals, which might have made the workout hard instead of moderate.
This was another pitfall. The ample energy that developed after a long
warm up when I felt lazy was false energy because it often ran out much
sooner than when I was feeling ready to run hard.

Changes in my energy not withstanding, I had to be clear about my
purpose on these interval workouts. For building my racing ability was
less important than being recovered for my next hard workout. Being
recovered meant having *sufficient* energy to do the hard workout. It also
meant having the *same* energy from hard workout to hard workout. In

other words, I wanted to feel *ready* for my hard workouts--not eager, lazy, tired or sluggish. After about a month, I had learned how to regulate my recovery runs for regular and adequate recoveries (see Figure 4.3).

Figure 4.3: A Typical Weekly Recovery Pattern.

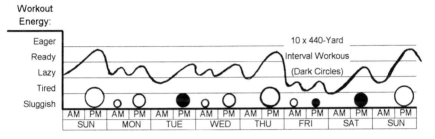

Though I was usually feeling ready for my hard workouts, I didn't always feel the same level of running energy during my 440-yard interval workouts (darkened circles). Sometimes I was tired (Friday pm), and sometimes I was lazy (Tuesday pm and Saturday pm). The worse I felt, the easier I had to run to avoid feeling burdened by my effort. Thus, the Friday pm effort-circle is smaller than the Tuesday pm or Saturday pm circles, indicating I ran easier on Friday than on the other days.

The game of running is made up of small gradations of effort and subtle differences in energy. To be successful I would have to listen to my body. In adjusting the pace of my intervals to accommodate my energy on recovery days I wasn't able to run very fast, but I was able to recover in time for my major workouts. And my easy tempo intervals in the park helped build my confidence for the races yet to come.

Recovery in Perspective: On Sunday June 5, 1994, I ran my first race since the Tamanaha 15-K, eight weeks earlier. It was a Mid-Pacific Road Runners Club event called the Lanikai 8-K, and I was pleased with my results because I did exactly what I'd intended. I felt eager to race, in spite of having trained hard the previous Tuesday. I also won my age division. And my time was a mere three seconds off my goal of thirty-two minutes.

I had done the race as a tune-up in preparation for the Hard Rock 10-K, which was coming up in two weeks. I wanted to know what it would take for me to run forty minutes at Hard Rock, and my thirty-two-minute, very hard effort at Lanikai indicated I could run a forty-minute 10-K. I reckoned I'd have to run at least forty minutes to beat my nemesis, Candy Smiley, who was training for Hard Rock, too. But I also wanted to win my age division, which--I was afraid--would take a much faster time and a much harder effort.

Unfortunately, I wasn't willing to run an all-out effort during the Hard Rock 10-K. I was apprehensive about having to run another excruciating effort like the one I had exerted during the Pro-Bowl 5-K in February. Though I wasn't willing to admit it to myself at the time, the discomfort of another all-out effort was too high a price for me to pay, even to win my age division at Hard Rock.

Nonetheless, I was feeling ambitious about the Hard Rock 10-K, and aggressive about my training the day after the Lanikai 8-K. The race had built my confidence to the point of arrogance. In fact, I was feeling downright invulnerable. I was also caught in a bind. Hard Rock was only two weeks away, yet I didn't have a plan for training up to it.

Thus, my arrogance was a cover for the insecurity I felt about training for my rapidly approaching goal race. I'd been in this situation before and I'd rarely handled it well. I needed to back off on hard training the week before Hard Rock, but I also needed to lay off for most of the current week until I recovered from Lanikai. I could have laid off of hard training for both weeks, but my ambition was egging me on, and I felt compelled to train.

I reckoned I'd have a window of time between Thursday and Sunday to do a couple of hard workouts. But on Monday, the day after Lanikai, my energy was so good I talked myself into starting a new regimen of tempo intervals on the grass in Kapiolani Park. Still on a high from the race the day before, I decided to run a moderate workout of five 880-yard intervals on my grassy half-mile circuit through the trees in Kapiolani Park. I'd forgotten how good my workout energy could be the first day after a race, and how exhausted I could feel the following day. Sure enough, on Tuesday I was feeling tired, but somehow I convinced myself I wasn't feeling *that* tired. I did another workout of five 880s, pressing my tempo instead of staying relaxed as

I would have earlier in the training period.

On Wednesday I went out again to do the same interval workout. It was a hot afternoon and I was rushing to get the workout in before my triathletes started theirs. They were already gathering at our usual meeting place adjacent to my course and--in my mind--I was performing for them, trying to look the part of someone who had just won his age division in a race the previous Sunday. However, I wasn't enjoying the part nor the effort, which, by the third consecutive day, had become a burden.

I was deluding myself with thoughts of how important these workouts were. I definitely wasn't enjoying myself. "But," I thought, "all I have to do is hang in there a *few* more days." When I woke up the next morning, I decided to do a hard interval workout on the UH track. It was Thursday, and I should have been recovered from having run the Lanikai 8-K the previous Sunday. I followed my usual routine of riding my motorcycle to the track, warming up for a mile at a very slow pace and jumping into my first 1200-meter interval at a quick, relaxed effort.

The first interval went okay, though I felt some tightness in the long hamstring muscles on the back of my right upper leg. My hamstrings had never given me problems so I expected the tightness to go away as I continued warming up. During the second interval, my energy was developing as usual, and so was my tempo. Suddenly, I felt a sharp twinge in the middle of the hamstring. I slowed down immediately, completed the lap but stopped without finishing the interval. I grabbed my water bottle and walked directly off the track to my motorcycle.

This was a nasty injury. I wasn't limping as I walked, but I couldn't have run without limping--definitely a bad sign. I'd had many injuries over the years so I knew when I was in trouble, and this was definitely trouble. It wasn't enough to say I'd known better than to train as hard as I had during the past several days. Obviously, the recovery focus that had guided me for months was no longer the most important thing on my mind.

As I headed home, I had to admit my ambition, my arrogance and my insecurities had gotten control of my better judgement. Competitively, my recent race had gone well, but I hadn't been satisfied with that. Moreover, I was only fooling myself if I thought I was on track to achieving my immediate goal. I would have to relax my compulsion to be the best in my age division, or I simply wouldn't be able to stay in the game long enough to do so.

Chapter Four Synopsis:

■ **The Main Issues:** How can I schedule my training for regular and adequate recovery from my hard workouts? What sort of mental focus is necessary to avoid injuring myself?

■ **Concepts:** (Note: "energy" is a generic term that refers to two major conceptual constructs: running energy and workout energy.)

1) Running energy is the amount of energy you feel at any moment during a run, measured as none, little, some, ample, and abundant.

2) Workout energy is the particular *pattern* of running energy that develops from the start to the finish of a workout. The five patterns are sluggish, tired, lazy, ready, and eager.

3) The "energy cycle" is the ebb and flow of energy as it changes from the beginning of a workout to the beginning of the next. It includes six phases: a transition from resting to running, a warm-up, an occasional extra spurt of energy, a period of fatigue (if the run is long enough), a contraction of energy after the workout, and a period of energy restoration or recovery between workouts.

4) Regular recovery means you experience the *same* pattern of workout energy during your hard workouts. And adequate recovery means you have *sufficient* energy to do a hard workout.

5) Scheduling is the activity of anticipating your recovery needs and allowing sufficient time to recover between workouts.

6) A "recovery focus" is the sensitivity to feel your energy level and train just hard enough to achieve regular and adequate recovery.

■ **Theoretical Tenets:**

1) It's possible to accurately measure your recoveries during a workout by focusing on your sensations of running energy.

2) In scheduling your workouts you must account for the time you'll need to recover from them. Too much effort or too little recovery time leads to irregular and inadequate recover-

ies.

3) Irregular and inadequate recoveries can lead to injury, illness and exhaustion. Conversely, regular and adequate recoveries can lead to injury free training and improved racing performance.

■ Relationships:

1) The more energy you feel, the faster your pace tends to be, and the longer you can run at that pace without becoming fatigued.
2) The harder a workout, the more time you'll need to recover from it.
3) The less energy you have during a recovery run, the easier you must run to recover in time for your next hard workout.

■ Questions and Answers:

1) What sort of mental focus is necessary to avoid injuring myself?

You have to focus on your running energy from moment to moment during a run. Running energy will always form a pattern from the beginning to the end of a workout. You should be able to recognize the five basic workout energy patterns: sluggish, tired, lazy, ready, eager. And you must be able to adjust your effort to your energy as it changes during a workout. In the long term, this is the only way to avoid severe breakdown.

2) How can I maintain my "recovery focus" in the face of blind ambition and the unbridled compulsion to overtrain?

This book is an inquiry into this issue, and, in my experience, there are no easy answers. Some people are dealing with deep seated insecurities and mental habits, such as perfectionism, which make it difficult to accept their ability in the training moment. These are problems that require constant surveillance to keep from overtraining.

3) How can I schedule my training for regular and adequate
    recovery from my hard workouts?

    Regular and adequate recoveries occur to the extent that you
    are disciplined enough to run no harder than the effort you've
    scheduled for yourself. In other words, if you are scheduled
    to run hard, then run hard, not very hard. If you run very
    hard in a hard workout time slot, you'll probably feel less
    energy during that recovery period than you would have with
    a hard workout, and thus you'll need a longer recovery
    period.

    You have to know how long it takes you to recover from
    workouts of varying degrees of difficulty, beginning with the
    hardest workouts you intend to run. Generally, I wouldn't
    recommend running very hard workouts on a regular basis.
    However, you can probably get away with running hard work-
    outs on a regular basis, though not more than three per week
    because you'll need a minimum of 48 to 60 hours to recover
    from each hard workout.

    A typical hard workout schedule would have you running hard
    on Tuesday and Thursday afternoon, and Sunday morning.
    This schedule gives you 60, 48 and 60 hours between each
    hard workout, respectively. If you repeat your workouts in
    these time slots from week to week, you maximize the time
    you have for recovery between each hard workout.

    You might also consider running hard every Monday,
    Wednesday and Friday afternoons. This schedule gives you
    only 48 hours between the first two hard workouts, but it
    gives you 72 hours between the next two. Sometimes that
    extra 24 hours can lift your energy and your spirits so you are
    ready for another hard week.

4) Can I train between hard workouts?

    By definition, it takes at least forty-eight to sixty hours to
    recover from your hard workouts. Therefore, you have to

give yourself at least that much time to recover from them. You may run easy or moderate workouts within your recovery periods, as long as they are easy enough to promote injury-free recovery from the hard workouts.

Chapter Five
Dealing with Injury

Most of my running injuries have been rooted in ambition. Whenever running ruled my life, everything became secondary to the all-important racing goal. Ambition demands improved performance, so I would push myself without mercy until the thought of doing another workout would make me cringe at the intense discomfort I was about to inflict upon myself.

By pushing too hard, I was risking injury--and I knew it. Yet obsession often made the risk of even severe injury seem inconsequential. If I had already developed a chronic injury, I'd be haunted by the thought that my next workout could be my last. And if I survived it, I'd breathe a sigh of relief for having again cheated severe injury. I was injured a lot during the early 1980s, so I learned the pitfalls of obsessive training.

Nonetheless, in June of 1994, I was once again caught in the grip of my ambition--this time to win my age division in the Hard Rock 10-K. With two weeks to go before the race, I was still feeling insecure about my ability. And though I'd just run a successful 8-K race, I felt compelled to start a new regimen of half-mile interval workouts. I withstood the stress of several consecutive moderate runs, but, by the fourth day after the race, I'd worn myself to a point of vulnerability. As a result, I injured my right hamstring.

My purpose here isn't to explain or recount my injuries, but to describe how to recognize and get rid of them. Being injury-free is an absolute prerequisite for effective training and racing. Yet for athletes with even a modicum of ambition, injuries are almost inevitable. And when an injury forces us to curtail hard training, we can expect our ability to eventually decline. Thus, it behooves us to understand both the nature of injury and some of its underlying psychological dynamics.

Running Under Injury: As a coach and runner, the last thing I need to know about an injury is what to call it. Fancy names such as achilles tendinitis, chondromalacia, or plantar fascitis are useless because they don't lead to a cure. Whenever I am dealing with pain, my first concern is not to name it, but to discover what is causing it.

An injury is a symptom of a problem in need of solving. And the problem is rarely where the pain resides. My hamstring injury, for example, had been caused by a worn pair of shoes and an overly ambitious frame of mind. Unfortunately, in the past I'd tried to treat my injuries with aspirin instead of dealing with underlying problems. Aspirin could reduce mild inflammation so I could run without pain. But there were injury problems for which the use of aspirin was either ineffective or based on wishful thinking.

Most injuries I encountered as a runner (and a coach) were shoe-related. As my shoes wore out or became compressed, I usually felt a tender spot develop somewhere. Tenderness was not a pain *per se,* but a tingling, annoying awareness that something was wrong (see the injury scale below). And since I rotated my shoes from workout to workout, I could usually tell which pair was bothering me. If I were thinking correctly, I'd dump those shoes immediately, get another pair and the pain would go away. In the current situation, however, both pairs I used for running intervals had worn out at once, and since I'd already spent more than $500 on shoes in the previous six months, saving money seemed more important than avoiding injury. I procrastinated and, with the combined stress of racing and training, the tightness in my hamstring developed rapidly into a full blown injury.

The Injury Scale

Tender: Not a pain *per se,* but a tingling, annoying awareness that something is wrong.

Twinge: A sharp, darting pain with each step that can disappear with gentle jogging, walking, stretching, or massage.

Deep, Dull Ache: Prolonged, recurring pain that can subside during a long warm-up, but usually returns during or after a hard workout, and is most noticeable when getting up from a chair and trying to walk. A sign of chronic fatigue.

Sore: A sharp burning sensation, which is often accompanied by swelling or discoloration. Soreness is a serious injury because it causes limping during running.

Severe: An acute, stabbing pain that makes jogging, running or even normal walking impossible.

Having injured myself, my first priority was to get rid of the pain by immediately backing off on effort. Not only did I abort the workout, I gave myself thirty-six hours before my next workout, jogging my hilly 3.74-mile course from home as slowly as possible. I felt the hamstring twingeing at various points of the run and I knew the pain would have been much worse if I'd tried to run faster. There was no doubt I was seriously injured, but the pain wasn't worse on my next workout the following day so I knew I could continue doing easy workouts.

My goal was to create a steadily declining level of pain from workout to workout until it went away. As long as I was injured, I would run only to keep track of the injury, not to keep in shape. I'd be okay as long as I ran slowly enough to feel the pain only at a tender or mildly twingeing level. During the next three days, I did six easy workouts and the hamstring pain slowly abated to the point where I could barely feel it when I was running at a slow pace. This was exactly what I'd wanted to achieve.

My next objective was to get rid of the injury so I could run the Hard Rock 10-K--still several days away. However, as long as I could feel the hamstring at a slow pace, I didn't think I could run the race without risking a severe recurrence of the injury. Thus, although the pain was much improved, it was still discernable on a jog with thirty-six hours to go, and I would soon decide not to run the race.

Back to Hard Training: At the time, my recovery had progressed to the point where I reckoned the pain would disappear the following week. Sure enough, by Tuesday afternoon I was pain-free and ready for a moderate interval workout on the grass in Kapiolani Park. Since I hadn't run hard in two weeks, I was feeling loose and eager for the workout, and the hamstring didn't bother me. Nonetheless, I could tell the potential for injury was still there.

Several days later, I did my first hard workout--a long slow run-- and during my next two easy workouts the hamstring bothered me again, slightly. I realized I could continue doing long runs and the injury would go away. But having upped the ante to running long, now I had to decide whether to further test the injury by resuming my hard interval workouts. After the original injury I had purchased a new pair of shoes, and I was looking forward to using them on the track. But my top priority was to avoid reinjuring the hamstring. And I knew running intervals would be risky business.

To complicate matters, I was thinking about doing another race in two weeks, the Mid-Pacific Road Runners Club's One-Hour Run on the track. I wanted to prepare for this race with interval training, but I didn't think that missing a few more weeks of intervals would hurt me. In fact, I wondered whether doubling up on my long runs each week would be of relatively greater benefit, considering the one-hour duration of the event. Thus, I decided to carry on with long runs in lieu of intervals. I wasn't out of the woods yet with regard to the injury, but I was willing--if necessary--to back off even on my long runs to get rid of a recurring pain.

I was proud of myself for being this conciliatory. But I was also aware that under different pre-race circumstances I might have tried to push myself with the long runs or the intervals in spite of further aggravation to the hamstring. I was fortunate in two respects. First, the pain was located in the meaty part of my leg rather than in a tendon that attached to a bone. Tendon injuries usually take a lot longer to heal than muscle injuries, so injuring a tendon would have really tested my resolve.

I was also fortunate because I wasn't feeling pressured to perform in the coming race. No one knew I was thinking about running it, and since it was a minor Mid-Pacific Road Runners Club event--similar to the Lanikai 8-K I'd run a few weeks earlier--I was willing to accept myself however I performed.

Training Through Injuries: Of course, if I'd been as caught up in the impending one-hour run as I'd been when I injured myself originally, backing off on effort or choosing a more prudent line of training might have been problematic, if not impossible. Still, I'd seen this movie enough to know when I was at risk.

During the early 1980s, for instance, my ambition was often more important than being injury-free. If I injured myself, I'd try to train through the injury, hoping it would go away rather than committing myself to getting rid of it. As far as I was concerned, minor aches and pains were inevitable side effects of hard training, so a twinge wasn't necessarily a sign of debilitating injury.

As long as I could cause a twinge to disappear with gentle jogging, I reckoned I was still injury-free. But I sometimes fooled myself with this attitude. For if the pain recurred from workout to workout, I was definitely injured, and deluding myself by thinking otherwise. Nonetheless, once I became familiar with a twinge, I could anticipate its pattern of inflammation--the particular ebb and flow of pain and how it would affect my running. By adjusting my schedule with fewer or slower recovery runs between hard workouts, I could continue training hard for a long time, even with considerable pain.

Meanwhile, I would have forgotten what it was like to run without pain. I would even come to accept the pain as normal. By compulsively concentrating on my pace or mileage, I'd overlook the violence I was doing to myself. Procrastination would set in and I'd fail to change my shoes, to restructure my training schedule, or--heaven forbid--to take a rest. Eventually, the pain would develop from a twinge to a deep, dull ache.

A twinge was bad enough, but a burning achy sensation in a muscle or tendon was a serious injury. If it were so sore that I had to limp while running, I could expect to have to deal with it for a minimum of several weeks, rather than having it disappear overnight. In fact, a deep dull ache usually worsened overnight and was most noticeable the morning after a workout. Whenever I felt an ache developing after several workouts, especially when the burning persisted for an increasingly longer part of my recovery periods, I knew I had a chronic injury.

Chronic injuries were difficult to heal, especially when I was training intensely and I wouldn't allow myself enough time between workouts to complete the healing process. Sometimes by jogging slowly for a while at the start of a hard workout, I could warm up an injured area enough so I wouldn't feel it during the rest of the workout. But the pain would usually return in spades a few hours afterwards.

Thus, I learned that the best test of an injury wasn't the way it felt during a workout, but the pattern of inflammation that developed later.

Psychological Dynamics: In addition to physical pain, the effects of abusive training included dreary emotions that colored my other activities and adversely affected my relationships. My training may have been soaring, but my work and marriage were failing.

As a result, I often felt guilty about my training, knowing the effect it was having on other aspects of my life. Unlike the myopic guilt I'd feel when I missed a workout, the guilt of self-abuse wouldn't go away unless I made a fundamental shift in my way of being. And that was just about impossible while I was obsessed with winning.

As long as a race was coming up, I'd willfully maintain excessive effort in spite of self-abuse. Willful training disregards the pleas of conscience and suppresses the inner voice that cries out for balance in my training. And although I could rationalize my willfulness by thinking it was necessary to my goal, rationalization would always take a toll in psychic energy.

I was often tired while training during the 1980s--bone weary from the combined effects of overtraining and constant denial. I denied my injuries and I denied the effects that too much stress was having on my work and marriage. In thinking about the ways my training was affecting me, I eventually learned to observe my "life energy," keeping track of my lowest level between workouts and entering it in my diary on the scale below.

My objective was to be rested or energetic most of the time, but often I'd hang out in the mid-range: able to do my work, but not winning friends or influencing people. Sometimes I would be so weary after my tougher workouts that I couldn't function until I'd had a nap. Fortunately, I was engaged in a forgiving line of work that permitted frequent napping. I worked long hours, but since I determined when I would work, I could take a nap whenever I needed one. Unfortunately, I sometimes needed more than napping to break the pattern of ambition, overtraining and denial.

Life Energy

Exhausted: Non-functional. Must go to sleep.
Weary: Stressed out, irritable and badly in need of a nap to renew one's energy.
Able: Can function at work or play, but not cheerfully. In need of a nap to make it through the evening.
Rested: Good energy through the day, but it falls off in the evening.
Energetic: Good energy and enthusiasm through the day and evening.

I eventually began to realize that the discipline of training affected me like a kettle under pressure. As I trained the pressure would build, either empowering me to achieve my goals or causing me to subvert them. I seldom injured myself severely without wanting to at some level. Sometimes my training could be so oppressive that severe injury came as a relief. It purged a guilty conscience and gave me an excuse to avoid continued self abuse. In this sense, a severe injury was anything that prevented burdensome training: the flu, a prior commitment, even an accident that might seem totally unrelated to my training.

I needed tremendous mental concentration to avoid severe injury. At the conscious level I was trying to succeed. Unconsciously, I was waiting for an unexpected moment when a lapse in concentration offered an avenue for escape. This had been my pattern in the early eighties, so having injured myself during my current comeback, I had to take a look at my behavior to see how it might be conforming to the model I've just described.

Recognizing Injuries in Perspective: I hadn't overtrained during the eight weeks leading up to the Lanikai 8-K. Yet there was no question I had overtrained the week after the race. Something shifted for me mentally that week, and it had to do with the conflict I was experiencing between my expectations for winning my age division in the June 1994 Hard Rock 10-K and the price I'd have to pay to do so.

Bottom line: I wasn't willing to race all-out. And rather than bring this issue to the surface and deal with it in a positive way, I let my ambition rule my better judgement. Thus, the hamstring injury allowed me to avoid adjusting my expectations. For I couldn't have been satisfied if the race had turned out differently from what I expected, even though what I expected may have been beyond my capacity. Having unreasonable expectations usually set me up for failure.

The week after Hard Rock, I recovered from the injury in time to train for the One-Hour Run on the track which, coincidentally, required a more moderate price in effort and, therefore, saved me from having to deal with my aversion to all-out racing. Of course, I could have dealt with my resistance to the Hard Rock 10-K without injuring myself, but at the time, my ambition had been screaming at me so loudly I didn't even hear my voice of reason.

And since I often expected to be the best in spite of competitive realities, I'd probably have to deal with this problem again before future races. Meanwhile, I avoided dealing with my aversion to all-out racing by telling myself I needed more time to train before I put myself on the line against the best fifty year-olds.

Chapter Five Synopsis:

- **The Main Issue:** What is injury? How can I recognize and get rid of my running injuries? What psychological dynamics lead to injury?

- **Concepts:**

  1) Inflammation is pain, heat, swelling and discoloration in a damaged area.
  2) An injury is a developing pain, measured as tender, twinge, ache, sore, severe. If you feel no pain, you aren't injured.
  3) "Training through" an injury is an attempt to improve ability by training hard, *with* pain. Training through is self-abusive.
  4) "Training under" an injury is running easy enough to avoid limping, while also steadily reducing pain within a workout and from workout to workout.
  5) "Life energy" is a gauge of the level of stress in your life, including the amount of rest you need to deal with it. Your life energy is the way you feel *between* workouts, measured as exhausted, weary, able, rested, and energetic (see page 59 for definitions to these terms).

- **Theoretical Tenets:**

  1) Most running injuries are rooted in ambition. You cannot train hard without ambition, but when you become overly ambitious, compulsion sets in and you lose your recovery focus.
  2) At any given moment, your are either training too hard, too easy or just right for your level of recovery. Training too hard increases your risk of injury.
  3) Injuries are rarely caused by a single training or racing effort. It is usually a combination of several overtraining efforts that lead to injury.
  4) Sometimes a muscle or tendon can be damaged yet you feel no pain until after the run. Thus the best test of an injury isn't necessarily the way it feels during a workout, but the pattern of inflammation that develops between workouts.

■ **Questions and Answers:**

1) How can I get rid of an injury?

    Back off immediately on training and racing effort. If you
    choose to run, go slow enough that you feel only tenderness
    or, at most, a mild twinge.

    You can run while even seriously injured, as long as you run
    only to know how the pain is progressing, not to increase
    your ability. The goal is to create a steadily declining level
    of pain from workout to workout, until it goes away.

    Take responsibility for injuring yourself. You caused the
    injury by overtraining, by rationalizing overtraining, by being
    insensitive to a growing pain, or by procrastinating about a
    worn pair of shoes. You wouldn't have hurt yourself if your
    goal wasn't more important than the pain or the threat of pain.

2) How does my thinking affect my risk of getting injured?

    Most injuries are rooted in ambition, especially being overly
    ambitious. In addition, if you are insecure about your
    training, or if your goals are unrealistically high, you'll tend
    to overtrain and injure yourself.

3) What are the warning signs of injury?

    Serious injuries (that cause limping) rarely happen without a
    warning. If you've been pressing too hard you'll feel
    burdened by your training, and that's a warning. Further-
    more, you'll usually feel a tenderness appear before a twinge,
    and a twinge before an ache.

4) What causes injury?

    It is very difficult to injure yourself with a single training or
    racing effort. Your body is much too resilient. Most injuries

are caused by a series of efforts that were too hard for the amount of recovery time you gave yourself between them.

Although too much running causes injuries, worn or compressed shoes can be a major contributing factor. The bottom line, however, is closer to the way you happen to be thinking about your training leading up to the time when you injure yourself. Watch out for ambition, compulsion, insecurities, dissonance, taking risks, chronic fatigue, denial, and misplaced priorities.

Chapter Six
Adaptive Value

I've always been a runner who could train for months before getting down to the business of racing. As long as I could tell my ability was improving, it didn't matter to me that I wasn't racing.

Of course, my training had to lead somewhere. And during my current comeback, there was nothing I wanted more than to run great races. However, none of the four races I had run since the beginning of 1994 was great. One had been poor, one was fair, another was fair-to-good, and only one had been a solid good.[6]

Unlike some of the less than satisfying races I'd run, a "great" race was one in which I'd have abundant energy and a strong competitive desire, because feeling that eager I could generally count on being willing to race all-out. And if I were to run all-out while feeling eager, I was confident my performance would take care of itself.

My primary objective, therefore, was to get to the starting line feeling eager to race. On the surface, this had always seemed a matter of backing off on hard training the last week or ten days before a race so I'd be well-rested. Of course, I also ate and drank the right foods so I'd have ample energy. Yet, as many times as I had tried to bring myself up for a race in this manner, I'd never discovered the combination of food, drink and rest that could substitute for right effort in my training.

My pre-race customs notwithstanding, I had always suspected that the way I trained would be the way I'd race. Thus, if I wanted to run great races, I'd have to run great workouts. But whether out of ambition, insecurity or stupidity, I'd often opted for tremendous workouts rather than satisfying races.

The distinction here is one of the most important in this book. For although tremendous workouts are the sort to brag about, great workouts

---

[6] I often ask my runners to rate their races on the following scale: bad, poor, fair, good, great. Their answers are important to me because they tell me how well I'm doing as a program director.

are simply in harmony with the way you feel. In my opinion, this is the most important principle of training.

Our Adaptive Limits: At the basic experiential level, every run consists of a certain amount of effort and a certain amount of energy. This is inescapable. Yet most runners--myself included--have been conditioned to focus exclusively on effort, often to the exclusion of effort's counterpart--energy.

Of course, no one can improve in running unless they exert an effort, and this is what makes the racing game so beguiling. It seems to be a simple matter of train and improve. Yet our racing results often belie this simple training model, which is why we sometimes seem to run great races by accident, as much as by design.

The "train and improve" model doesn't work because our workouts are contained and limited by workout energy. In the scale on page 46, we already have a way of measuring changes in workout energy: sluggish, tired, lazy, ready, eager. In my own training, I expected my energy to expand and contract from day to day, with drastic effects on what I was able to do. In 1994, for instance, I could do a hard interval workout when I was ready, but all I could do was an easy jog when I was tired (see Figure 6.1).

These workouts not only indicated dramatic changes in my capacity for exertion, they also represented astonishing differences in performance. After all, a hard/ready workout was a bigger effort than an easy/tired workout. It produced a faster pace for a longer duration, and it took more out of me, requiring 48 to 60 hours for recovery.

However, my performances were only indicative of my individual ability. Some runners are much more talented than others, meaning they have a larger capacity for exertion and, therefore, their hard workouts yield much better performances. Yet we are all limited by a unique capacity for exertion, otherwise anyone could become a world record holder by simply training harder than everyone else.

Nonetheless, we can all build on our natural ability as long as we respect our adaptive limits. For in any running moment, we are either running too hard, too easy, or just right for the amount of energy available to us.

Thus, rather than the simplistic train-and-improve model, it is more accurate to say that the adaptive value of an effort depends on how well we coordinate it with our constantly changing feelings of energy.

Figure 6.1: Capacity's Potential to Contain Exertion.

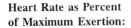

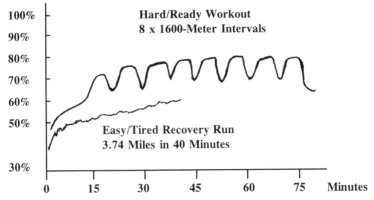

It was all I could do to cover 3.74 miles during a forty-minute, easy/tired recovery run, with my heart rate averaging 53% of maximum. During a hard/-ready workout of eight 1600-meter intervals, however, I could cover nine miles in sixty-five minutes, with my heart rate averaging 74% of maximum.[7] The limiting/enabling factor in these workouts was my workout energy, from tired to ready. The better I felt, the greater my capacity for exertion.

The Building Blocks of Adaptation: In my system, the adaptive value of an effort is its potential to expand capacity for exertion. A slow warm-up jog expands capacity. And so does recovering from a hard workout. But these are short term, temporary changes in one's capacity.

Adaptation is a long term, noticeable change in capacity that improves racing ability. In other words, adaptation enables you to race faster with the same effort because you have more energy. In part four, I'll describe some ways to measure adaptation. Here I'm concerned with describing the fundamental building blocks of adaptation.

----

[7] Average heart rate for this workout includes the eight 200-meter recovery jogs.

Every workout is potentially an adaptive workout, depending on how well you coordinate your effort with your energy. As we have seen, effort and energy have five and six distinct levels respectively. Thus, any workout you can run falls into one of thirty possible combinations of effort and energy (see Figure 6.2). At the basic experiential level, these effort/energy combinations cover the gamut of workout possibilities, including those that are either too hard, too easy, or just right for adaptation.

Figure 6.2: Optimum Effort/Energy Combinations (Shaded).

	Sluggish	Tired	Lazy	Ready	Eager
All-Out	AO/S	AO/T	AO/L	AO/R	**AO/E**
Very Hard	VH/S	VH/T	VH/L	VH/R	**VH/E**
Hard	H/S	H/T	H/L	**H/R**	**H/E**
Moderate	M/S	M/T	**M/L**	**M/R**	M/E
Easy	E/S	**E/T**	**E/L**	E/R	E/E
Very Easy	**VE/S**	**VE/T**	VE/L	VE/R	VE/E

WORKOUT EFFORT (left axis)

WORKOUT ENERGY (bottom axis)

Each cubby-hole in this matrix represents a unique experience of effort and energy. However, only the ten shaded combinations are "adaptive," i.e., they expand capacity and they can lead to improved performance. The combinations below the shaded diagonals are too easy for adaptation and the ones above it are too hard.

Moreover, the optimum, adaptive workouts each have a common characteristic: your workout effort is in harmony with the way you feel. By "harmony" I mean a sense of agreement, accord and compatibility. In my own training, I measure harmony and discord by asking the following question: Is this workout oppressive, burdensome, satisfying, enjoyable, or exhilarating? The key is how much energy I have. For example, I can enjoy a hard workout if I'm feeling ready for it. But even a moderate workout will be burdensome when I'm tired.

For example, the reason I was having so much trouble summoning the courage to run an all-out racing effort in mid-1994 was because I had forced myself in February to run an *all-out* 5-K, while I was feeling *lazy*. Five kilometers is a tough racing distance under the best of circumstances, but the Pro-Bowl 5-K had been an oppressive experience for me because all-out/lazy is a disharmonious and incompatible effort/energy combination.

Ideally, I would have run a very hard 5-K feeling eager, which would have made it a tough race, but a good race because I would have had the energy to beat Candy without running all-out. Under the circumstances of incomplete recovery, however, I had to run all-out in order to win because--feeling lazy--my capacity was smaller than it would have been if I were feeling eager. Thus my energy limited my potential to perform and required a much harder effort of me than I wanted to exert.

Realistically, I had no reason to believe I could run a good Pro-Bowl 5-K that day anyway. I had jumped into the race at the last moment with questionable motivation and inadequate preparation. I had declared my intentions ahead of time and I had overtrained the week before. Under these circumstances, I was fortunate to have beaten Candy--even with an all-out effort. Yet I had paid a heavy price.

One thing leads to another in this game. Thus, my race in February was still affecting my mental attitude in June. For although I shouldn't have been afraid of running an all-out/eager Hard Rock 10-K, emotionally, the thought of running all-out under any circumstances was so undesirable to me that I was forced to take myself out of the running.

This wasn't difficult to do. Too much effort always strikes a distinctly discordant note that can result in injury, illness or exhaustion. I was doomed by my inability to choose the middle path between too little and too much effort. Effective training is a mental game and I was still learning how to run great workouts.

A "great" workout would have been in harmony with my running energy. The quality of my performances was secondary because I adapted to the stress of effort, not pace or mileage, *per se*. For this reason, even my easy/tired workouts could have had adaptive value.

Adaptive Value: Dr. Jim Gallup was one of the best runners in Hawaii during the 1980s. He used to run by my neighborhood six days a week on his way to and from work, often so slowly that even my grandmother could have kept up with him. When I asked Jim about his pace, he said it was usually slow because he was tired from an intense noon-time, five-mile workout.

Gallup ran the 1985 Johnny Faerber 10-K, winning the 50-54 with a Hawaii state age-group record of 34:16. He was a strong runner, yet on his seven-mile commuter runs he always jogged very slowly when he was tired. The slow pace was part of his discipline and the only way he could survive his regimen, running back and forth to work--six days and eighty-four miles a week, not counting weekend races and noon-time workouts.

In my opinion, those seven-mile commuter runs were the mainstay of Gallup's incredible running ability. Yet most of his mileage was much slower than his pace for 10-K, so how was he able to build his ability from such light-exertion running? Considered in isolation, his individual commuter runs were not tremendous workouts, but, together, they each added their small increment of adaptive value to his ability.

Similarly, in my own running, whenever I had taken the time to build a broad base of mileage, my subsequent training and racing had soared. In this regard, Jim Gallup was one of my running heroes. And it was his example I planned to emulate by building my mileage with twice-a-day workouts in the autumn of 1994.

Meanwhile, I didn't want to take the time to build a wider training base because I was too eager to satisfy my ambition in the short term. Thus, the few easy recovery runs I was doing to boost my weekly mileage into the low fifties were only marginally effective for building my current racing ability.

Starting in the fall, however, I planned to run a slew of easy workouts, believing that each would add its small amount of adaptive value to my training regimen.

Adaptive Value in Perspective: The most common mistake in training is to believe that all-out training is the best way to practice all-out racing. I personally saw myself racing an all-out/eager 10-K before the end of the summer, but I didn't need to train all-out in order to prepare for it.

My hard/ready workouts would be my main adaptive vehicles. They were hard enough to simulate some aspects of the race I planned to run, but they weren't so hard that I'd need more than a couple of days to recover from them. My intention was to string together a series of these workouts, making them hard enough to stimulate improvement, but easy enough to continue indefinitely without injury, illness or exhaustion.

Early in the five-month training period, I had gotten into the habit of entering information about my major workouts into a data base in my computer. At the time, however, I was so cavalier about my training I didn't bother to record information about my easy workouts. After I injured my hamstring, however, I realized how vulnerable I was to the scourge of overtraining. From then on, I recorded information on all my workouts, whether hard or easy in an effort/energy log (see Figure 6.3).

Figure 6.3: An Effort/Energy Log.

Date: am pm	Workout:		Duration:	Mileage (Workout/Cum): /	
Workout Effort:	Very Easy	Easy	Moderate	Hard	Very Hard
Workout Energy:	Sluggish - 0 +	Tired - 0 +	Lazy - 0 +	Ready - 0 +	Eager - 0 +
Attitude Re Effort:	Oppressed	Burdened	Satisfied	Enjoyed	Exhilarated
Workout Pain:	Tender	Twinge	Ache	Sore	Severe
Life Energy:	Exhausted	Weary	Able to Work	Rested	Energetic
Comments:					

This effort/energy log has spaces for information about a single workout, including five scales that measure workout effort and workout energy, your attitude about the workout effort, injury, and the lowest level of "life" energy experienced between this workout and your last workout. The top right space is a slot for cumulative weekly mileage.

Making written entries in an log forced me to be aware of how I was performing on various effort/energy scales. Of course, these were subjective judgements on my part, subject to misinterpretation or even denial. But usually I marked the form honestly and correctly, and every week or so I'd enter the data into my computer.

My computed results told me that, for the most part, I was training within my adaptive limits (see Figure 6.4). In fact, I ran 131 workouts during the nineteen-week training period between April and August, and only ten (7.6%) were too hard for the way I felt at the time. I also ran fifteen easy/ready workouts, eight of which were on the easy side of optimum because I was recovering from my hamstring injury and I couldn't have run harder without exacerbating the problem.

Figure 6.4: Distribution of Effort/Energy Combinations For a 19-Week Training Period.

WORKOUT EFFORT	WORKOUT ENERGY					
---	Sluggish	Tired	Lazy	Ready	Eager	Totals
All-Out						0
Very Hard				1	3	4
Hard			4	19	2	25
Moderate		4	21	13	2	40
Easy	1	5	31	15		52
Very Easy		5	4	1		10
Totals:	1	14	60	49	7	131

Any workout is always a combination of variable levels of effort and energy. This matrix summarizes my effort/energy combinations during the 19-week training period between April and August, 1994. Most of the 131 workouts I ran were clustered within the adaptive (shaded) cubby-holes of the matrix. The fifteen easy/ready workouts are an exception because most were run while I was injured.

When I began training in April, I'd planned to run two hard workouts per week in specific time slots each week. In fact, not counting those periods when I was racing, I ran hard in twenty-five out of thirty-two scheduled time slots (78.1%). I'd skipped or aborted some hard workouts because of injury or because I wasn't ready for them. As I surveyed these numbers before another goal race in mid-August, I couldn't help wondering whether my training indicated I could run a great race.

I still hadn't proven that I could run a great race--at least not in this comeback. The Lanikai 8-K I had run in early June had been a good race, which told me I was on the right track, but injuring myself the next week pointed at problems needing my attention. Thus, I didn't think I would run a great race until I'd made a mental breakthrough.

Looking Ahead: As I'll describe in the next part, my main concern in mid-1994 was how to build specific racing abilities by structuring the exertion of my workouts in characteristic ways. For instance, long slow running would build my stamina, and short fast running would build my speed.

Nevertheless, the structure of a workout was secondary to the fundamental activity of matching effort and energy to produce adaptation. In other words, I aimed to build my ability within the context of my hard/ready workouts. In the process, I'd use specific racing abilities to expand my capacity while exerting just enough effort to recover in time for my next scheduled hard workout.

In other words, I had to control my efforts for regular and adequate recoveries. Though all of my workouts were separate in time, they were nonetheless connected by my ability to recover from them. And, ultimately, every workout in the five-month training period was connected to my goal race.

Since the racing effort I would run in August would be different only in degree from my training efforts along the way, if I wanted to run a great race I'd have to run great workouts.

Chapter Six Synopsis:

- **The Main Issue:** What is a great race? In any running moment, how much effort will result in injury-free running and improved racing performance?

- **Concepts:**

    1) A "great race" is one in which you exert a very-hard to all-out effort, having abundant energy and a strong competitive desire.
    2) A "great workout" is one in which your effort is in *harmony* with the way you feel. Great workouts are never "all-out efforts" in the sense that you run as fast as possible for the workout as a whole.
    3) In running, "harmony" is a sense of agreement, accord and compatibility between your effort and your energy. You can measure harmony and discord by asking the following question: Is this effort oppressive, burdensome, satisfying, enjoyable, or exhilarating? It's okay to be merely satisfied

with your effort/energy combinations, but feeling burdened or oppressed is a sign that you are running too hard.

4) An effort/energy combination is one of the thirty ways that you can experience workout effort and workout energy during a race or workout. The more energy you have on the workout energy scale and the more effort you exert on the workout effort scale, the more powerful the combination you'll experience.

5) Capacity for exertion is both the limiting and the enabling factor in endurance athletics. Your capacity is the limit within which you can exert an effort. The outer limit is defined in terms of the on-set of extreme fatigue and the inability to continue running without a crashing slow-down.

One way to measure your capacity is to feel the pattern of running energy that develops during a workout: sluggish, tired, lazy, ready, eager. The more energy you have, the more running you can do and thus the greater your capacity. By this measure, your capacity can change from day to day as you recover from different workouts on your schedule.

Capacity is also a measure of talent. If you have good natural ability, you may be able to perform better than someone else in a 10-K race. Thus, both of you may have felt eager-to-race, yet the one with greater capacity will run the faster 10-K with the same overall effort.

Besides being measurable, your capacity is also dynamic, elastic, and malleable. It changes from week to week and month to month, growing and shrinking in response metabolic forces which are stimulated by your training efforts (see part four on adaptation).

6) Adaptation is a long term, noticeable change in capacity that improves racing ability. In other words, adaptation enables you to race faster with the same effort and the same energy, because you have greater capacity for exertion.

7) Adaptive value is the potential of an effort to expand your capacity for exertion, either during a run or during a training

period of up to several months.

8) An "adaptive limit" is the amount of workout effort you can
    exert harmoniously, given a certain level of workout energy
    (sluggish, tired, lazy, ready, and eager).

9) Right effort is the middle path between too much effort
    (marked by a feeling of dissonance) and too little effort
    (marked by the feeling that you haven't trained enough).
    Right effort changes according to the amount of running
    energy you feel at any moment during a workout.

■ **Theoretical Tenets:**

1) Effort and energy are opposite sides of your running experi-
    ence. Thus, every time you run a workout you exert some
    level of effort and you experience some level of workout
    energy. You cannot experience one aspect of running without
    the other.

2) You adapt to the stress of effort, not to pace or mileage, *per
    se*. The better your natural ability, the faster you can run a
    race or workout compared to other athletes. But at the funda-
    mental, adaptive level, everyone experiences effort and energy
    in the same way. For this reason, certain workouts can have
    adaptive value regardless of your training pace and mileage.

3) There are thirty combinations of effort and energy, but only
    a third of those lead to injury-free adaptation and improved
    performance. The other combinations are either too hard or
    too easy for the amount of energy you feel.

4) Every athlete has a unique capacity for exertion, which deter-
    mines that athlete's performance potential.

■ **Principle:**   Every workout is potentially an adaptive workout,
depending on how well you coordinate your effort with your energy.
An "adaptive effort" is in harmony with the way you feel.

■ **Relationships:**

   1) The better you feel (i.e., the more workout energy you have) during a workout, the greater your capacity for exertion.

   2) The greater your capacity for exertion, the more effort you can exert while staying within your adaptive limit.

   3) The larger the proportion of adaptive workout combinations you run during a training period, the better your chances of being able to run a great race.

■ **Questions and Answers:**

   1) What is the most adaptive level of workout effort?

      It depends on how you feel. The more energy you have, the harder you may run and still expand your capacity. The less energy you have, the easier you must run to avoid injury, illness and exhaustion.

   2) How can I manage my training so I can run hard workouts on a regular basis?

      You should run a series of great workouts, meaning workouts that are hard enough to increase your racing ability, yet easy enough to continue for several months without injury, illness or exhaustion.

Part II
Building Ability

I gave myself a heart rate monitor for Christmas in 1993. It was my first step in eight years toward serious training, and I was very excited. It had been so long since I'd been committed to competitive running that I couldn't recall what it had been like to force my pace into heavy breathing. With my new heart rate toy, I was about to test myself again at the full range of effort to see what I might learn about the training process.

A few days into the new year, I headed out to measure my maximum heart rate. It was early evening as I jogged from my home down winding Sierra Drive and through the bustling Kaimuki business district. People would still be on the University of Hawaii's newly resurfaced track when I arrived, but the lights would be off, the runners would be gone, and I would have it to myself for the 10-lap (4,000-meter) time trial I was about to run.

I was warmed-up and feeling ready when I jogged onto the track. I went immediately to the nearest turn where a white line marks the start of the metric mile. I pressed the memory button on my heart rate monitor and took off at a quick, relaxed pace--just slow enough during the first four laps that my breathing remained inaudible. I was very interested in the heart rate readings showing on my monitor (see Figure II.1). On the way down the hill from my home they had ranged between 95 and 112 beats per minute (bpm), and, later, as I approached the track at a brisk pace, they had risen into the 140s. Now, at steady state exertion, my heart rate was in the low 150s. I was running by feeling and using the heart rate monitor simply to observe my heart rate. I was amazed and delighted at what it was enabling me to see.

Every half-lap I pressed the large red memory button to record my heart rate and time. Later at home I would put this information into my computer to see what I could make of it. For the moment, however, I was simply focused on my running. During the second mile, I began pressing the pace and my breathing became slightly audible. Within 200 meters my heart rate shot up into the mid-170s, and, as I pressed onward, it continued inching up until, by the end of the eighth lap, it

was 180 beats per minute. The second mile had been tougher than the
first, but I still hadn't begun to force my pace. With two laps to go,
however, I started charging. I hadn't run this hard in years and it was
exhilarating to pound along on the back stretch, feeling the rubbery,
resilient surface fly by as it had many times before.

About 250 meters into this portion of the run I suddenly noticed my
breathing was no longer merely audible--it was downright labored. I
glanced at my heart rate monitor, saw 199, and pressed Big Red again.
I had a hunch 199 bpm was going to be my maximum, and that I
wouldn't be able to sustain my initial charge. Sure enough, I discovered
later from the times recorded in the monitor that not only had I slowed
my pace by a second on that 200-meter leg, but my heart rate had also
dropped to 193 bpm with a lap to go.

Figure II.1: Maximum Heart Rate Time Trial

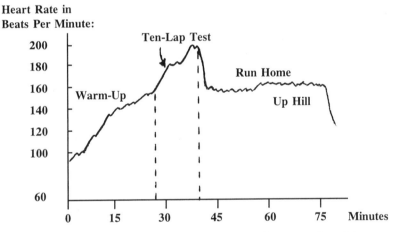

My heart rate moves through several stages for this
75-minute hard workout, including a warm-up, the
ten-lap time trial, the return to the bottom of my hill,
and the steep uphill mile to my home.

Two hundred meters later my heart rate was at 189 bpm, and at that
point I bore down again, thinking I might squeeze out another maximum
heart rate before the finish. But my legs were wobbly and I wasn't
willing to kill myself, knowing I still had to jog several uphill miles to
my home. Nonetheless, my last 200-meter leg was my fastest and,

interestingly, my heart rate at the finish had risen to only 195 beats per minute.

Running home was a struggle. I was tired and pressing slightly with my heart rate in the 150s as I jogged back through Kaimuki. When I hit Sierra Drive and started up the moderately steep last mile to my home, my heart rate rose into the low 160s. And even though I had slowed considerably by that point, the effort had become a burden. Once indoors, I treated myself to a tall glass of apple juice and watched the monitor as my heart rate dropped into the 120s.

It had been a seventy-two minute run and the first hard workout of my comeback. I wondered what my heart rate and performance would be like the next time I did this run, say, four months from now. I was delighted to have a tool I could use to accurately measure, record, and compare future performances. Analyzers love data, and I now had the means for generating a slew of meaningful data.

Perhaps the most important piece of information I would learn from the time trial was my "threshold" heart rate. It was the exertion level I associated with a rapid tempo and audible breathing between eighty and ninety percent of my maximum heart rate. Those ten percentage points turned out, in my case, to be a range of twenty heart beats per minute. While I was running at the upper limit of this threshold range, my breathing slipped from merely audible to heavy as my body labored to deal with the lactic acid being produced by my fast, sustained pace. I called the heavy breathing level of exertion "ragged edge" to distinguish it from threshold.

The ability to run at ragged edge was what highly competitive endurance racing was all about. And if I wanted to be able to endure ragged edge exertion, I would have to practice running at that level. Nonetheless, I planned to do most of my race-specific training for the 10-K in my threshold target range.

Threshold was a lower level of exertion, but I could build a broader base of threshold running with less risk of injury and exhaustion. And now that I knew my threshold range, I could use my heart rate monitor during subsequent training runs to keep myself on target.

Chapter Seven
The Target Ranges

While I was attending the University of Oregon, the assistant track coach, Charles "Chuck" Bowles, was working on his doctorate in exercise physiology, and I was one of eight runners in a heart rate study he conducted in the fall of 1964. Chuck wanted to find out what happened to our heart rates during a fast mile on the track. This was years before commercial heart rate monitors became common, and there was little knowledge of what actually happened to the heart rate under competitive conditions.

Chuck had us run a series of three one-mile time trials over a period of several weeks. He wanted to see if there was a correlation between our heart rate under various pacing conditions and our ability to sprint on the fourth lap. We ran on the Oregon practice track and he monitored our heart rates from the infield with a radio receiver that picked up and recorded transmissions from a box and antenna contraption strapped to our backs. It was a crude and heavy instrument that rattled around as we ran, and--in spite of the scientific possibilities--I was happy to be rid of it after every mile trial.

Chuck discovered that each runner's heart rate rose to a near-maximal level within the first half-lap and remained there for the rest of the trial, regardless of our pacing. And apparently our ability to sprint at the finish was not related to our pacing, but perhaps to psychological factors beyond the scope of the study. I was one of two runners who ran all-out at the end of each trial, and from my point of view that minute of extreme discomfort was simply part of the price I was willing to pay to become a top competitive miler. I was vaguely interested in the scientific issues Chuck was studying, but I thought of his mile trial as only the first part of a workout in which I would also be doing difficult intervals in the hills.

I did a lot of successful running in those days, but I never bothered to measure my training heart rate. My coach, Bill Bowerman, would occasionally check it--usually when he had a question about how fatigued I was. He would press a calloused thumb against my jugular vein and stare intently at his watch, but I don't recall him ever saying what the results were. I personally didn't know how to take my heart rate, and even if I had, I wouldn't have known what to do with it. I paced myself by an intuitive sense of "right effort," which I now realize was based on my breathing, as well as sensations of power, tempo and intensity.

Even years later, when I became a high school coach, I used a similar sense of right effort to judge my runners' pace. I would observe how much effort they were exerting by paying attention to their breathing, their running form or the look on their faces. If my milers were supposed to run fast 220-yard intervals, I looked for signs that they were forcing their pace, but not straining. If they looked intensely focused but composed, they were in the right range. But if their faces were contorted with intense discomfort, I knew they were running too hard. Again, these judgements were largely intuitive on my part. I looked and I saw and I coached, but I doubt I could have articulated exactly what I was seeing or why I made certain coaching decisions.

High school runners generally didn't care to know why I was telling them to speed up or slow down, so I could get away with my intuitive method of coaching. However, when I began coaching adult runners for a living in 1979, I soon realized that many wanted to understand the training process. Unfortunately, since I'd never had to articulate it, I found myself scrambling both to comprehend and explain what I had only dimly intuited until then.

My Ignorance Shows: I was saved in my professional ignorance because most recreational runners knew even less than I did. They were usually easy going and willing to learn, but many were also inclined to train according to personal whim. Lacking clear parameters from me, they were happy to set their own pace, which was often harder than optimal. Thus, a significant number would become injured or exhausted, and thereby fail to race effectively. In my early days of coaching adults, I learned a lot from my runners' mistakes.

Of course, I was aware of the problem I'm describing. In order to bring wayward runners under my control and place my training program on "scientific" footing, I would have a new group of runners pace themselves by using their heart rate as a guide. If they were doing "tempo" intervals on our grassy course in Kapiolani Park, I would teach them how to determine their heart rate by counting their pulse for six seconds and multiplying by ten. Since they couldn't do this during an interval, I would have them do it immediately afterward, before they began their recovery interval. Assuming they had counted correctly, this was a fairly accurate way of determining an "ending" heart rate, i.e., the heart rate as it was at the end of a tempo interval.

I would also instruct my runners to aim initially for a heart rate of 150 beats per minute (bpm). In my coaching experience, 150 bpm was a steady state level of exertion, quick and relaxed for most runners, but usually not slow or fast. Since my runners were willing to at least try the target heart rate approach to training, they were generally close to the heart rate I wanted instead of endangering themselves with a much harder effort. Thus, I had some time to observe each runner and adjust target rates if I thought they were too high or too low in relation to the ideal training tempo I had in mind.

I'd observed many runners over the years and I had a good idea of what they looked like when they were training correctly. When my fastest runners were practicing the specific tempo of a 10-K race, they would appear to be running at a rapid, pressing tempo--one they were capable of holding for the entire 10-K distance. But if certain runners appeared to be running slower than I wanted at 150 bpm, I would ask them to raise their target heart rate. Thus, I was still coaching by observation and intuition--much as I had with my high school runners.

Furthermore, I was in the habit of incorrectly using the terms "quick and relaxed" instead of "rapid and pressing" to describe 10-K tempo for my fastest runners. A quick, relaxed tempo was more appropriate for a longer racing distance or a group of joggers who, because they were slower than the racers, would be on the 10-K course for a longer time. Clearly, I was still struggling with the problem of how to describe exertion, and in the early 1980s I often raised this problem with my student runners during our seminars on the training process.

Heart Rate and the Target Ranges: I taught my training seminars by raising problems for discussion, the first of which was how to develop a set of terms to describe exertion. We began by dividing it into five components: heart rate, breathing, power, tempo and intensity (see "The Components of Exertion" below). We also "scaled" the components from high to low, using terms that described our sensations as we learned to recognize and interpret them from our experience.

Next, we combined the components of exertion to form a single exertion scale. This scale described the effort necessary to sustain a training or racing pace, and it went through extensive revision during the 1980s. For instance, we added a new level called "threshold," which I had formerly included with ragged edge as part of audible breathing. I eventually realized that there were several distinct levels of audible breathing, including just audible, heavy, and labored. Thus, by the 1990s, we were using the pace exertion scale (below) in our training to describe six distinct levels of pace exertion.

The most difficult problem we encountered in setting up the exertion scale was how to correlate each runner's unique heart rate with the various target ranges. In the fitness literature, target heart rates were based on a calculation of maximum heart rate, which was usually estimated as 220 beats per minute minus a runner's age.

I resisted using this formula, however, because it didn't work to measure my personal maximum heart rate. In my own training during the early 1980s, I had run hard enough to measure my maximum heart rate as fifty-five beats per minute above my theoretical maximum. Furthermore, many of my runners at the time were recording training heart rates as fast as their theoretical maximum, and they were clearly not running at maximum exertion.

Measuring Pace Exertion

Mild Exertion: A very slow, gliding tempo. Breathing is normal and heart rate rises to approximately double the resting rate: 45 to 59% of maximum. A very comfortable, soothing effort ideal for the first few minutes of any run.

Light Exertion: A slow and restful tempo. Heart rate is 60 to 69% of maximum, and breathing is unconscious and conversational. Light effort is appropriate for extended warm-ups--especially during the first part of a very long run. A runner has to hold back at this level, especially before the halfway point of a race or workout.

Steady State: A quick, relaxed tempo. Heart rate is a steady 70 to 79% of maximum. Breathing is deep, slow and inaudible, but steady state exertion makes conversation more demanding than when running at a light exertion. Steady state is a comfortable effort, ideal for practicing the tempo of races between half-marathon and marathon.

The Components of Exertion

Heart Rate[8]	Breathing	Power	Tempo	Intensity
Maximum 96-100%	Labored	Strained	Very Fast	Very Uncomfortable
Ragged Edge 90-95%	Heavy	Forced	Fast	Uncomfortable
Threshold 80-89%	Audible	Pressed	Rapid	Tolerable
Steady 70-79%	Inaudible	Relaxed	Quick	Comfortable
Light 60-69%	Conversational	Held Back	Slow	Very Comfortable
Mild 50-59%	Normal	Gentle	Very Slow	Soothing

---

[8] The target ranges are computed as percentages of maximum heart rate.

Threshold: A rapid tempo, pressed beyond the level of relaxed running. Breathing is conscious, controlled and just audible to someone running nearby. Heart rate is between 80 and 89% of maximum. The perfect effort for building tempo ability for the 10-K. Tolerably uncomfortable.

Ragged Edge: A fast, forced tempo on the border between uncomfortable and extremely uncomfortable exertion for the 10-K. A maximum aerobic effort perfect for building endurance. Heart rate rises between 90 and 95% of maximum; breathing is heavy and labored. Can be very uncomfortable.

Maximum: A very fast sprint or surge. If the effort is sustained for a minute or more, the heart rate rises above 95% of maximum, breathing becomes hyper-fast and uncontrolled, and the runner soon begins to strain. This level of effort is extremely uncomfortable and very difficult to sustain.

Since the scientific formulas didn't consistently predict maximum heart rate, I finally decided to put my runners through a testing protocol that would. The all-out, sprint-to-the-finish time trial I described in the introduction to this part became our accepted way of assessing maximum heart rates. In the process of directing many runners through it, I discovered that some runners, regardless of their age, had a relatively low maximum heart rate--commonly in the 160 to 170 bpm range. Thus, their target zones were proportionately lower in beats per minute than runners with average or higher-than-average maximum heart rates.

By contrast, I personally had a maximum heart rate of 199 beats per minute, which was high for my age of fifty in 1994. Thus, my target ranges were higher in beats per minute than someone whose maximum might have been 180 beats per minute. Nevertheless, I found that any runner could experience the same gradations of effort as a percent of his or her unique maximum. And once we computed those gradations in beats per minute, they could use their heart rate to keep their running effort within a specific target range.

With this as our understanding, heart rate monitors soon became an important tool in my training programs. Unlike the innovative but cumbersome equipment Chuck Bowles had been using in 1964 to test runners at Oregon, commercial heart rate monitors in the 1990s had become as simple as a chest strap and a wrist watch. Our equipment was enabling us to conveniently and accurately assess our running effort without stopping to take our heart rate.

Moreover, the POLAR VANTAGE XL® monitor I'd purchased in late 1993, came equipped with a memory for automatically recording my times and heart rates at regular intervals during a run. Using the POLAR® computer program, I could use this feature to graph even small changes in exertion. And with a graphic record of my heart rate during a workout, I could visually see how long I had been running within a target range. This was important information because the time I spent within the target ranges would determine the racing abilities I would build.

The Five Racing Abilities: In my training system, there are five racing abilities: stamina, power, tempo, speed and endurance. Even by my current out-of-shape standards, I still had each ability in small measure. I could run slowly for a long time (stamina); I could use my muscle strength to exert a powerful running motion (power); I could comfortably hold a 10-K racing pace (tempo); I could sustain uncomfortable exertion (endurance); I could even accelerate to a level that was faster than my 10-K racing pace (speed). But since I hadn't practiced using these abilities in a long time, I was deficient in each of them.

In order to build a specific racing ability, I would have to use it during my workouts to expand my capacity for exertion. Each workout would have a distinctive structure that would become apparent when I graphed the heart rate record of a workout (see Figure 7.1). A *stamina* workout, for example, would be a long duration effort at mild to light exertion. A 10-K *tempo* workout, by comparison, would be half as long as a stamina workout, but would raise my heart rate to my threshold target range for a series of five-minute intervals, each one separated by an 80-second recovery jog that was slow enough to lower my heart rate to light exertion.

As I began my racing comeback in 1994, I wanted to concentrate on racing ten kilometers. With my natural speed I might have been more competitive at shorter distances, but Hawaii's major races were 10-Ks, and I wanted to be where the action was. I had to structure my workouts to build abilities for ten kilometers--not the mile as I had years before at Oregon or the marathon. as I had in the early eighties. I will allude to

my training at Oregon in this part, but I'll mostly describe my 10-K
training during mid-1994. Nonetheless, the general principles I used in
setting up my 10-K workouts apply to any racing distance. A "tempo"
workout, for instance, is always one in which I practice the specific
tempo of the race I want to run.

Figure 7.1: Two Different Heart Rate Structures.

**Heart Rate Ranges as
Percent of Maximum:**

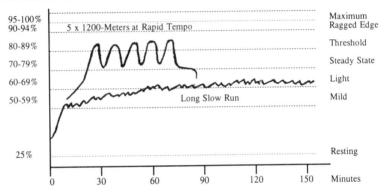

My heart rate curve during a long run appears
markedly different from a tempo interval workout.
Each type of workout has a different ability-building
purpose. The long run extends capacity in the horizontal direction, while the interval workout builds
capacity in the vertical direction. Since I have limited
capacity (energy) to do either type of workout, my
exertion has to be relatively light for the long run and
relatively short for the tempo run.

If I had been training for the mile in 1994, my tempo intervals
would have been about as fast as my current pace for a mile. Obviously,
since I couldn't sustain my current mile pace for five-minute intervals,
my tempo intervals for the mile would have had to be much shorter than
my tempo intervals for the 10-K.

Thus, the shorter the racing distance, the shorter and faster the
bouts of race-pace running needed to build a specific ability. But there

were also definite parameters within which I could apply this principle. And these parameters are the focus of each of the following chapters on the five racing abilities.

The Target Ranges in Perspective: My main purpose in part two is to describe the process of developing workouts to build five racing abilities. Anyone can purchase a heart rate monitor, but few people know how to use one to build ability. The following chapters explore my first attempts to use a sophisticated heart rate monitor for my own ability-building purposes.

I was also bringing my personal history with me into my 1994 comeback. I'd been a miler and half-miler in college and my experiences at the University of Oregon were valuable in formulating my thoughts on endurance training. I've described some of those experiences in this part, especially as they relate to my current comeback.

Though I was coming back to running in middle age with my natural ability diminished, nonetheless, I had extensive experience in the competitive game, a sound theoretical grounding in endurance training, and a fresh mental attitude.

Chapter Seven Synopsis:

- **The Main Issue:** How can I structure the effort of my hard workouts to build racing abilities specific to my racing distance?

- **Concepts:**

  1) Racing ability is your cumulative proficiency in the use of five race-specific abilities: stamina, power, tempo, speed and endurance.

     A. Stamina is the ability to run for long duration at light exertion. ("Long" is defined as that point in a light exertion, hard/ready workout when fatigue sets in.)
     B. Power is the ability to run at race pace using every major leg muscle, and without undue quickness in leg turnover.
     C. Tempo is the ability to run comfortably at race pace for at least half your racing distance.

      D. Speed is the ability to sprint or surge at a faster pace
         than you can average for your full racing distance.
         Speed is used sparingly in tactical situations during a
         race.
      E. Endurance is the ability to endure uncomfortable race
         exertion. Endurance usually becomes a factor when you
         try to sustain your racing tempo beyond the mid-point of
         a race.

2) "Exertion structure" is the specific pattern of exertion that
develops from the beginning to the end of a workout. This
book makes extensive use of heart rate curves to detail
changes in exertion.

3) A workout is "race specific" when its exertion structure
closely duplicates some aspect of the race you want to run.
Similarly, an ability is race specific when you can use it to
simulate some aspect of the race you want to run.

■ Theoretical Tenets:

1) In competitive distance running, every workout has an ability-
building purpose, which is inherent in the exertion structure
of the workout and the racing distance it is designed for.

2) Depending on how a workout is structured (e.g., long/slow or
short/fast), you can build various racing abilities with it.

3) The only way you can build a racing ability is by using it to
expand your capacity for exertion.

■ The Principle of Specificity:
The best way to prepare for a race is
to simulate in training some aspect of the specific exertion of the
race you aim to run. Since exertion is made up of five components
(heart rate, breathing, power, tempo, and intensity), you can
structure your workouts to focus on each component in turn.

■ Relationships:

1) The shorter your racing distance, the faster your racing pace
and the higher your exertion level will have to be to race
effectively.

2) Similarly, the shorter your racing distance, the faster your
training should be to simulate the specific exertion of the race
you want to run.

3) The faster your training pace, the shorter your training bouts
should be to stay within adaptive limits.

4) The more energy you have for a race or workout, the higher
you can push your heart rate towards maximum.

■ **Questions and Answers:**

1) What are the target ranges?

You can think of target ranges in two ways:

A. As distinctive levels of exertion, measured as mild,
light, steady state, threshold, ragged edge, and maximum. You should know how to distinguish each of
these from the others, using the five components of
exertion: heart rate, breathing, power, tempo and
intensity.

B. A "right effort" heart rate range is measured in beats per
minute. They are narrower than the six levels of perceived exertion described in this chapter and they represent levels of exertion that simulate specific aspects of
the race you want to run.

2) How can I determine my maximum heart rate?

Aside from blitzing an 8 to 10-lap test effort (as described on
pages 76), you can try slowly increasing your effort from
mild to threshold, paying strict attention to your heart rate as
you pass from one level of perceived exertion to another.
Each level is different from the others, so you can mark the
borders using a heart rate monitor.

For example, your "threshold" range begins when you first
hear your breathing at approximately 80% of maximum.
Thus, you can infer your maximum heart rate by noting your
heart rate when you slip into audible breathing. If, for

example, you first hear your breathing at 160 beats per minute, then you would divide 160 by .8. According to this calculation, your maximum heart rate would be 200 beats per minute (160/.8 = 200).

My experience indicates that the more energy you have for a race or workout the higher you can get your heart rate up. Another way of saying this is the greater your capacity, the higher your potential maximum heart rate. For example, I've "maxed out" at 193 beats per minute during a hard/ready time trial the week before a very hard/eager 15-K race in which I was able to run at 196 bpm during the last mile. In other words, you'll be able to push yourself harder when you are eager rather than tired.

3)   How can I structure my workouts to build five racing abilities for the race I want to run?

First you have to be clear about the racing distance you are aiming for, whether the mile, the 10-K or the marathon. You can train for more than one distance at once (say, 5-K and 10-K), or you can train for different distances within a yearly cycle (say, from the marathon to the mile). But since the structure of your workouts will depend on your racing goal, you should have some rationale for deciding how and when to change the structure of your workouts.

Also, you should be clear about the pattern of exertion you will experience during the race you want to run. A heart rate monitor would be an invaluable tool for determining your actual exertion during a practice race. Will you hold 75% of your maximum heart rate for 90 minutes, or 90% for 30 minutes? In general, a relatively long/low heart rate pattern during the race will indicate a relatively long/low heart rate pattern during your hard workouts. In other words, your goal race should have a direct bearing on the exertion structure of your hard workouts.

Then, you should break your race into its various components of exertion. For example, you may have to practice a rapid tempo for a 10-K, while a quick tempo might be more appropriate for a half-marathon. Similarly, a pressing sense of power might be appropriate for the 10-K, while a relaxed level would be more appropriate for the half-marathon. Thus, you would structure your workouts differently for tempo and power, depending on your racing distance.

The following five chapters focus on ways of structuring effort to build the five racing abilities for the 10-K racing distance.

Chapter Eight
Power, Form and Balance

I transferred from the University of Hawaii to the University of Oregon in the middle of my sophomore year. My father had been corresponding with Bill Bowerman, and they had arranged for me to connect with the team at a track meet in Sacramento, California. I was thrilled to be on the mainland U.S.A. for the first time and to have an opportunity to be in the big leagues of university track and field.

I ran the mile at the track meet in Sacramento and came in second behind one of the Oregon runners. My time was slower than it had been in a race the week before, but Bowerman didn't seem to mind and my new teammates were friendly and supportive. That afternoon, we were bused to Hamilton Air Force Base near San Raphael, where we would spend the rest of the week in training for the coming track season. The next day, when I asked Bowerman what I should do for my first workout with the team, he looked around for a veteran who could lead me through a workout. At that moment, a gangly kid in green shorts jogged by with his knees knocking and a contented smile on his face.

"Kenny," Bowerman said. "How about taking Brian here on a run in the hills." Kenny Moore gave Bowerman a laconic, "Ho-kay," and we were off, exploring along a highway that wandered through some hilly dairy land. I had never seen country like this. Unlike the jagged, rocky slopes I was used to in Hawaii, the hills in northern California were rounded on top, with clumps of trees scattered between acres of ankle-deep grass. They were steep hills but they looked runnable, and I was immediately interested in exploring beyond the confines of the highway.

Before we headed into the hills, however, Kenny wanted to know whether I had ever done a twenty-mile run in training. Those were the days when Peter Snell, the New Zealand world record holder in the mile, was known for his twenty-mile training runs. Most middle distance runners in the nation, myself included, were busy trying to emulate Snell's training. So I was relieved to answer Kenny in the affirmative, which seemed to satisfy him that I was indeed worthy of his respect, and thus I wouldn't be tested with a twenty-miler that afternoon. However,

I was dismayed by his next question. "What about hills?" he asked.

"Some," I hedged. I had run back and forth over the moderately hilly approaches to Diamond Head during my *one* twenty-miler. Otherwise, I had kept assiduously to the flats. But I wasn't willing to tell Kenny that. He was sizing me up and I wasn't about to expose my weaknesses. There was something about the guy that told me he would run me into the ground if he could without jeopardizing his ego. I didn't know Kenny or his background, but these guys from Oregon were supposed to be the best.

I knew I was good, but I wondered if I was good enough to stay with Kenny in the hills. Of course, I was taking Kenny's measure, too, and I would have tried to dominate him if I could. But at that moment I was mostly interested in surviving the run. The pace seemed easy enough, but we had already agreed we would stay out for two hours, which was about as long as I had ever run, and I had no idea what the hills would be like.

An Early Milking: When Kenny felt we had warmed up long enough, he said, "Let's go up *there!*" stabbing the air with a skinny arm pointed in a nearly vertical direction at the top of the nearest hill. "Hokay," I said, feigning the nonchalance of someone who'd run hills all his life. It was a muddy slope, so steep in places that we had to pull ourselves up by grabbing grass and small shrubs along the way.

I noticed immediately that Kenny took short steps on the balls of his feet. On the steepest slopes, his heels never touched the ground. He wore ripple-soled shoes that dug in to the hillside but soon became clogged with mud. When he stopped to clean them, I caught my breath and marveled at the view of a herd of cows grazing on the other side of the hill. "Let's chase them home for an early milking," Kenny said. "You take that group and I'll take the ones above." He was off immediately and the next thing I knew he had four big cows stampeding downhill in my direction. I scrambled behind a tree as Kenny hooted at my predicament.

I chalked this incident up to on-the-job training, while harboring my resentment and looking for an opportunity to get even. Letting Kenny and his herd go by, I maneuvered my way to a group of cows he had missed on his initial sweep. They were still grazing placidly, though they cast wary glances at me as I coaxed them into position above the unsuspecting Mr. Moore. Before he realized what was happening, I had my herd rumbling towards the barn in the valley below the now frantic Kenny, whose ripple-soles--which must have weighed a ton by then-- were slip-sliding for the safety of higher ground. He took his comeuppance well, as I learned he always would, and one of the patterns of our friendship was established.

A week later the team returned to Eugene, and another new acquaintance, steeplechaser Bruce Mortenson, invited me on his easy run through the hills of Hendricks Park. The first hill was only a half-mile from our dorm and it seemed that Bruce had chosen the steepest way up. Lagging behind, I gazed in wonder at the size of his bulging calf muscles. I noticed he also ran uphill on the balls of his feet, with short bouncy steps, like a roller-coaster being ratcheted to the highest point of its ride.

It was only a thirty-minute jog, but I was still recovering from my run in the hills with Kenny, and my calves were burning in protest. As Bruce and I finished the run, I realized I had some getting in shape to do if I wanted to keep up with these guys in the hills.

Making the Grade: I maintained my training as well as I could during the rest of the spring term. Being a recent transfer, I was ineligible to be on the track team so I did my own workouts or tagged along with whomever seemed to be doing something close to my ability.

My mission in coming to Oregon that spring was to earn a track scholarship for the next school year. At the end of the spring term, I ran the mile in an all-comers meet, taking the lead and pressing the pace from the half-mile point when I realized my competitors, who'd had pacing duties on the first two laps, had run too slowly. I ran a 2:03 second half and just managed to meet the 4:12 qualifying standard for a track scholarship.

The following week, I visited Bowerman in his office. I still wasn't certain whether I had my ticket back to Oregon in the fall, and somehow I felt I'd never know for sure unless I asked Bill himself. He swallowed hard, but readily confirmed my scholarship, which immediately brought me under his tutelage for the foreseeable future. However, when I asked him what I should do to train during the summer, Bowerman must have realized the impossibility of long distance coaching. "Why don't you run that hill you have over there?" he said. I had no idea what hill he was referring to, but I knew him well enough to suspect he didn't either. I said, "Diamond Head?" He said, "Yeah, that's the one. Go run

Diamond Head. You'll be okay when you get back."

I knew Diamond Head--the extinct volcanic crater at the edge of Waikiki--wasn't the hill he intended me to run. But I got the message. Do hills. I flew back to Hawaii and spent the summer running long, slow eighteen milers on a mostly flat course. Hill training was integral to the Oregon system, but I felt I needed a base of distance running at the time. And I wasn't open yet to doing long runs with hills.

My Hill: When I returned to Oregon in the fall, my perspective shifted. I had my base of stamina and I knew enough about the training process to realize I needed now to build my power in the hills. I don't recall making a conscious decision to do hill workouts, it was simply impossible to train at Oregon without being in the hills.

Eugene, Oregon is nestled at the southern end of the Willamette Valley with hills on three sides. And although the campus is in a relatively flat area, it takes only minutes to be in hilly territory. Furthermore, Bowerman wrote our training schedules, and there wasn't a day when he wouldn't have us doing something in the hills. For instance, my morning and afternoon easy runs were scheduled for a hilly course through Hendricks Park, and even my hard workouts often included periods of running in the hills, as well as on the track.

There was also a strong tradition of hill-work among the runners on the track team. My buddies told me about our famous predecessors, implying they'd become famous in part because they trained in the hills. In fact, the measure of their greatness was in having a hill named after them, such as "Burley's Hill" or "Forman's Hill." Wanting to be famous myself, I looked around for a hill I could call my own.

I found it while exploring one day along the main road through Hendricks Park. I was running past the menagerie in the upper region of the park where a narrow, inconspicuous road comes out of the forest and meets the confluence of several other roads, most of them leading downward. I had run past it many times, but now I turned and noticed how it bent immediately out of sight, swallowed by the dense foliage, but definitely heading upward.

Several runners had told me the road led nowhere, meaning it ended at the top of the hill and there were no trails out. While Kenny Moore tried to talk me out of going up there because of the legendary "wild man" who roamed the area, Bruce Mortenson and his pals scoffed at the notion of a wild man in Hendricks Park. "That's where all the lovers hang out in their cars," Bruce said. My interest peaked, I took the opportunity to explore the place. The one-lane road led to the highest point of Hendricks Park, and though it was only a few hundred yards to the top, it was steep enough beyond the initial turn to offer significant resistance to a run. There were cars with lovers in them parked in a lot at the top, but the road was clear on the way up and I immediately saw the possibilities of running intervals on it to build my power.

I usually began a hill interval there by lifting my knees as high as possible on the gentle incline around the first curve. Past that point, I shifted into a powerful bounding motion for the moderately steep middle section. My breathing soon became heavy, and the exertion felt like a fast quarter-mile on the track. I would sustain the bounding motion as long as I could, usually shagging the last fifty yards at ragged edge while doing my best to hold my form against the onset of rigormortis. I would stop before the parking lot at the top and force myself to jog immediately down. The first fifty steps, while my lungs were bursting and my legs were aching, were the toughest. The rest of the way down was a cake walk, cool and shady under a dense canopy of evergreens.

I never ran more than four of those intervals at a time. There were plenty of hills to run on the outskirts of Eugene, and I liked to make the rounds. It was a playful, two-hour run with lots of ups and downs on trails through the forests, back woods and farming areas. I ran at an easy lope most of the time, but occasionally I'd take the opportunity of an interesting hill to do several intense repeats, generally trying to simulate the specific intensity of the mile and the half-mile. The workout also took me through Laurelwood golf course, where I would run downhill intervals on a 200-yard fairway to practice getting my legs moving at a very fast tempo. At the club house end of the golf course, I would charge several times up a short, steep hill before heading back to the campus.

I did this workout throughout the autumn and winter terms, and I'm certain it built a base of leg strength which enabled me to lower my mile time to 4:06 and my half-mile to 1:51 during my junior year at Oregon. By the time I returned to Hawaii for the summer, I had become a true believer in the value of hill training.

A Summer in the Hills: The previous summer, I had run a series of long workouts every Monday, Wednesday and Friday afternoon. There were some hills in the middle section of this eighteen-mile run, but most of it was flat. Having just returned to Hawaii, I was having trouble getting back to the long-run regimen of the year before.

This would have been my third summer of training on Kalanianaole Highway, and I was tired of the cars, the noise and the exhaust fumes. Moreover, the state was widening the road that year and there was virtually no shoulder for me to run on. After several close calls with cars sweeping by at less than arm's length, I decided to change my route. I recall coming to the realization that I could do a long run, get away from traffic and combine my new love of hill training by running Waialae Iki Ridge to the top of the Koolau Mountain Range.

The Koolaus had been a live volcano at one time. As the lava flowed, a huge mountain was formed in the shape of an immense shield. As volcanic action shifted eastward along the Hawaiian Island chain, the lava cooled, the rains came and the mountain began a long process of erosion. The heavy rainfall on the northeastern side of the volcano eventually eroded that side of the mountain, forming a long, steep, windward-facing cliff. On the leeward side, there was less rain and therefore less erosion. Thus, a hundred thousand years after the last volcanic eruption on Oahu, the leeward side of the Koolaus--where I lived--was marked by finger-like ridges with deep valleys on either side that extended away from the top of the mountain range.

Waialae Iki was one of those ridges, rising from sea level to 2,000 feet in less than four miles. On my first run up the ridge, I was in awe of the ritzy houses that had sprung up in recent years. People were using the best architects and the finest materials and, unlike the standard subdivision homes I was used to in Waialae Kahala, their creations were each unique and fascinating. Above the subdivision, an old jeep trail wandered into a wind-swept meadow. It rose in stages, steep in some places and gradual in others, but always heading upward.

As I ran away from the coast towards the top of the ridge, the dry grass and shrubs turned to rain forest, with unseen birds singing exotic melodies through a screen of greenery. Running Waialae Iki was a welcome respite from the stressful highway running of the previous year and the equally stressful running of the recent track season. It was a long steep climb, however, that could have become stressful, too, if I had attacked it at ragged edge. There were a few very steep hills along the way, and I ran them hard enough to hear my breathing, but for the most part I poked along at a relaxed pace, springing gently off the balls of my feet with most of the action concentrated in the flex and extension of my ankles, not the lift of my knees or the flip of my heels.

Running up Waialae Iki Ridge was similar in exertion to the steady state runs I had done the year before. I would adjust my pace so I was breathing steadily going up. If a particular hill was steep, my actual pace would be very slow, but my pace was unimportant to my power-building purpose. I would concentrate on maintaining my form while taking short, quick steps. I worked hard getting to the top of the ridge, but the way back was a cake walk. I knew intuitively that the pounding my legs would take with fast downhill running would be injurious, so I took my time and enjoyed the view while suffering the boredom of putting one leg in front of the other for forty minutes of mild, downhill running.

I was concerned about wasting my time running downhill for such a large portion of my major workouts. Nonetheless, by the time I returned to Oregon in the fall, I'd built tremendous leg power. With virtually no speed work, I ran a 1:54 half-mile in the early fall on a muddy track through huge rain puddles. I can still recall how strong my calves and quadriceps felt as I powered away from my Oregon team-mates.

Ever since then, I have always incorporated hills in my training regimen. I'm convinced that running hills builds the power necessary for faster running. Hill training also breaks the tedium of running constantly on the flat.

Hills and Power at Fifty: In 1994, there were few things I enjoyed more about running than training in the hills. Even during my lay-off between 1986 and 1994, I had run exclusively on a 3.74-mile course that had only a few short level sections. It was an enjoyable workout, but it wasn't enough hill activity to maintain the sort of muscle power I once had.

Thus, in mid-1994, I was in the hunt again for power. After years of relatively sedentary living, I missed the power I'd had in college. Instead of bursting with strength, my calves, butt muscles and quads felt weak and hollow, and I had difficulty walking up stairs I once sprang up two-at-a-time with ease. I wanted to run Waialae Ike as I had when I was younger, but I was much more susceptible to injuries. Thus, I was forced to develop my ability in the foothills near my home.

My wife and I lived on Maunalani Heights--a few ridges west of Waialae Iki. Viewed from a distance, the face of our hill looked like a huge table top tilted at a thirty-five degree angle. It was covered with trees and homes, and bisected by Wilhelmina Rise, which rose straight as an arrow from Waialae Avenue at the bottom of the hill to Maunalani Circle at the top. Our home was situated in the middle of the hill--a mile from the top via Sierra Drive, which took a more meandering and gradual downhill route.

Everywhere there were spectacular views of Diamond Head and Waikiki, framed against the azure blue Pacific. The bottom of Mauna-lani Heights was actually the top of a massive promontory connecting Diamond Head at the ocean with the inland Koolau mountains. I was surrounded by hills and opportunities to train on them.

Building Power, Form and Balance: I stayed away from hard hill workouts until mid-September of 1994, which is after the training period described in this part of my story. Before then, I had decided to run only two hard workouts a week from April to August, and I'd passed up doing a hard hill workout in favor of a long, relatively flat run and an interval workout.

Every time I did a hard workout of any kind, the bursa of my left achilles would ache for several hours until the aspirin I took with my first post-workout meal quelled the pain. This was the same injury that had taken me out of running in 1986, and I was leery of coming down again with a more serious case of bursitis. Since hill work would have stressed the achilles bursa directly, I decided to stay away from serious hill training until September, when I could take my time about adjusting to it.

After my goal race in late August my attention shifted to ways I could prepare for Hawaii's major road races the following spring. I envisioned a four-month base-building period of high mileage, hills and intervals. And as I jumped into this new regimen, I decided to risk doing a moderate hill workout to segue into the longer hill workout I planned to do beginning in mid-September. This transition workout was a simple sixty-five-minute hill run, starting with a downhill mile from my home.

I liked running downhill at the beginning of a workout. It took little effort compared to uphill running, and since I always warmed up at mild to light exertion anyway, it didn't matter that I was running downhill. The mile to the bottom of Sierra Drive took me about twelve minutes. From there, I jogged for twenty minutes on a gently rolling course through the residential neighborhood of Kaimuki. This middle section gave me an opportunity to continue my warm-up and to prepare myself for the climb back to the top of Maunalani Heights.

I had chosen the steepest route to the top via Paula Drive, which rises nine hundred feet in less than two miles. The ascent would take twenty-five minutes--about the same time I would have spent doing intervals if I were preparing for a 10-K. I wanted my exertion on the hill to simulate the pressing effort of a 10-K, but not its rapid tempo. In other words, I was isolating the power component of the race I wanted to run. I settled into a relaxed pace on the first long incline, and despite the increased metabolic resistance I encountered, I soon felt my energy expanding. As it did, I pressed a little harder, noticing my heart rate rise from 125 to 138 bpm (see Figure 8.1). I couldn't hear my breathing at 138 bpm, but I could definitely feel the stress of the hill work on my achilles tendons, my calves and my quads.

The first few times I did the run, I had to resist the urge to attack the hill, reminding myself to relax while my body adjusted to the shock of steep uphill running. But sometimes I'd think my pace was too slow to be doing me any good, and without thinking further, I'd find myself leaning into the hill and shagging toward the top with my heels on the ground, instead of sitting back on my hips and getting up on the balls of my feet so I could bring the power in my legs into play.

Once I got my ambition into the background, however, I was able to bring back memories of old routines I'd developed years before to help me up a hill. I repeated the phrase I'd learned at Oregon, "Short and quick, short and quick," to help me balance the powerful bounding motion of my legs with the efficiency of short, quick steps. Similarly, I played with the tilt of my head to find the right measure of power and efficiency for any change in terrain. The steeper the hill, the more forward tilt I employed to get onto the balls of my feet.

At Oregon I'd discovered I could maintain my balance--as a gymnast would during a routine--by focusing on an imaginary spot on the ground six or eight feet ahead of me. Using the same technique, I was also able to see and adjust to minor bumps in the road, thereby saving myself from stumbling, which would have needlessly sapped my energy.

At the same time I thought about my running form, keeping my chest open by loosely bringing my shoulder blades together and swinging each arm back in a throwing motion to match the powerful, backward action of the opposite leg.

I kept my hands close to my chest, moving them in a relaxed, curving arc from just below my sternum to just below my lowest rib.

I visualized myself as an elite athlete leading the pack on heartbreak hill in the Boston Marathon.

Figure 8.1: Hills and Heart Rate.

Heart Rate Ranges as Percent of Maximum:

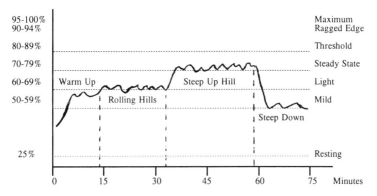

There is no characteristic heart rate structure to hill training, except that downhill running should be at a considerably lower heart rate than uphill running. In this workout, I ran downhill during the first twelve minutes, and on gently rolling terrain during the next twenty minutes while I completed my warm-up at light exertion. About thirty-two minutes into the run I started up a long steep hill which took twenty-six minutes. I held my heart rate down to mid-steady state on the hill by running at a very slow pace. My heart rate dropped precipitously during the last eleven minutes because I followed a steep downhill route from the top of the hill to my home.

Hill Running in Perspective: These mental and physical routines worked on several levels, not only to maintain my physical balance but my psychological balance as well.

I'd often thought that competitive running was mostly a game of balancing my ambition with my sense of play. As long as I could play with the structure of my workouts, or even my running form, I could keep from becoming obsessed with winning my next race.

Still, I often found it emotionally difficult to accept that I could build my muscle power by running slowly. I could recall training in the hills during the early eighties when I had sometimes acted as if I was still at Oregon training for the mile. I would slip unconsciously into forcing my pace.

But I could only force it for a short time before my effort became a burden. Though I was capable of withstanding a lot of burdensome running, I would eventually take myself out of it with an injury, a cold, or a seemingly unrelated accident. I recall injuring myself several times before I finally learned to regard burdensome running as a sign of impending doom.

At the start of 1994, I'd resolved to avoid burdensome running. I wanted to enjoy my training or at least be satisfied with it, so I held myself back as I ran to the top of Maunalani Heights. Even though it would take a few minutes longer to reach the top, a slower pace would decrease the threat of injury, while making a major difference in my attitude. Whenever I approached 160 bpm, I could hear my breathing, and the effort definitely began to wear on me. But I could remain relaxed at 150 bpm, so I decided to use that as an upper limit for the run.

There was a flat area at the top of the heights, and I could have amazed myself with my speed by applying as much muscle power on the flat as I had in coming to the top. I resisted the urge to sprint, however, because I wasn't warmed up for tempo running. I jogged the flat area and heading down by the shortest, steepest route to my home.

My downhill pace was quicker than my uphill pace, but soon my heart rate was registering thirty or forty beats per minute less than it had coming up. To my way of thinking, the workout had ended at the top of the hill, and now I wanted to get home, take a shower and get on with my day.

Chapter Eight Synopsis:

- **The Main Issue:** How can I structure workouts to build leg strength for faster running?

■ **Concepts:**

1) Power is the ability to run at race pace using every major leg muscle, and without undue quickness in leg turnover.[9]

2) Your "sense of power" is the relative degree of effort you generate while running, measured as: gentle, held back, relaxed, pressed, forced, or strained

3) "Striding" refers to the length and tempo of your steps while running. "Overstriding" occurs when your heel lands before your lower leg has become perpendicular to the ground.

■ **Theoretical Tenets:**

1) To be effective in distance running you'll need a stride that balances power and efficiency. A quick, efficient stride is essential when you have to compete at long distances, and the more power you have the more ground you'll cover with each stride.

2) The power muscles are the prime movers on the back of the legs and butt, including the calves, the ham strings and the gluteals. Certain types of exercises build strength in these muscles, including squats, lunges and stair climbing. But the best strengthening exercise is running uphill.

3) You don't have to run uphill at race pace. The hill itself offers sufficient resistance to simulate the sense of power you'll experience in the race, even while you are running at a relatively slow pace.

4) Correct running form is important in the hills because poor form is exaggerated when you isolate the power component, and poor running form leads to inefficient running, as well as injuries.

5) You can practice faster running without having built a prior base of power, but you might leave yourself vulnerable to injuries because you may not have the leg strength yet to sustain a faster pace.

---

[9] Notice how a good runner appears to be relaxed and within himself at a relatively fast pace, while a weaker runner appears to be forcing the pace and moving his legs at a faster tempo to keep up.

■ **Principles:**

1) Cumulative Stress: You can build power and tempo in the same training cycle, as long as you realize that both activities stress the same muscles, and thereby increase your risk of injury. It's especially risky to try to run uphill at an up-tempo pace.

2) Power and Specificity: Your hill work should prepare you for the specific power of the race you want to run. To find this sense of power, you would have to pay strict attention to the power component of exertion while running your race, and duplicate that sense of power in your hill training.

■ **Relationships:**

1) The shorter and faster your racing distance, the more power you'll need for effective racing.

2) The longer your racing distance, the less power you'll use with each stride. On the other hand, the longer the race the more power you'll need to keep from losing your running form as fatigue sets in.

3) The longer and steeper a hill, the slower your training pace should be to stay within adaptive limits.

4) The longer your race, the slower and longer you should run uphill to simulate the power of the race you want to run.

5) The steeper the hill, the closer your running comes to simulating the bio-mechanics of fast running.

6) The more power you have, the longer your stride will be at any given tempo.

■ **Questions and Answers:**

1) Why should I run hills?

The main training purpose of uphill running is to build leg strength for racing. However, variety is the spice of life, and hills can also make a run interesting and enjoyable by forcing you to adjust your pace and form to changes in terrain.

2) How can I get a sense of power on a hill?

Focus on whether the your effort is gentle, held back, relaxed, pressed, forced, or strained. The longer the hill, the lighter the effort should be. Under no circumstances should you strain in training.

3) How does power convert to pace?

Try running an uphill course at approximately 75% of your maximum heart rate. Then notice how much faster you run at the same heart rate when you're running on the flat. The hill isolates the power component of the race you want to run, while forcing you to run at a relatively slow pace. Once you are stronger in the hills, you can be faster on the flats because you can take a longer stride at the same tempo as before.

4) How fast should I run uphill?

Race-specific uphill running should be fast enough to simulate the specific sensation of power you'll experience in the race you want to run. The shorter the race, the more power you must generate, even up to forcing the pace if you're a miler.

If you are building a base of power with long duration hill running, however, then your pace should be slow enough for you to run for a long time without becoming burdened by the effort, regardless of your racing distance.

5) How do I know when I'm running hills too hard?

You are running too hard if you are getting injured, if you find the effort burdensome, or if you are afraid of repeating the hill workout.

6) What is good running form?

Good running form begins with a relatively quick, efficient stride. Pick your feet up and put them down quickly, instead of letting them drag out behind or forcing them to reach ahead for the longest possible stride. The more power you have, the longer your stride will be without appearing to overstride.

Learn to play with the tilt of your hips and head to find the right balance of power and efficiency for your particular racing distance and the type of terrain you encounter. For example, the steeper the uphill, the more you should tilt your head forward so you can bring your calf muscles into play by getting up on the balls of your feet.

Let your legs do the work. Your arms have little to do with forward movement, so avoid reaching out or "punching" with your arms. Bring your thumbs up to your sternum and back to your lowest rib in a vigorous, yet relaxed and easy, arc. Keep your gaze down on the road a few meters ahead to assist with maintaining your balance.

7) Is there any value to downhill running?

Unless you are training for a downhill race, downhill running is next to worthless for building racing ability because you can't get your heart rate up without running dangerously fast. Downhill running increases the risk of injury due to excessive pounding. If you are running downhill to practice faster leg turnover, it's best to do it on a grassy course that reduces the shock of landing.

8) How do I know when I have enough power?

Some runners have strong legs and a long powerful stride. If you were a sprinter in high school, you may be in this category. Otherwise, you can probably benefit from building power in the hills. Rather than asking when you have enough power, ask how much time you have to build some added power.

9) How can I structure my hard workouts to build leg strength for faster running?

A lot depends on the hills you have to run on. Obviously, you'll have to "make do" with whatever hilly terrain your surroundings offer.

Assuming you haven't run hills before, begin with short and easy hills inserted within an easy workout. Once you are adapted to this as a regimen, you can build to a series of rolling hills within a long run.

Next, if you have a mountain nearby, do a forty to eighty minute run to the top, and then jog back down. You shouldn't hear your breathing on a run like this. Just go at a slow pace and concentrate on good running form.

Once you have increased your basic strength on a long hill, set up another workout doing hill repeats at a pace that's quick enough that you can almost hear your breathing. The slope should be just steep enough that your heels kiss the ground and lift off lightly. In other words, you are landing mostly on the balls of your feet. The longer your race, the longer these repeats may be, up to four or five minutes.

Chapter Nine
Stamina--The Base Ability

It was one of those proverbial "pea soup" foggy days in Oregon. Steeplechaser Bob Williams and I were sharing a fifteen-mile run on the farming roads around Spencer's Butte outside of Eugene. It was beautiful country, but we saw only the shadows of nearby objects through the grayness, chatting as we ran and heartened to have one another for company on such a dismal afternoon.

We were there to witness an incredible feat of mental toughness. At that moment--approaching us somewhere in the fog ahead--Kenny Moore was in the final stages of a thirty-mile run. Thirty miles seemed like a long way to Bob and me, but not an impossible distance. I had run twenty-four miles on my long run the week before. What was notable about Kenny's run, however, was the way he was doing it. That week he had declared his intention to start at the fire hydrant in front of MacArthur Court, run fifteen miles around Spencer's Butte, touch the fire hydrant and run the butte again.

Bruce Mortenson and his buddies on the track team were outraged. They disliked Kenny for his defiant style. While they were secretive about their own training, Kenny was open and cocky. He took pleasure in provoking a reaction. One of his favorite ploys was to do more hanging-bar pull-ups than any of the UO football players, much to their embarrassment. And his present challenge to the runners on the track team was another case in point. He relished an opportunity to make them squirm, and this time he had struck a sensitive cord. If they spurned Kenny for his brashness, he disdained them for their "weakness of spirit." None of them were weaklings. (Bruce would win the national championship in the steeplechase that year.) They simply seemed intolerably wishy-washy to the stouthearted Kenny Moore.

Bob and I were constantly entertained by this clash of personalities. I liked Kenny and I liked the others, but I didn't take sides. I appreciated an outstanding performance and, in this case, Kenny was challenging the runners on the team to a truly demanding performance. Imagine how difficult it would be psychologically to run a fifteen-mile loop, and then to turn around and have to run it again.

By contrast, once a runner makes it to the fifteen-mile point of an out-and-back course, he has no choice--psychologically--but to run back. But running two fifteen-mile loops presents an unavoidable moment of decision--to run it again as Kenny proposed, or to head for the showers. This was a moment only the most resolute could savor.

We Miss Our Turn: Bob and I had dispensed with these concerns early in our run, and were enjoying another line of talk when we saw Kenny's orange cap emerge from the fog ahead. A moment later the rest of him took form--the light-blue wind breaker and the green cotton long-johns that were standard issue to all the runners on the team. He was there and past us before we could say a word--a ghostly figure scattering gravel with his footfall on the unimproved road.

We had timed our run to pass Kenny beyond the point of no return on his second loop, so we knew in that moment what he'd accomplished. We were silent for several minutes before continuing our conversation. Darkness was rapidly falling, and with the fog hampering our vision and the discussion occupying our thoughts, we completely missed the turn which would have taken us back around the butte to Eugene. We knew we were in trouble when we asked for directions to Eugene and a farmer shouted back, "It's straight ahead." We had gone so far beyond our turn that, now, the shortest way back was to complete a much longer loop around the butte than we'd intended.

By the time we got back to Bob's apartment, we reckoned we had run nearly as far that afternoon as Kenny had. But as I continued on to my dorm, I realized the two runs were in no way psychologically comparable. Bob and I might have matched Kenny's mileage, but neither of us was willing to brag about our accomplishment or the embarrassing circumstances surrounding it.

I had one more weekend before the end of the fall term, however, and I decided to test myself by running twice around the butte. I kept my goal to myself. To have declared my intention publicly would have required more clarity and confidence than I could muster.

Acting on My Resolve: It was raining when I headed out the following Sunday afternoon. This was my eighth consecutive week of running the same three-mile approach to the Spencer's Butte loop. I was bored with the streets along the way, but I was definitely challenged by the thought of what I was about to do.

I had discovered early in the game that a long run could be a piece of cake if I started at light exertion. I took my time, even holding myself back as I ran past the cemetery on the long Willamette Street hill. From the highest point of the loop, the road curves and undulates like a roller coaster through beautiful ranching areas with nothing but an occasional tethered horse, an angry watchdog, and tall evergreens for company.

On my longest previous workout around Spencer's Butte, I had gone around the nine-mile loop that encircles the butte, then I'd doubled back on the loop again. That made eighteen miles, and the addition of the three-mile approach and return legs made a total of twenty-four. I figured the easiest way to run my 30-mile distance was to duplicate my previous run, then double back with the approach and return legs. It would be tough enough, I thought, with rain pouring down and night setting in, to turn around at Mac Court--having done twenty-four miles--and repeat the boring six-mile distance out to the butte loop and back. At the time, I was most concerned with taking the path of least mental resistance.

Nevertheless, I can recall the feeling of exhilaration that came over me when I finally headed back from the butte, splashing deliberately into the biggest puddles to punctuate the victory I was claiming for myself. I had run a measured thirty miles, the culmination of months of training begun the previous June with a steady regimen of three 18-milers a week. Throughout the fall term, I had been building my long Sunday runs from the basic fifteen on my schedule to the twenty-four I had run two weeks previously. I was definitely pleased with my accomplishment.

Reality Sets In: The next day, Kenny caught up with me on my afternoon recovery run. Bob was the only person I had told about my thirty-miler, but Kenny had heard immediately that I had done the butte twice and he wanted to know *how* I had done it. I told him the truth about saving the approach and return legs for last. "That's not the same," he said. "I know," was my reply.

It would never be the same. The following year, I returned to Oregon after a summer of doing long hill runs in Hawaii. They were tough workouts, but they were not the same as the 18-milers I had done the previous summer. My calves and quadriceps were very powerful, but I was afraid I didn't have the base of stamina that had been the foundation of my strength and confidence the previous year. Then I

compounded my concern by jumping immediately into a thirty-mile run--
as if I could pick up where I had left off the year before. I was doomed
from the get-go, injuring myself during the run just enough to hamper
further progress.

Since then, I've come to believe that competitive running is
fundamentally an adventure in personal learning. My times had
improved in high school and college because I'd had excellent coaching
and because, from year to year, I had learned the lessons running had to
teach me. When I took myself out of running in 1966, I still had more
to learn from the sport. Years later, as a coach and a runner, I realized
my experience at UO had taught me many of the realities of distance
running.

In my marathon training program, I would share what I'd learned,
orienting my runners to the technique of building stamina. Ironically, in
my own training I often had to relearn old lessons. The following story
from my comeback in 1994 illustrates the pitfalls of disregarding the
physiology of marathon running.

Facing Up to a Lack of Stamina: Endurance racing requires a
solid base of stamina--the ability to run for a long time at light to steady
state exertion. Even as a miler at Oregon, I never regretted spending
half the year doing long slow runs of 105 minutes or more several times
a week. But in the spring of 1994, stamina was only one of several
racing abilities I needed to build, and I was struggling with the question
of which to focus on first.

I had recently purchased an excellent book, which was helpful in
solving this problem. Entitled, *Oxygen Power: Performance Tables for
Distance Runners,*[10] it was written by noted coach and physiologist Jack
Daniels, whom I had recently met. Jack had been graciously willing to
share his extensive knowledge about the training process, and in
discussing the problem of which abilities to build first, he'd suggested I
compare my racing performances in relation to performance standards in
his book. I discovered that my time of 19:12 for the Pro-Bowl 5-K I'd

---

[10] *Oxygen Power, Performance Tables for Distance Runners,* by Jack
Daniels and Jimmy Gilbert, for copies or information write Oxygen Power, P.O.
Box 5062, Cortland, NY 13045.

run in early February rated a 52.3 on Daniels' performance tables.[11] However, even after two more months of training, my time of 63:20 for the Tamanaha Memorial 15-K rated only a 50.2. Thus my 5-K was a relatively better performance than my 15-K.

My nemesis, Candy Smiley, had beat me by a minute in the 15-K. Yet I'd come in a few seconds ahead of her in the 5-K two months earlier. There was no doubt in my mind that we had different abilities. My natural gift was speed, so I was most competitive at racing distances between the mile and the 5-K. At progressively longer racing distances, however, I lost my competitive advantage to runners who either had greater distance running talent or a better base of stamina. During the early part of my comeback, Candy and I had done a two-hour run in the hills and I'd had great difficulty keeping up with her. She'd been doing long runs consistently for the previous several years, while I hadn't run longer than thirty-five minutes in eight years.

Based on the Daniels tables and my performances relative to Candy, I reckoned I still had speed, but I couldn't use it to sustain a competitive pace in a race longer than a 5-K. Knowing I would need a better base of stamina for the races I wanted to run in the summer of 1994, I decided to commit myself to a training regimen of long runs. My goal was to do them once a week for seven weeks, after which I would assess the effect they'd had on the Hard Rock 10-K I aimed to run in mid-June.

Setting Up the Long Run: Having set a general direction for building my stamina, I was ready to decide how long and how fast to run. Looking back from the perspective of several months, I can see the pitfalls I brought to the project: my personal history and misconceptions about the training process, as well as my current ambitions, anxieties and insecurities.

Training is rarely a simple matter of running textbook-perfect workouts. Each of us brings our mental baggage to the game, which makes competitive running fascinating and dynamic. Eighteen miles, for instance, had been my standard long-run distance during my previous forays into competitive running, and even as a fifty year-old, I still wanted to run eighteen miles on my long runs. I was certain I could run

---

[11] The higher the number, the greater a runner's aerobic capacity. The best runners have numbers in the seventies.

the distance, but I wasn't willing to run it at a significantly slower pace than I had years before. I was vested in looking good, knowing I'd be running in plain view of hundreds of passersby.

In addition, I felt myself in competition with an associate who--though in a younger age group--was someone over whom I had enjoyed racing dominance more than a decade earlier. He was now racing successfully, with 10-K times several minutes faster than mine. His training secret, he had told me, was a series of bi-weekly eighteen-mile runs he had done over a period of six weeks. He said he had started each eighteen-miler with an easy pace during the first nine miles, building the effort during the last nine and finishing with a rapid, pressing tempo. I was considering using his regimen as a training model, but I had my doubts about my ability to build to a rapid tempo during the second half of an eighteen miler, no matter what the pace on the first nine.

I was also very ambitious. It was mid-April of 1994, and I had run three races since early February, placing in the top four of my age division in each. Nonetheless, I was still several minutes behind the best fifty year-olds, and I could see I had my work cut out for me if I were to win my age division in a major race before the end of the summer. I was willing to put in the work, but my compulsive desire to succeed from the get-go definitely conflicted with the path of moderation.

Training Long by Feeling: With the exception of a recent two-hour run in the hills with Candy, I was in uncharted territory as I headed out for my first solo long run. I had decided to do a double out-and-back course around Diamond Head. Running out and back twice would minimize my chances of having to run a long way back if I misjudged my energy and became unexpectedly fatigued in the middle of the run.

In spite of my history of exceeding my limits at the start of a training regimen, and in spite of my strong desire to complete eighteen miles my first time out, I held myself back to thirteen and a half miles the first day, feeling satisfied to run that far and no more. The workout took two hours and three minutes, and I felt moderately fatigued at the finish. The next week, I ran two miles farther in 2:15, feeling tired at the finish, though not quite at a point of total collapse. I chalked up my fatigue to being low on stamina, and I expected that to change soon.

During these first two long runs, I had paced myself in relation to hazy memories of long runs in my former years of training. I was

carrying my heart rate monitor with the intention of observing my heart
rate for a few runs before establishing an "appropriate" heart rate
structure for the workout. Ironically, I knew I should do the same thing
I tell my marathoners, "Warm up for an hour at a pace that's slow
enough to talk casually with a friend." But as I got into the first two
runs, that effort seemed too slow compared to the effort my ambition and
vanity were dictating in the moment.

And since I could feel myself developing ample energy early in the
run, I reckoned I'd be able to complete two hours at that pace. I was
correct on that score, but I hadn't considered the intangibles. There was
a measured mile about twenty minutes into the workout and I couldn't
resist my desire to run it at a "respectable" pace. As I ran, I kept an eye
on my heart rate monitor, and noticed the readings were creeping up to
150 bpm, which was mid-steady state for me and definitely high enough
to allay casual conversation. Seeing what was happening to my heart
rate and intuiting that my effort--still in the first half-hour of the run--
was too hard to sustain for two hours, I consciously backed off a few
beats per minute, all the while feeling the conflict between the time I
wanted for the measured mile and my better judgement.

The slightly slower pace notwithstanding, I became increasingly
fatigued during the last half-hour of the workout, and I had to slow down
to mid-light exertion. Afterward, I felt uneasy with the way my effort
had progressed, and also with the way my running energy had failed to
develop during the middle of the run. But I was finding it difficult to
respond appropriately through the static of my ambition.

My pride still wouldn't let me accept thirteen miles as the better
distance for me to run than eighteen, especially at that point in my
comeback and at the level of exertion I was choosing to run. My lack
of self-honesty on this issue was soon to become a source of trouble.

Hitting the Wall: I was ready for a hard workout as I started my
third long run, and my heart rate followed the same early pattern it had
during the previous workouts. Since I still had ample energy as I started
my second out-and-back loop, and in spite of knowing my energy had
been flagging at the end of the two previous runs, I decided to try for
eighteen miles.

I probably could have run the full distance without crashing, but not
at steady state. I still couldn't appreciate how high that level of exertion
was. But as I pressed beyond ninety minutes, I could sense my attitude

deteriorating.   Up to that point, I hadn't particularly enjoyed the workout, but now I could feel a shift from barely satisfied to burdened. My ambition was leading me into dangerous waters, and--sure enough-- two hours into the run and four miles from home, I suddenly ran out of energy (see Figure 9.1).

Figure 9.1: Hitting the Wall

**Heart Rate Ranges as
Percent of Maximum:**

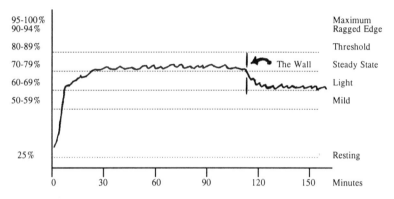

I started this long run with too much effort. And
though I had enough energy to sustain steady state
through the first hundred minutes, my energy was
definitely flagging by the two-hour mark. Since the
graph shows my effort, but not my energy, the "wall"
is only apparent in that my heart rate dropped to low-
light exertion during the last thirty minutes. That was
all the effort I was able to sustain without excruciating
discomfort in my arms, legs, and torso.

Heavy-legged and sluggish, I was forced to trudge four miles back, with my heart rate slowed to 124-128 beats per minute and my pace at eleven minutes a mile. Other runners were sweeping past me and there was no way I could have stayed with them. I tried once to pick up the pace to see what would happen to my heart rate. It went up slightly as my pace increased, but the burning in my arms and legs immediately escalated from tolerable to intolerable and I had to back off, as it was all I could do to keep from being overwhelmed by extreme fatigue.

Without a doubt, I had bitten off more than I could chew, yet I was convinced my experience was an aberration. I had hit the wall because I'd extended the distance of the long run before I was able to. Thus, the following week, I backed off to 13.5 miles, running it in two hours, while keeping my heart rate to the previously established pattern. And I finished with little energy.

I thought I was fatigued because I was out of shape. It still hadn't occurred to me that I might be breaking the first rule of distance running: Don't go out too fast. I would need graphic evidence before submitting to a more moderate approach to building stamina.

The First Rule of Distance Running: I was feeling lazy from some tough interval training as I started the long run the following week. But I decided to do it anyway, reckoning I'd have enough energy to last a while, though I didn't expect to perform well because I had significantly less energy than at the start of the previous runs, and I anticipated running out of it even sooner.

Nonetheless, I was committed to running for two hours, so I held myself back to mild exertion for most of the first half-hour. This was definitely an easier starting effort than during the previous runs. And since I continued having only some energy, I kept my effort mostly on the low side of light exertion for the next thirty minutes. Then, an hour into the run, my energy suddenly and unexpectedly improved.

I was going up the steep approach to Diamond Head and I'll be darned if I didn't begin feeling ample energy. I was tempted to pick up the pace, but with another hour to go I was wary of collapsing, so I held myself back. Ninety minutes into the run, however, I still felt ready to hold a harder effort so I increased it to the mid-range of steady state. The way my energy had developed during this run was the exact opposite of my several previous long runs, when I had felt ready to run hard almost from the outset but began running out of energy between ninety minutes and two hours.

When I got home, I printed out a composite graph of my heart rate for my previous workouts (see Figure 9.2). The graphic evidence indicated a major difference between my most recent workout and the run when I hit the wall. I had to acknowledge a tangibly improved sensation of energy as a result of going out slower on the recent run. It was as if my muscles had been suddenly greased with energy. After an hour at a slow pace, everything had begun to flow with power.

Figure 9.2: Finish Strong or Finish Weak.

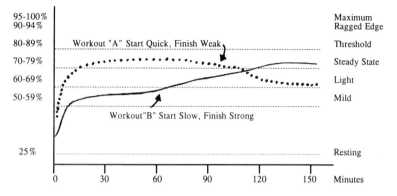

**Heart Rate Ranges as
Percent of Maximum:**

In workout "A" (the dotted line) I started at light to
steady state exertion and finished by struggling in at
light exertion. In workout "B" I started at mild to
light exertion--a slower pace--but I had enough energy
during the last fifty minutes to raise my effort into
steady state. By going out slowly, I not only con-
served my energy, I expanded it during the second
hour to the point where I *enjoyed* running at steady
state. By contrast, I was barely satisfied with my
exertion early in workout "A" and I found the effort
late in the run to be oppressive.

As I thought about my experience, I could see an application for my
new heart rate monitor. I had purchased the model with an alarm feature
that would tell me whenever I ran outside of two pre-set heart rate
ranges. I had thus far resisted the idea of using the alarm to determine
my level of exertion--not knowing what I was doing, for one thing--but
also because I insisted on indulging my ingrained preference for training
as I wanted, rather than letting reason and a machine dictate my pace.
I was quickly coming to the opinion, however, that using the monitor's
"bells and whistles" would be an excellent way to discipline myself to a
workable long-run effort.

I had to correct my habit--acquired from recent years of running
much shorter workouts--of pressing the pace from as early as ten or

fifteen minutes into a run. During subsequent long runs, I set the first alarm range to tell me when I was outside of light exertion. It would beep reassuringly early in the run to tell me I was warming up at mild exertion. The beeping would stop as I slipped into light exertion and remain quiescent for the rest of the first hour as long as my heart rate didn't rise above 125 beats per minute. After that, I could simply press a button and shift to the second alarm range, assuming I felt ready to run at a higher level of exertion until the finish.

Using this technique to manage my pace, I became increasingly energetic during the second hour of subsequent long runs. The better I felt the harder I could run, even to the point of picking up my effort to the top of my steady state range, while still not running out of energy before two hours.

Long Runs in Perspective: Some of my associates, when looking at Figure 9.2, have commented that I must have become fatigued during the second hour of workout "B", otherwise my heart rate wouldn't have risen so dramatically. Actually, the opposite was true. I became increasingly energetic and capable of handling a harder effort through the workout, especially after the first hour at light exertion.

Of course, I was definitely becoming fatigued during the last thirty minutes, with my fatigue showing up in various ways. Whenever I resumed running after a water break, for instance, I found it difficult to build my effort up again. My feet would slap the pavement and my legs would feel logy. And I'd also be tired on my easy runs for the next day or so. Nonetheless, going out very slowly had allowed my capacity for exertion to expand to the point that even as I became fatigued late in the run, I still had more energy available than I'd had previously.

Unfortunately, this capacity for faster, harder running wasn't always there. Sometimes during subsequent long runs I would go out slowly, expecting my energy to develop during the second hour of a run, and I'd be distressed to find myself remaining physically and emotionally flat. I'd blame it on the weather, inadequate rest, insufficient carbohydrate loading, or the stars, but when my energy wasn't flowing I knew that picking up the pace would only be exhaustive. Indeed, I found it downright difficult to run hard when I wasn't feeling ready to do so. At such moments I simply kept a light, slow pace until the finish, without getting down on myself for something I couldn't help.

For similar reasons, I eventually decided to forget about running eighteen-milers until I'd established my capacity to run with strength and confidence for two hours. In reflecting on my personal history, I realized that two-hour runs had been a constant in my training, dating back to when I was twenty and could cover twenty miles in a little more than two hours. Later, in my mid-thirties, I was doing eighteen miles in the same time frame. And as a fifty year-old, I would have to live with running an even shorter distance in two hours.

Nevertheless, I expected my stamina to grow as a result of the two-hour regimen, and at some point I would use that added energy to extend the duration of my long runs to eighteen miles. Also, I was confident the long runs would form a base from which I'd be able to run shorter, faster workouts more in line with my racing goals. I had a way to go, but I was beginning to accept my current ability and I was enjoying the prospect of watching it grow.

Chapter Nine Synopsis:

■ **The Main Issue:** How can I structure workouts to build a base of stamina? How should I pace myself for a long race like the marathon?

■ **Concepts:**

1) Stamina is the ability to run for long duration at light exertion. ("Long" is defined as that point in a light exertion, hard/ready workout when fatigue sets in.)[12]

2) "Base work" refers to exertion that is lower level than race exertion. Thus, a "base workout" is generally slower than race specific running. Base work can include long runs, as well as hill and tempo training, or even easy recovery running.

3) "Marathoning" refers to training for the marathon distance of 26.2 miles, which is generally considered long to very long duration, depending on your natural ability.

---

[12] There is nothing wrong with using the term "endurance" to mean stamina. I prefer to give separate meanings to the two words, using endurance to imply *uncomfortable* race exertion instead of mere staying power.

■ **Theoretical Tenets:** The game of marathoning can be summed up in one word: pacing. You must have the patience to go slowly at the beginning of a run when you feel you can go a lot faster. Here's why:

1) Your body runs on two types of fuel: fat and glycogen (which is a kind of sugar). Most people can store enough fat to survive the marathon. But even well-trained athletes cannot store more than 90 minutes worth of glycogen for race-pace running. The only reason you can survive a three- to five-hour run is that you can run for a long time on a *combination* of fat and glycogen.

2) When you are out of glycogen you hit the wall, which is no fun. You'll feel so fatigued that you won't be able to maintain your pace. Even walking can feel like drudgery. The trick is to conserve your glycogen by running slowly at the start of every run.

3) It takes about an hour for your body to completely turn on fat metabolism. Meanwhile, it burns a lot of glycogen. The faster you run, the more glycogen you burn. This is true for the beginning, middle or end of a run, but especially the beginning.

4) After an hour of light exertion running, you can pick up the pace while maintaining light exertion for a much longer time than you could have if you went out at a quicker pace.

■ **Relationships:**

1) The longer your racing distance, the more stamina you'll need to race effectively.

2) The longer the duration of a workout, the lighter your exertion needs to be to stay within the bounds of adaptive training.

3) The more adapted you are to a base training regimen, the more energy you'll have for running shorter faster workouts during the sharpening phase of training.

■ **Questions and Answers:**

1) What's the difference between stamina and endurance?

    Stamina is the ability to run long and slow. Endurance is the ability to sustain uncomfortable race exertion. When you use these abilities as defined, you create two distinct running experiences (see chapter 11).

    For example, if you do a long, slow workout, "slow" means that you run comfortably, and "long" means that you end the workout before fatigue-related discomfort becomes a major factor. Therefore, endurance never becomes an issue, unless you happen to define long/slow running as endurance running.

    On the other hand, if you are running at an uncomfortable level of exertion, it doesn't matter how long you run because "uncomfortable" is uncomfortable. And the longer you sustain uncomfortable exertion, the more unpleasantness you have to endure.

2) How much stamina do I need?

    This is one of the most hotly debated issues in running. The trend in the United States is to focus on short, intense workouts. But U.S. runners have not shown well in international marathons for some years now.

    I believe in building a broad base of stamina, no matter what your racing distance. A broad base means fourteen or more workouts and fourteen or more hours of running a week. The faster you are, the more miles you'll cover--up to 140 or more miles per week for elite athletes.

    Of course, it's difficult to race effectively when your mileage is high. You've got to cut back on mileage after having adapted to your base milage before you can reap the benefits of enormous stamina. At this point, with your energy high, it makes sense to run workouts at higher levels of exertion.

The real question is how much stamina do you need for what racing distance? Obviously, if you are a marathoner or an ultra marathoner, you'll need more stamina than someone training for the mile.

3) Of the five racing abilities, which should I focus on building first?

To some extent, this depends on how much you want to race well immediately. Intense training will rapidly develop your inherent ability. But you'll eventually reach a plateau beyond which you'll see little or no adaptive progress.

On the other hand, the higher your mileage, the slower you'll race initially because you'll be so tired from your mileage that you won't have the energy to train at the necessary, race specific levels (see part four). If you have time and patience, however, it makes sense to build your stamina before moving on to other abilities. Eventually, you'll race faster if you have built a huge base of stamina.

Your training should proceed in periods. The first might be a base building period of mostly long, slow running in the hills and flats. The next period could include shorter hills and tempo training, and the next might focus on race specific tempo running, speed work, endurance training and tune-up races. During a peak racing period, you would cut back on hard training and focus on moderate, up-tempo efforts and major races.

Your objective during each training period would be to develop race-specific abilities. This involves adapting to the stress of training effort, which is the subject of part four.

4) How can I structure a long workout to build my stamina?

Stamina is the ability to run long and slow. "Slow" is the operative word. The issue of how long to run will take care of itself once you've slowed down to at least light exertion.

If, for example, you can discipline yourself to jog at your fastest walking pace, you can probably build to two hours within several weeks. But this pace will seem very slow--too slow for some athletes to tolerate. Nonetheless, if you can run for two hours at that pace, your stamina will grow and you'll eventually be able to run a little faster. (Note: two hours is a long run for some athletes, so do them regularly, but not more often than once a week at first.)

No matter how good an athlete you are, you should discipline yourself to run the first hour of a long run at your slow tempo. That's light exertion, which is between 60 and 70 percent of maximum heart rate. Slow means conversational breathing. If you are talking to someone and you hear a "huff" in your conversation, you are running at 70 to 80% of maximum, which is too hard.

The toughest part of running long is to maintain your light exertion, slow pace until you have become moderately fatigued. At that point, you will have run a hard workout. The more stamina you have, the longer you will have run. If you aren't used to running for two hours in a workout, that should be your first objective. Even if you are an out-of-shape jogger, you can jog for two hours within several weeks of starting a base building regimen, as long as you are willing to run slowly.

Be willing to repeat the workout, looking at your results. Remember, you should be able to recover from a long, hard run in 48 to 60 hours, just as you do from your shorter hard workouts.

Chapter Ten
Tempo Intervals

Most of my novice runners associate interval training with intensity and heavy breathing. They've heard that they aren't doing intervals correctly unless they are pounding an oval track, so they're generally surprised to discover that interval training in my system consists initially of comfortable running in a pastoral setting.

I'm grateful to Stan Hattie, my coach at the University of Hawaii, who got me away from running intervals exclusively on the track. When I joined the UH track team in 1963, Hattie was training milers on a grassy quarter-mile straightaway in scenic Kapiolani Park. Our small group of runners did twenty quarters twice a week on that course, with Hattie standing stoically at one end calling out times as we finished.

Alan Birtles was our fastest miler and the center on the UH basketball team. When Birtles was there, he decided when we were ready to start each interval. With Hattie standing at the other end of the straightaway, the six-foot-six-inch Birtles would slowly raise his arm and we'd come to a set position on either side of him. Then with a long, sweeping motion he'd signal the start and we were off.

As we approached Hattie, he could often tell exactly what our pace was by seeing how fast we were running. Once at the end of a workout we decided to run an all-out quarter--unbeknownst to Hattie. As we approached him, he could see we were running a lot faster than usual, but when he looked at his watch for confirmation, our times were several seconds *slower* than he expected. A quarter-mile was far enough away that he couldn't distinguish our forward motion at the start. We had fooled him by running in place for several seconds, laughing like kids in anticipation of the look of astonishment we knew to expect on Hattie's face.

My runners and I have run thousands of intervals on Hattie's quarter-mile straightaway. Even in my third competitive comeback since the early sixties, there were few activities I found more invigorating than running ten to sixteen quarters at a brisk tempo on the grass in Kapiolani Park.

The course is nestled in the lee of Diamond Head with banyan and kiawe trees all around. A root snakes out from a tree at one end, and runners who finish the quarter there are treated to a panoramic view of the distant Koolau mountain range with its emerald valleys and majestic ridges shimmering in the late afternoon sun. At the other end of the straightaway, the park comes to a point at the confluence of several well-traveled thoroughfares. There, the endless flow of passersby adds human interest to the run.

The grass is usually short enough for fast running yet long enough to offer protection from injuries due to pounding. In the early years, I always ran barefoot--braving occasional encounters with half-inch kiawe thorns. By the 1980s, the thorny keawe trees were gone, but the grass had patches of nasty stickers so I used a pair of shoes without heels to simulate the feeling of running on the balls of my feet. I had experienced the grass in many states of growth, from short and dusty to long, thick and luxurious. I preferred the feeling of my feet striking hard ground like a tightly-strung racket hitting a new tennis ball.

Occasionally, we've had to skirt around outfielders playing softball on a nearby field, but usually we've had the course to ourselves. And although there were minor grooves and bumps along the way, wary beginners could keep their balance by watching an imaginary spot on the ground ahead.

Sometimes during stormy weather, we had to spot on the surface of puddles so large it was easier to run through them than around. I used to love the sensation of hitting the water bare-footed, of feeling it fly apart in a glorious splash.

Tempo Training for Beginners: I've always introduced my novice runners to tempo training on Hattie's quarter-mile straightaway. My 1994 New Year 10-K training program, with twenty-five runners in it, was no exception.

During our first interval workout, I taught them the basics of where to start and finish, how to time themselves and how to measure their heart rate. This was the easy part, as pacing is always more difficult to teach.

Prior to their first interval workout, I'd had them run a low-key 10-K race so I could determine their current ability. Their times ranged from forty to seventy minutes and, based on their performance, I assigned each runner a target distance for the "two-minute intervals" they would do during the next several weeks.

They ran their intervals to different points of Hattie's quarter-mile straightaway. The most talented runners--we called them racers--ran somewhat farther than 440 yards in two minutes, the middle group--the runners--did 330 yards in the same time frame, and the slowest group--the joggers--did 275 yards in their allotted two minutes. As long as they finished their designated distance in close to two minutes, their stride appeared to be about as long and fast as it had been during the recent 10-K.

During a tempo interval, their heart rate would rise to about seventy-five percent of maximum. The fastest athletes were generally on the high side of steady state, and the joggers were on the low side. But individual heart rates were so diverse that it was impossible to assign a standard heart rate in beats per minute for the group as a whole. Besides, I wanted them to know what their 10-K tempo felt like before I assigned training heart rates. Generally, it felt quick and relaxed for the joggers and the slower runners, while the fastest athletes experienced their 10-K tempo as rapid and pressing.

After every tempo interval, they rested by jogging for a minute. The object was to recover as quickly as possible, so I had designated trees just far enough away from the finish points that it took about a minute to get around and back at a very slow pace. These one-minute recovery intervals enabled them to lower their heart rate into light exertion before beginning the next tempo interval.

Thus, the beginners learned to choreograph their intervals with regular bouts of 10-K tempo running interspersed with very slow jogging. At this point, each athlete was set to explore the limits of their tempo ability.

Rebellion in the Ranks: The workout consisted of sixteen two-minute intervals, which is a lot of tempo running for one workout. Fortunately, their rest intervals kept the overall workout from becoming as hard as it would have been with a flat-out, thirty-two minutes at 10-K tempo.

Yet a few of my athletes felt constrained by two-minute intervals. The tempo seemed too easy for the distance they were running so they began pushing their effort into audible breathing. When I failed to slow them down in time, they soon discovered that a minute wasn't long enough to recover from a tempo interval. No matter how slowly they tried to run succeeding intervals, their heart rate would continue rising into threshold instead of topping off at steady state.

I had seen this phenomenon many times with athletes who were not used to interval training. One woman, who seemed to be running from Jack the Ripper, thought she had to train faster than her current 10-K race pace if she wanted to improve. "Isn't steady state for long runs?" she asked. What she meant was, "Shouldn't I be running faster?" There was no denying her logic: If you want to get faster, you should train faster than your present racing pace.

I pointed out to her, however, that she didn't have to force her effort to run faster than race pace. In fact, her relaxed, steady state tempo *was* a little faster than race pace, even though it felt only quick and relaxed. While it took a minute or more for her heart rate to rise to steady state, her tempo was quick from the start. And by the time her heart rate reached steady state, it was time for her to slow down. If she ran too fast, however, or if she ran longer than two minutes, her heart rate rose above steady state.

Two-minute intervals were thus a way to isolate the tempo of a 10-K, without having to breathe audibly or endure the intensity of longer intervals. "But," I cautioned, "two-minute intervals can also give you a false sense of confidence. You may be used to running two minutes at 10-K tempo, but you won't be prepared to sustain that tempo for a full 10-K unless you practice longer intervals."

After several weeks, my runners began showing signs of mastering two-minute intervals, and at that point I raised the ante, first to four-minute intervals and then to five. From then on, they would have to contend with 10-K tempo and moderate intensity, too.

Setting Up My First Interval Workout: I had run a variety of tempo workouts with my runners by the time my 10-K program ended in early April, 1994. I had divided my running time among the groups, teaching, coaching and encouraging them as they trained, so as I began training on my own, I was confident I wouldn't blow myself away with the tougher tempo workouts I was about to do.

I set my sights on beating Candy Smiley and winning my age division in the Hard Rock 10-K in mid-June. I reckoned I'd have to run a forty-minute 10-K so I planned to practice that specific tempo in my training. I envisioned a series of interval workouts, using a sustained and rapid pressing tempo, with audible breathing and tolerable intensity between 80 and 89% of my maximum heart rate. And I was curious as to how the workout would evolve.

I planned to run on the University of Hawaii's track so I wouldn't be distracted by broken or uneven ground. I liked the resilient feel of an all-weather track, but the measured distances created a built-in temptation for me to push my times down from week to week with progressively harder workouts. I'd gotten into trouble doing this years before, but now for the first time in my running career I had a heart rate monitor to keep myself properly focused.

I wanted to keep my heart rate within my threshold range, assuming, in my particular circumstances, that threshold would most closely simulate the tempo of a 10-K race. But my threshold heart rate range was twenty beats per minute wide and I didn't know exactly what my target should be within that range. Nor was I clear about the length of the intervals I should run. Being a regular and avid reader of *Running Research News*, I knew their writers recommended five-minute intervals at ninety percent of maximum heart rate as an effective way to increase capacity for the 10-K.[13]

And since I was looking for the quickest route to glory, in the back of my mind I was aiming for intense intervals in the five-minute range. But would that be consistent with my purpose of building a base of 10-K tempo ability? I wouldn't know until I gave the workout a try. I started with intervals of 800, 1600 and 1200 meters at a rapid pressing tempo. They raised my heart rate to about 165 beats per minute (the low end of my threshold range). That seemed easy enough so I decided to finish the workout with three 1600-meter intervals, during which my heart rate occasionally crept up to 170 bpm (the middle of my threshold range and 85% of maximum).

Sixteen-hundred meters is the equivalent of a mile, and I was accustomed to that distance from my training years before. But these intervals felt harder than the ones I remembered. In fact, the workout wiped me out for several days, and I decided that mile intervals were longer than I wanted to run. I needed almost seven minutes to run a mile interval, and, at my current age and ability, six mile-intervals at that pace would have made the workout too long and too hard.

The next week I cut the interval to 1200 meters, running six of

---

[13] *Running Research News*, Volume 9, Number 6, pg. 2, or Volume 9, number 4 pg. 3. For subscription information, write *Running Research News*, PO Box 27041, Lansing, MI 48909

them at the same tempo I'd run the week before. Afterward, I decided that this workout was still too stressful. My energy was low on the last interval, and during the next several days I was irritable, achy, and tired during my recovery jogs. Obviously, I wasn't used to the stress of running six 1200s at threshold, so I decided to cut back to five the following week.[14]

I was feeling eager as I began the first interval that Sunday afternoon. I ran it more aggressively than I had the previous week, and my heart rate rose immediately into the high 160s--eight beats per minute faster than the week before. The next several intervals followed suit, rising into the mid-170s. Yet my heart rate on the fifth 1200 was identical with the fifth of the previous week, so at least I was being consistent at that point of the workout. And since I was able to recover from the workout inside of sixty hours, I decided to stay at five 1200-meter intervals during succeeding workouts.

Thus, nearing the mid-point of my training period leading to the Hard Rock 10-K, I'd settled on an interval distance (1200 meters) that had me running at a rapid, pressing tempo for about five minutes per interval. Based on my prior reading in *Running Research News,* this was exactly what I'd wanted to do. Nevertheless, having established the workout, I immediately had my qualms about it.

In a Quandary About My Purpose: In my opinion, the workout was too short and too intense, to be a "tempo workout." I was running for a total of twenty-five minutes (at tempo) while approaching ninety percent of my maximum heart rate. I would have preferred to run for thirty-five minutes at eighty-five percent because a longer, slower workout would have simulated the actual duration of a forty-minute 10-K and the sort of tolerable intensity I could expect during the first half of the race.

My objective was to start a race at the right tempo, which would bring me to the mid-point with enough energy to endure the intensity of the second half without having to slow down. But I was concerned that the current workout was teaching me to start a race at a potentially

---

[14] Note that all of the above intervals were followed by rest jogs of 400-meters. I would soon cut back to 200 meters because my heart rate, breathing and desire indicated I was recovered at that point.

suicidal pace. Nonetheless, I was obsessed with the idea that intensity was the most potent adaptive stimulus. In the short term, I was willing to endure some discomfort, as long as I thought I could achieve my goal of winning my age division in the Hard Rock 10-K. But it was hard to deny the picture my exertion was drawing for me.

For instance, my guideline for 10-K tempo running was the same one I gave my runners, "No heavy breathing." Audible breathing (the next lowest level) was okay for athletes who could finish a 10-K inside of fifty minutes. But heavy breathing was in the realm of endurance training, which wasn't the purpose of a 10-K *tempo* workout. And although my heart rate indicated I was still in my threshold range, I was definitely fudging on my no-heavy-breathing rule.

My threshold range was about twenty beats per minute wide, and there was a big difference in exertion between the high and low ends. At the low end, I could barely hear my breathing, and there was little sensation of the discomfort I anticipated during the last part of a 10-K race. But I was often running at the middle to high end of threshold during the intervals (see Figure 10.1). I told myself as long as I didn't take my heart rate into ragged edge, I was still running a "tempo workout." But it was a delicate balancing act, considering my heart rate would have risen into ragged edge if the intervals had been longer or if I'd tried to run a sixth or seventh interval in the workout.

Figure 10.1: Five Times 1200-Meters

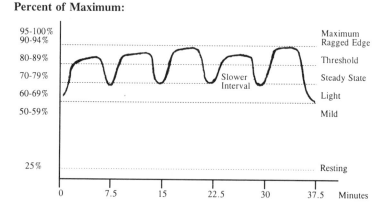

After a fifteen minute warm-up jog (not shown), I ran five 1200-meter tempo intervals within my threshold range. I took something off the fourth interval, running it eleven seconds slower than my average for the first three. The effort seemed too easy to simulate the intensity I anticipated during the Hard Rock 10-K, even though it was exactly at the level that would have made the workout a more legitimate 10-K "tempo" run.

I could tell I was training too fast, even though I denied it to myself. And, as events would soon reveal, I would have a difficult time training before the 1994 Hard Rock 10-K because my ambition was in conflict with reality. Ultimately, I managed--unintentionally--to resolve the conflict by taking myself out of the race with the hamstring injury I described in chapter five. Yet I didn't need to hurt myself to resolve the conflict. All I needed was to adjust my expectations for the race.

Tempo Training in Perspective: Part of the problem was my dearth of recent 10-K racing experience. Since I didn't know exactly what to expect from my current racing ability, I decided to test myself under race conditions with the Lanikai 8-K on June 5--two weeks before Hard Rock.

I also decided to run an interval workout the Tuesday before Lanikai. During this workout, I wanted to actually simulate the tempo of the 8-K race I was about to run, instead of pushing for intensity as I had been during my recent interval sessions. The workout would consist of three 1200s, with a single 2400-meter interval tacked on for perspective (see Figure 10.2).

As I started the first 1200, I pretended to be running a full 8-K, rather than a 1200-meter interval with an eighty-second rest period to recover. This was a radically different attitude from the one that had driven my recent training, and it managed to tone down my aggressive spirit, making the interval slower, less intense and more relaxed than during my previous workouts.

I was certain as I finished each of the first three intervals that I could continue for a distance longer than 1200 meters without having to force my pace. Then, for confirmation, I doubled the interval distance, running 2400 meters (1.5 miles) to better simulate the feeling of having to sustain the same tempo for eight kilometers (4.97 miles).

I was definitely into heavy breathing during the 2400-meter interval, but I wasn't forcing the pace, and I was confident I could sustain that forty-minute tempo during the coming race.

I ran this workout in mid-May, but it would be late July before I would finally accept that this was the right effort for my 10-K tempo intervals.

Figure 10.2: Tempo Workout and 8-K Race.

Heart Rate Ranges as
Percent of Maximum:

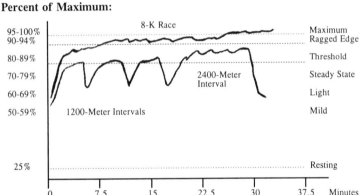

This workout clearly shows the difference in heart rate between a tempo workout and an 8-K race. Even though the workout heart rate was lower, the tempo felt about the same because, in fact, my training pace was approximately the same as the race pace. The reader may be interested in comparing the gap between my training and racing heart rate here and the narrower heart rate gap which is evident between the same race and the endurance workout in Figure 11.3 on page 144.

Chapter Ten Synopsis:

■ **The Main Issue:** How can I structure workouts to build tempo ability for the race I want to run? What's the difference between tempo training and speed work?

■ **Concepts:**

1) "Tempo" is the ability to run comfortably at race pace during the first half of the race you are training for.

2) "Race pace" is the pace you can currently average for the whole racing distance you are training for. Your goal pace for the race may be somewhat faster than your current racing pace, but, in my system, race pace is what you can currently average for the whole distance.

3) A "sense of tempo" is the relative quickness of your arms and legs in motion, measured as very slow, slow, quick, rapid, fast, and very fast. Having a sense of your racing tempo is the ability to repeat the specific cadence of your race pace during a race or during training.

4) A "sense of pacing" is the intuitive ability to judge your pace in a race or workout, i.e., to bring yourself past an intermediate distance in exactly the time you intend.

5) "Tempo training" is the activity of practicing the tempo of the race you want to run. There are two essential marks of this sort of training (no matter what your racing distance): it is comfortable and it feels like the tempo of the race you are training for.

■ **Theoretical Tenets:**

1) You should be able to run at race pace for at least half your racing distance before it becomes difficult or uncomfortable to sustain. Of course, if you never practice a specific racing tempo, you'll be unprepared for it in a race, and thus it's unlikely that you'll be able to hold the pace comfortably until the mid-point of a race.

2) There is nothing inherently difficult or uncomfortable about racing tempo. Going out too fast in a race raises your level of exertion above a level you can sustain for the whole distance. Thus, you could become fatigued early in the race, and make your initial racing effort more difficult and more uncomfortable than necessary.

3) You can improve your tempo ability by practicing it. Generally, tempo training should be intervalized to prevent

you from running so far that the effort becomes uncomfortable.

■ **Principle:** You will rarely have as much energy for a workout as a race. This is the same as saying your metabolic engine is smaller for a workout than a race. Therefore, you can't go as fast in a workout as a race, without over-taxing your engine. And thus, if you want to simulate the specific tempo of your race, you should run a little slower than race pace.

■ **Relationships:**

1) The shorter your racing distance, the faster your racing pace will be, and the shorter your bouts of tempo running should be to remain within the bounds of comfort.

2) The longer you sustain racing pace, the more difficult and uncomfortable it becomes.

3) The better your running energy during a tempo workout, the faster you can run and still be comfortable.

■ **Questions and Answers:**

1) How are tempo intervals different from sustained tempo runs?

Tempo intervals give you frequent breaks to recover between bouts of tempo running. Frequent recoveries enable you to run at a faster tempo. They also enable you to keep your average level of exertion at a lower level, which in turn keeps your overall workout effort at a lower level than it would be if you ran the same tempo without taking breaks.

A sustained tempo run more closely simulates the overall effort of the race you want to run because it has no recovery breaks. Sustained tempo efforts become endurance runs to the extent that they become uncomfortable. Thus, you would have to put time or exertion limits on your sustained tempo runs to keep them within the realm of tempo running, and within the realm of hard, adaptive training.

2) How do I know when I'm sufficiently recovered from a tempo interval?

You are sufficiently recovered when your heart rate drops into your light exertion range. If you are in good shape, this may take a minute or less, even if you continue jogging during the recovery interval. Note: Tempo intervals are different from "full recovery" speed intervals, where the walking or jogging breaks are as long as five to seven minutes and your heart rate drops to a mild level of exertion during the recovery break.

3) How is tempo running different from long slow running and speed work?

Tempo running feels like race pace, so it will feel quicker than your pace on a longer, slower stamina run. Similarly, speed work feels quicker than race pace running. In my system, speed work is a "notch up" from your racing tempo in terms of pace and effort. For example, if your race is the 10-K, then your speed work should be closer to your 5-K tempo, which is a notch up from 10-K tempo.

4) Why is tempo running necessary?

The purpose of tempo running is to develop an efficient stride at your racing pace. In distance running, efficiency is important because, without it, you would soon become fatigued from having to rely too much on power to run at race pace. Since your stride at race pace is a combination of power and efficiency, you've got to prepare for both parts. Hill work builds power, and tempo training builds an efficient turn-over at race pace.

5) What should my tempo feel like when I'm running at my racing pace?

The shorter your racing distance, the faster your tempo will be on a slow/fast tempo scale. But there are five components of exertion, and tempo is only one way to experience exertion at race pace. Your heart rate and breathing, as well as your sensations of power and intensity can also guide you to the right tempo. For example, I experience my pace during the first half of a 10-K as rapid and pressing, with my heart rate in the high 170s, my breathing slightly audible, and intensity at a tolerable level.

6) What's the difference between my race pace and my racing tempo?

In terms of the specific cadence, there is little difference. If you take 180 steps a minute in a race, then you should take 180 steps a minute in your tempo training.

Conceptually, "race pace" is the average pace you can sustain for a given racing distance, such as six minutes per mile for the 10-K. "Racing tempo" is the specific cadence you're able to sustain throughout a race, such as 180 steps a minute. You can measure the way your racing tempo feels on the following scale: very slow, slow, quick, rapid, fast, and very fast.

Since you will rarely have more energy for a workout than a race, your training pace should be slower than your racing pace. In other words, tempo training in a hard/ready workout should be somewhat slower than a very hard/eager race. This is one of the toughest principles to abide by in training because it's so easy to run faster in training. And because, it seems so much more effective to train at a faster, more intense pace.

7) Are there any tricks to building tempo?

You'll find it a lot easier psychologically to run at tempo for a short distance. If you start a workout with a series of short intervals and then progress to longer intervals, you'll get used to the quicker pace and transfer some of that proficiency to the longer intervals.

Similarly, if you start a training regimen with short intervals, you can get used to your racing tempo without having to deal with the added burden of sustained tempo running, at least not until you've had a chance to adjust to tempo running *per se*.

8) How can I set up a tempo workout for myself?

First, you've got to know what race you are training for, and what pace you can hold for the whole distance. Perhaps you should try a test-effort race or workout at that distance to get yourself in the ball park. Otherwise, try estimating your ability based on other racing distances you've run.

The length of a tempo interval will be the distance you can run *comfortably* at race pace (or a little slower). Remember, the shorter your race, the shorter your tempo intervals will have to be to stay within this "comfort" framework.

Next you have to place your intervals within the context of the workout you are planning. Will it be an easy workout, a moderate workout, or a hard workout? Obviously, you can do a lot more tempo training in a hard workout than an easy workout. So decide how hard this workout will be.

Finally, you've got to play with the number of intervals you are running to find the number that will create the effort of the workout as a whole. And, remember, no matter how hard you think you've run, if you are trying for a "hard" workout, you have to recover within 48 to 60 hours.

Chapter Eleven
The Endurance Cornerstone

During my 10-K training program in early 1993, I talked my runners into doing a weekly quarter-mile interval workout. As a group, they ran a total of 1700 intervals, and their times went into a data base in my computer. I wanted to see whether there was a connection between their training pace for the intervals and their racing pace for a 10-K they would run at the end of an 8-week training period.

Some runners ran their quarters faster than they raced, and some ran them slower. Figure 11.1 shows the results for the seventeen runners in my study. The horizontal line in the middle of the graph represents each runner's average 10-K pace. The vertical bars represent each runner's average training pace for the quarter intervals, with the bars above the middle line indicating a faster training pace, and vice versa. The longer the bar above (or below) the middle line, the faster (or slower) the training pace.

Clearly, individual runners varied widely in their training pace. At one extreme, Ron P (RP), who was recovering from the flu during the race, trained an average of twenty-two seconds per quarter faster than he raced. At the other extreme, Pam R (PR), an over-weight jogger who was "trying to keep her quarters slow," trained an average of nineteen seconds per quarter slower than she raced. Pam was one of six runners in my study who did their quarters slower than their 10-K race pace.

What was most interesting to me about these results was the difference in the way the runners rated their race on a questionnaire I gave them afterward. The number at the end of each bar is the rating they gave their race on the following scale: 1 = great, 2 = good, 3 = fair, 4 = poor, and 5 = bad.

On the average, the six runners who trained slower than they raced rated their race between great and good (an average of 1.16). The other eleven runners--those who trained faster than they raced--rated their races between good and fair (an average of 2.63). These results seem to suggest that runners who want to feel good about their racing should do their tempo training at a pace which is slower than they can race.

Figure 11.1: Average 10-K Pace And Average 440-Yard Interval Pace. Comparing the Way Seventeen Runners Rated their Race Experience.

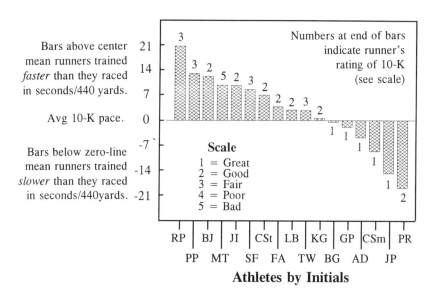

Bars above center mean runners trained *faster* than they raced in seconds/440 yards.

Avg 10-K pace.

Bars below zero-line mean runners trained *slower* than they raced in seconds/440yards.

Numbers at end of bars indicate runner's rating of 10-K (see scale)

Scale
1 = Great
2 = Good
3 = Fair
4 = Poor
5 = Bad

RP | BJ | JI | CSt | LB | KG | GP | CSm | PR
PP | MT | SF | FA | TW | BG | AD | JP

Athletes by Initials

Expecting Race Results: Some commentators have questioned this conclusion, claiming the ratings were influenced by the runners' expectations. Their argument goes this way: those who trained faster than race pace "down-rated" their race experience because they *expected* to race that fast, and they were disappointed when they didn't. The other runners were so "thrilled" by the *unexpected* quickness of their 10-K pace that they rated their race at a higher level.

I replied that some runners may have expected to race as fast as they trained, but their expectations were not necessarily warranted. Most runners can push short intervals--like a quarter-mile--at a faster pace than they can sustain for longer distances. That's why I also had my runners doing another workout of three 1.5-mile repetitions. Figure 11.2 indicates that only two runners ran their 1.5-milers barely faster than they raced. So the "expectations" argument tends to break down on the basis of these longer intervals, because the runners would have had conflicting expectations based on their long and short interval workouts.

Nonetheless, it is apparent from figure 11.2 the runners who had a "great race" were still grouped at the slow end in relation to their 10-K race pace. And although these results might not hold up against rigorous statistical analysis, they seem to indicate that running tempo and endurance intervals faster than race pace doesn't necessarily translate into satisfying race results.

In fact, often a blistering pace makes the overall effort of a workout too difficult for regular and adequate recovery. And, therefore, overtraining can cause exhaustion at a point when being well rested is the only way to ensure top performance and a great race.

Figure 11.2: Average 10-K Pace and Average 1.5-Mile Repetition Pace. Comparing the Way Fifteen Runners Rated their Race Experience.

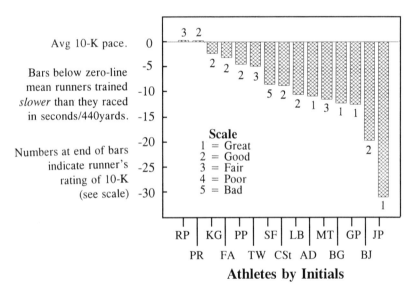

My Personal Experience: I have often struggled with this principle in my own training and racing. I've known the gamut of racing experiences from great to bad, and I've drawn my own conclusions about what creates those experiences.

I agree with most experts that, when a runner is already training at a high level, less training effort generally leads to more race satisfaction.

But like many runners of good ability, I've often overused it in vain attempts to become the best. My training for the 1994 Hard Rock 10-K was a case in point.

In recent years, the Hard Rock 10-K had become the most competitive 10-K in Honolulu. I didn't know whether I'd be ready to challenge the top runners in my age division for the gold medal, but I aimed to do my best. Thus far, I'd established a workout of five 1200-meter intervals, running it on the UH track every Sunday evening for the previous four weeks. In mid-May, however, I decided to inject an endurance workout of three 2400-meter repetitions into my schedule to supplement the tempo workout.

As I described in the last chapter, I suspected I was running my 1200-meter intervals at a faster pace than I could sustain for a whole 10-K. If the 1200s were too fast, I'd know it during the endurance workout because doubling the distance from 1200 to 2400 meters would force me to run long enough at racing tempo that I'd get into trouble from fatigue, especially if I were lacking endurance.

A 10-K Endurance Workout: The summer sun was just breaking over the baseball stadium next to the UH track as I began the endurance workout. It would be hot by the time I finished, but the early morning conditions would be about the same as I could expect on race day.

I planned to build my effort up during the 2400-meter (1.5-mile) repetitions. I wanted to run the same rapid tempo throughout, but I'd breathe inaudibly during the first half-mile, audibly for the middle half-mile, and heavily on the last half-mile. By getting up to ragged edge, I expected to teach myself how to endure exertion beyond my maximum aerobic capacity.

Theoretically, my maximum capacity for running aerobically (with oxygen) was about 90% of my maximum heart rate (in my case, 180 bpm). If I were just below that level, I would hear my breathing, but it wouldn't be as heavy and uncontrolled as it would if I were above 180 bpm, and thereby forcing my body to produce additional energy anaerobically (without oxygen). Thus my target range for 10-K tempo training was just within my maximum aerobic capacity, and my target range for endurance training was just outside of it.

My mistake in years past had been to push most of an endurance workout at ragged edge. After building my exertion up to threshold during the first half-mile of each repetition, I used to press immediately into heavy breathing and hold it for the rest of the repetition. That had made the workout unnecessarily hard because I ended up running three miles at ragged edge when my actual racing distance at ragged edge was usually closer to 1.5 miles. These endurance workouts were often more grueling than a race, and in running them I often became injured, exhausted, or psyched out.

With this in mind, I decided to temper my exertion, while also simulating the endurance feature of the coming race. Mentally, I divided the 10-K distance into four 2400-meter segments. During the actual workout, I pretended the first and second repetitions were the first and second segments of the race, which would bring me to its hypothetical mid-point, feeling strong and ready for another 5-K at the same tempo.

As I ran the last half-mile of the second repetition, my heart rate rose to 180 bpm--90% of my maximum. At that level, I was breathing heavily, though I wasn't straining. And my three-minute recovery jog gave me enough of a break that I was able to lower my heart rate and renew my desire to push hard again on the last repeat. During the last half-mile of the workout, I pushed the pace to simulate the heavy breathing and intense discomfort of the last mile or so of the race itself.

Afterwards, I entered my times into the computer, looking for a certain pacing pattern. If I had run the repetitions correctly, the first one should have been the slowest, the second faster by fifteen seconds or so, and the last slightly faster than the second. However, if I had run too hard on the first or second repetitions, fatigue would have set in early, and the last repetition would have been slower than the second, though my exertion would have felt about the same in either case. My times for the three repeats were a textbook perfect 9:31, 9:19 and 9:16.

The workout was in the hard to very hard range, but it wasn't so hard that I ran into early fatigue. I was tired a day later, but not blown away by it. Nonetheless, I was afraid the tempo had been too fast for me to sustain for ten kilometers. I was so close to my capacity for the workout that I didn't think I had enough energy to allow for running a full ten kilometers.

It even occurred to me that the pace was faster than I wanted to run for the Lanikai 8-K, which I planned to run in early June. Lanikai--the race I described in chapter 5--would be a low-key, club event, and my purpose was to enjoy the race, test myself competitively and get a sense of how I might perform during the Hard Rock 10-K.

Endurance Training In Perspective: Happily, the Lanikai 8-K was a good race. I had abundant energy throughout, I paced myself correctly and I won my age division, beating several younger runners who'd been ahead of me in earlier races. Afterward, I was eager to get home and use the information from my heart rate monitor to analyze my performance.

I began by juxtaposing my heart rate for the race with my heart rate for the recent 2400-meter workout (see Figure 11.3). The heart rate curves for both activities followed parallel paths. According to my heart rate, the race was higher level running, but interestingly much of it felt like the workout. My breathing, for example, was as audible and controlled during the middle of the race as it had been during the middle half-mile of each 2400-meter repetition.

My average heart rate during the race was 180 bpm, which was 90% of maximum heart rate and, theoretically, 100% of my aerobic capacity. Yet I'd hit 180 bpm eight minutes into the race. And from that point until the finish, I averaged 185 bpm, indicating I'd spent most of the thirty-two minute race between 90% and 92.5% of my maximum heart rate, or, theoretically, somewhat beyond my aerobic capacity. Yet, for most of that time, I was breathing audibly, not heavily.

I didn't get into heavy breathing until about twenty-four minutes into the race, at which point my heart rate was 188 bpm, which was also my average heart rate during the last eight minutes of the race. I hit several highs of 191 bpm during the last mile and I was definitely suffering intense discomfort. But I was still able to sustain the pace, even picking it up enough to drop my competition in the last three hundred meters. All of this seemed to indicate I had good endurance, which is also what my training had indicated.

With Lanikai fresh in mind, I projected myself into the Hard Rock 10-K, still two weeks away. I reckoned it would take an all-out effort, but I was reasonably sure I could finish the Hard Rock 10-K in forty minutes, maintaining the same pace I'd run for Lanikai.

Next, I used Jack Daniels' performance tables to calculate how I would have performed for ten kilometers based on my Lanikai 8-K performance. According to the tables, I would have run 10-K in 40:31, which was certainly possible given my sense that I would have had to "gut out" another mile and-a-quarter at the pace I'd run Lanikai.

Figure 11.3: Three Endurance Repeats And an 8-K Race.

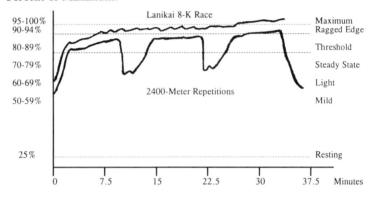

Heart Rate Ranges as Percent of Maximum:

The graph shows my heart rate for a hard workout of three endurance repetitions and a very hard Lanikai 8-K (the same race graphed in Figure 10.2 on page 132). These heart rate curves are closely parallel, but the cushion of exertion between the race and the endurance repeats is smaller than the cushion between the tempo intervals and the Lanikai race. Obviously, I ran at a higher level of exertion for the endurance repeats than I did for the tempo intervals.

These were devastating realizations because I'd previously reckoned on having to race Hard Rock in forty minutes to beat Candy Smiley, and faster than forty minutes to win my age division. As it turned out, the actual winning time in my age division for the 1994 Hard Rock 10-K would be 39:10, which was slower than the 6:14 per-mile pace I had run during my 2400-meter repeats. But at the time I wasn't sure what the winning time would be, and not knowing added to my anxiety.

Furthermore, I didn't think I could hold my 2400-meter training pace for 10-K, and now my 8-K performance, which had been ten seconds slower per mile than the 2400s, seemed to confirm it. And even though I probably could have run forty minutes with an all-out effort, I wasn't willing yet to race that hard. Thus I was faced with the intolerable possibility of not achieving my goals.

The following week, in a vain attempt to squeeze in several "quality" workouts before Hard Rock, I injured my right hamstring. The injury was serious enough to force me out of the race, and I had to wonder about the precipitating mental factors.

Chapter Eleven Synopsis:

■ **The Main Issue:**   How can I establish a hard workout to build endurance for the race I want to run? Is there a connection between my training pace and my ability to run great races?

■ **Concepts:**

1)   "Endurance" is the ability to sustain uncomfortable race exertion. Endurance is marked by durability and perseverance in the face of rising levels of intensity.

2)   "Intensity" refers to the degree of discomfort associated with the build-up of lactic acid and fatigue. Intensity can be measured as soothing, very comfortable, comfortable, tolerable, uncomfortable, and very uncomfortable.

■ **Theoretical Tenets:**

1)   Of the three major training stimuli (frequency, duration and intensity), intensity is the most powerful. Unfortunately, when you train intensely you limit the duration of the work-out, as well as the number of times you can repeat the workout because intensity causes early fatigue and it increases your risk of injury.

2)   You don't necessarily have to be fatigued in order to build endurance. If you are building endurance within the framework of a hard workout, the fatigue of the workout itself is sufficient for adaptation. An endurance run is simply intense enough to simulate the exertion of the second half of the race you want to run.

3)   Your endurance training heart rate doesn't have to be as high as it will be during a race. There should be a cushion of five to ten bpm between your training and racing heart rate because you're rarely as energetic during a workout as a race.

■ **Relationships:**

1) The longer you sustain your racing tempo, the greater the intensity you will probably have to endure.
2) The faster your racing pace, the more intense your exertion will be after the mid-point and at the finish of a race.
3) The longer your racing distance, the lower your sustained level of exertion must be to keep from becoming seriously fatigued long before the finish.
4) The longer your training distance, the less likely you are to train faster than your actual race pace.

■ **Principles:**

1) Endurance training should be intense enough to simulate the specific discomfort of the second half of the race you want to run.
2) Too much endurance training can have negative psychological repercussions which inhibit effective racing.
3) Even pacing contributes to a gradual build up of intensity throughout a race.

■ **Questions and Answers:**

1) Why do I get sick or injured just before a big race?

You are probably adding too much intensity to your training regimen, which lowers your resistance to colds and injuries.

Increasing intensity in your training as you approach a goal race is an effective way to build speed or endurance, but too much intensity leads to injury, illness and exhaustion.

The problem usually arises when you try to add intensity to your hard workouts by running them progressively faster. There is no problem when you are faster because you have increased energy due to progressive adaptation. In that case your times will come down within the context of a hard workout. However, faster running usually leads to harder workouts, which is the real problem. If you exceed your capacity for hard training, there will be a breakdown somewhere, especially when you are adding effort to several workouts at once.

The more effective way to add intensity is to restructure a tempo workout with fewer, longer tempo intervals and less overall distance so you stay within the bounds of hard training. Otherwise, you'll have to increase the duration of your recovery periods between workouts so you have time to adequately recover.

2) What level of exertion should I try to sustain during a race?

You should try to sustain a tempo and a heart rate which will enable you to run the second half as fast or faster than the first. If you go out too hard, you'll become fatigued too early, and fatigue will force you to slow down even if you try to run harder.

It's better to sustain a slowly rising level of exertion or one that is just below a threshold, which, if you went above it, you would become too fatigued to maintain your pace until the finish.

If you can finish a 10-K in less than an hour, you can probably run close to 90% of your maximum heart rate after taking ten minutes or so to get up there. This is assuming you have good endurance.

3) Does having endurance make me a faster runner?

Yes, to the extent that you can sustain your race pace without having to slow down because of fatigue. With less endurance, you would have to slow down earlier in a race.

You should be clear, however, that endurance training won't make you a faster racer unless you repeat an endurance workout enough to show some adaptive progress, i.e., your times come down in training at the same effort. This is the subject of part four on adaptation.

4)   How can I build endurance for the marathon?

If you can run a marathon in three hours or less, try running three 3-mile repeats at your half-marathon racing tempo. Or simply run a sustained twelve mile run at marathon tempo. Remember, these workouts have to be easy enough that you can recover from them in a reasonable period. Your recovery will be reasonably quick if you have previously practiced tempo running with shorter intervals of, say, a mile, so you don't blow yourself away with a sudden infusion of sustained race pace running.

If you are slower than four hours for the marathon, cut back on the distance of the repeats from three miles to two. You may be able to do four of them for a total of eight miles, which is one third of your racing distance--enough to simulate the discomfort of the marathon near the end of the workout. Remember, you don't have to feel uncomfortable for your whole endurance workout.

5)   How can I build endurance for a short race like the mile or 1500 meters?

During training, anything that's longer than a quarter mile can get uncomfortable at 1500-meter racing tempo. Two or two-and-a-half lap repeats at racing tempo are very effective endurance building distances.

16)   Is there a connection between my training pace and my ability to run great races?

Technically, no. Great races are a function of running great workouts (see chapter 6). However, the position I've taken in this chapter is that tempo and endurance training should be a little slower than race pace to prevent overtraining.

Chapter Twelve
Speed--The Icing on the Cake

Archie San Romani, Jr. was the only four-minute miler on the track team when I got to Oregon in the spring of 1964. Archie was a good looking, all-American boy, with a hint of a pompadour to go with his guitar and his rock and roll image. He was also a trickster who delighted in playing with the crowd at Oregon track meets.

There was a stand of bleachers on the field in the mid-sixties, and it hid the south end of the track from spectators sitting in the main stands. As Archie disappeared behind the bleachers on the last lap of the mile a hush would descend on the crowd of six thousand. Last seen dawdling along in second or third place, Archie's trick was to burst into view again in the lead by twenty yards with the home crowd going wild.

Archie was a talented athlete, and yet the Oregon system was designed to develop speed in talented athletes. Coming from the University of Hawaii, I had never seen runners train as fast as the middle distance men at Oregon. The 1964 NCAA Track and Field Championships were held in Eugene in June, and I recall sitting in the stands one afternoon and watching Archie train for the meet. His whole workout consisted of four or five 220-yard sprints at close to twenty-two seconds flat. Even with a running start, those were outstanding times for a miler, but they were common among the better UO runners.

When I was on the track team at the University of Hawaii, my fastest running had been during a weekly workout of twenty-five 220-yard intervals, averaging about 29 seconds at my best. This comparatively slower training at UH notwithstanding, I was no stranger to fast running. As a youth, I had always been into activities that required sprinting. I played football nearly every day of my youth, and until the tenth grade I'd had a bicycle paper route, which must have developed the power necessary for fast running. In the eleventh grade, I played varsity football and, later, I took up cross country and track.

When I got to Oregon, I noticed immediately that the middle distance runners did fewer 220s than I had at UH, but they ran them a lot faster. Beginning in the fall, Bowerman had us on the track with six or eight 220s at well under thirty seconds. Then, after forty minutes of running in the hills, we would finish the workout with four 110-yard sprints at "7/8ths effort." I recall returning to the track, putting on my spikes and gathering with several of my teammates at the top of the turn for a running start into the 110s.

There was nothing in my training experience to match the exhilaration of turning on the after-burners as we flew off the curve and onto the straightaway, our feet pounding the cinder track, each of us screaming for breath, yet somehow managing to control our form through the finish before coming to a halt. We'd catch our breath, walk back to the top of the turn--talking all the while--and then do it again, three more times before hitting the showers.

Speed and Injuries: The speed work Bowerman had me do at Oregon was like the icing on the cake of my earlier training. Of course, there was a lot more than speed work to the Oregon system, so I can't say exactly what effect it had on my times or my overall racing ability. I do know I reveled in the speed I developed at Oregon.

Teammates such as Archie San Romani, Jr. and Wade Bell had outstanding natural speed. And though my natural ability was not as good as Archie's or Wade's, even I learned to accelerate past a pack at the 660-yard mark of an 880-yard race. I'd trained in the hills and on the track to develop my ability to sprint at the end of a race. But I paid a hefty price in pain whenever I trained for speed.

Getting out of bed the morning after a hard workout, and for the first ten minutes of my morning jog, the pain in my legs and feet would be severe. In those days, I didn't know how to use stretching, ice and aspirin to quell the aches and pains of fast training, so I had to move very gingerly to loosen up. But soon the pain and stiffness would disappear and I'd be running as though nothing had happened. Those were the days when I was young and resilient.

I'd never injured myself in running, and even when I finally did, it wasn't directly because of training. I was finishing a long hill run in the summer between my junior and senior years at Oregon and some neighborhood kids challenged me to race them to the end of the block. They rode their bikes and easily dusted me. But I wasn't warmed up for the sudden acceleration, and in the middle of the sprint I heard and felt a groin muscle pop. It would bother me for months and would eventually lead to another injury that took me out of competitive running at Oregon.

Since then, most of my running injuries have been related to fast running. In my youth, I ran fast all the time, but the older I got the less I did. So fast running often came as a shock to my system and I'd end up injuring myself. For this reason, I was gun-shy at 50 when it came to training for speed, preferring instead to rely on my natural ability, and on the power and tempo abilities I'd developed in my hill and interval workouts. Yet there were times when I was anticipating a competitive finish to a major race that I'd risk doing some speed work.

Speed Kills: In mid-July of 1994, I had a month to prepare for the Hawaiian Style 8-K, one of the top competitive races in the islands (see part three). I aimed to make it my last race of the year before retiring temporarily from racing to build a base of mileage in preparation for races the following year.

At the time, I was coming off the hamstring injury which had prevented me from running the Hard Rock 10-K the month before. My only hard workouts in the interim had been twice-weekly long runs, which hadn't aggravated the hamstring as badly as the intervals would have. Nonetheless, it had now been six weeks since my last interval workout and I was eager to get back to training on the track.

I'd been toying with the idea of running a new interval workout to develop my speed. I'd even written a schedule for a series of weekly 200-meter interval workouts, starting at a moderate pace and slowly bringing my times down from week to week. But I scrapped the schedule because I didn't have the time to train so systematically before my goal race, nor did I currently have the patience to hold myself to a strict schedule.

Moreover, I assumed that running 200s in lieu of my usual 1200-meter interval workout would be of marginal value to the Hawaiian Style 8-K. I still needed a tempo stimulus in my training, and in my estimation the 1200s were best suited for that purpose. Thus, I decided simply to add six 200-meter intervals to the end of my usual workout of five 1200-meter intervals. I was wary of jumping into the 200s and reinjuring myself, but since I'd previously run some fast 200s during my easy workouts, I thought I could handle them in this context.

Unfortunately, after my recent lay-off from interval training, I was too eager during the workout to hold myself to a reasonable tempo. As a result I ran much too fast, and though I felt nothing during the workout, that afternoon I discovered I'd reinjured my hamstring.

What is Speed Work? Naturally, the new hamstring injury threw me into a reflective mood. I was concerned about having to stop training, but my sense was I'd recover quickly from the injury. I was more concerned about how I could adjust future interval workouts to include some speed work, while not hurting myself again.

I started by thinking about the heart rate and performance data I'd gathered during the workout. Running without the benefit of a stopwatch, I'd deluded myself into thinking I was running slower than I was, especially for the 200s. I'd averaged 6:10 per mile during the 1200-meter intervals, but my pace for the 200s had been close to 5:08. There was a big gap between my 1200 and my 200 times, and the latter were much faster than I could expect to run at any point of the coming 8-K race.

In running the 1200/200 workout, I'd intended to raise my heart rate during the 200s to the same level I'd reached during the 1200s. And although I could see from my heart rate graph that I had achieved my objective, unfortunately the 200-meter distance had been so short I'd had to run very fast to raise my heart rate from 140 bpm to 180 bpm. I could tell I was blitzing the 200s and it occurred to me to slow down, but since I couldn't feel an injury developing I kept the pace up-- compulsively. I was saved from serious injury because I'd been well rested and injury-free going into the workout. Nonetheless, my 200s were still much too fast.

It took me ten days to get over the hamstring problem, and with time running out before the Hawaiian Style 8-K in August, I was determined not to injure myself again as I prepared for another interval workout. My first task was to slow myself down on the 1200-meter intervals, so instead of running five as I had previously, I planned to run six (see Figure 12.1). I would set the tempo based on the distance I planned to cover during the workout. And since six intervals was a longer distance than five, I reckoned I'd automatically slow down enough to simulate the tempo of the race I was about to run.

For similar reasons, I decided to run three fast 400s instead of the six very fast 200s that had contributed to the recent injury. The total distance at speed would be the same, but running twice as far during each interval would have the effect of slowing me down to a more realistic pace than the 5:08 per mile I'd hit on the 200s. Of course, my main concern was to slow myself down enough to survive the workout without getting injured. I decided to hold myself to a range of 6:40 to

6:20 per mile for the 1200s, and to use a stopwatch for the first time that year to help me stay on pace.

It was a hot morning when I got to the track, and I took an extra lap of jogging before starting the first 1200. My pace on that interval was a relaxed 6:40 per mile, and during the next several intervals I gradually built up my heart rate to my predetermined target range of 160 to 170 beats per minute. By the last 1200, I'd brought my pace down to 6:20 per mile, which was close to the 6:18 pace I would actually average for the coming race. My average pace for the 1200s was 6:31 per mile, which was significantly slower than the 6:10 I'd averaged for the previous workout, but it felt like something I could manage for the race itself.

Figure 12.1: Six 1200-Meter Intervals And Three 400-Meter Intervals.

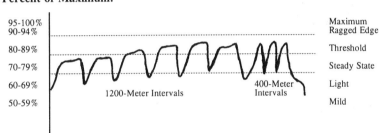

The 1200-meter intervals were a little slower than my average 8-K race pace, but the effort of the last three felt about the same. My exertion for the 400-meter intervals only reached the same level as the last three 1200-meter intervals, but my pace for the 400s was as fast as my last mile, and twenty-five seconds per mile faster than I averaged for the race.

After running the six 1200s, I was warmed up and ready for the three 400s. Since I was concerned about reinjuring myself, I'd set a strict limit of 88 to 90 seconds for my 400 pace, aiming for about the same intensity/heart rate as I'd run on the 1200s. The 400-meter distance was short enough that I automatically adjusted my tempo, picking it up to approximately 5:50 per mile--only two seconds slower than my actual pace for the last mile of the coming race.

These 400s at a fast, forced tempo were definitely a step removed from the tempo of the recent 200-meter intervals. But I got my heart rate into the mid-170s, which was high enough to sting. And since the 400 pace was significantly faster than my average 8-K race pace would be, in my opinion running it qualified as speed work.

Speed in Perspective: To recapitulate, in mid-July I'd resumed interval training after a six-week layoff. I was preparing for the August 1994 Hawaiian Style 8-K at the time, and I wanted to develop a full complement of 8-K racing abilities, including speed.

I wanted to be able to close a gap between myself and a competitor in the late stages of the coming race, and also to be able to sustain a fast quarter-mile drive to the finish. I decided to simulate the conditions of the end of the race when fatigue and intensity would be major factors, and thus to run three fast interval quarters at the end of a tempo workout.

I did this interval workout three and a-half weeks before the race and a variation of it nine days before the race. Running a few 400-meter intervals at the end of a couple of workouts didn't qualify as a lot of speed work, but I also intended to follow through with a new speed workout I'd begun earlier in the week. I had decided to shift my focus from tempo and endurance intervals to a workout of ten fast 400s, bringing my pace down from ninety to eighty-five seconds during the workout.

This workout raised my heart rate into the low 160s on the first few 400-meter intervals, and into the high 170s on the last few (see Figure 12.2). I could have run harder and faster, but I had to be realistic, given the short time I had to train before the race and the added risk of injury I would have assumed with faster running.

In fact, I wasn't interested in running faster. A workout of ten quarters was similar to what I saw other runners doing on the track, but my level of exertion was not as hard as theirs. I was definitely forcing it, but I wasn't straining as most of them appeared to be. And yet my tempo was definitely a notch above the tempo of the longer intervals I'd been running. Thus, I felt that I was taking the edge off the rapid pressing tempo I planned to hold for most of the race itself.

I ran this 400-meter workout on Sunday, Tuesday and Saturday during the penultimate week before the race. And, as I'll describe in the next part on racing, I may have done one-too-many workouts, because I seemed to exhaust myself during the Saturday workout, with only a week to recover before the race.

Figure 12.2: 400-Meter Intervals
For Speed and Tempo.

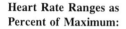

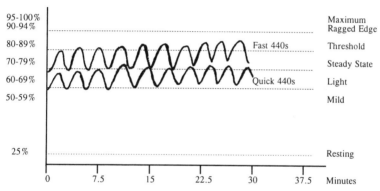

The graph shows two workouts: A moderate-to-hard workout designed to build my finishing speed for the Hawaiian Style 8-K (the top curve), and an easy workout designed to increase my training tempo on a day when I was feeling tired (bottom curve). I ran the fast quarters at the pace I ran the last mile of the Hawaiian Style 8-K, and I ran the slow quarters much slower than my 8-K race pace, but still quicker than I would have on a steady-paced, recovery run.

Chapter Twelve Synopsis:

■ **The Main Issue:** How can I structure a hard workout to build speed for a specific racing distance?

■ **Concepts:**

1) Speed is the ability to sprint or surge at a pace that's faster than your average pace for the race you want to run.

2) Sprinting is an attempt to beat a competitor to the finish line during the last few hundred meters of a race.

3) Surging is an attempt to lose or discourage a competitor during the middle portion of a race.

4) Speed work is training that is specific to the sort of pace and effort you may be forced to generate during a highly competitive race.

■ **Theoretical Tenets:**

1) You can run a lot faster when you are fresh than in the middle or at the finish of a fatiguing race. Thus, in distance running, sprinting is not the fastest possible pace you can hold for a short distance when you are fresh. It's the pace you can reasonably expect to generate when you are fatigued.

2) Unless you are a sprinter or a miler, speed work doesn't have to be a major part of your training regimen. Just a small and constant part of it during your base training, and of increasingly greater importance as your goal race approaches.

3) Speed takes a relatively short time to develop, as compared with the other racing abilities.

4) Speed work is riskier than long, slow distance running. You should do it in small doses, set up in relation to the distance you can actually expect to generate at speed during a race.

5) Speed work is better placed at the end of a hard workout than the beginning, especially if you are better warmed up at the finish. Speed work at the finish of a hard workout also simulates the experience of having to accelerate when you are fatigued.

6) Speed work is of little value for improving overall performance at racing distances of five miles or more (see #3 below).

■ **Relationships:**

1) The shorter your interval distance, the faster your pace must be to raise your heart rate to the same level you can achieve during a longer tempo interval.

2) The shorter your racing distance, the faster you will have to run in training to simulate your actual sprinting pace during a goal race.

■ **Questions and Answers:**

1) What's the best distance for a speed interval?

Think of taking your racing tempo up a notch from your tempo level, e.g., quick to rapid, or rapid to fast. How long do you have to run at that increased tempo to get your heart rate up to your tempo training level? The answer is: quite a bit shorter than your tempo interval distance. Whatever that distance is, it's a good starting distance for your speed intervals.

2) How fast should I train when I'm training for speed?

Fast enough to simulate the fastest tempo you can reasonably expect to achieve during the middle or end of a highly competitive race.

3) Will speed work make me faster?

Yes. It will make you faster in a sprint or surge. But it won't necessarily make you faster in a distance race. Speed work is a small part of training for events longer than five miles. If you want to be a faster distance runner, concentrate on building the other four racing abilities. Speed is the icing on the cake.

4) How can I structure a hard workout to build speed for a specific racing distance?

Every time you run faster than the average pace you can hold for your whole racing distance, you are training for speed. If you add a little speed work to the end of a hard workout, you'll build your speed. But if you run a hard workout consisting exclusively of speed work, you might be doing more than necessary.

Remember, your speed work should bear some relation to the distance you are aiming for. If you are training for the marathon, for instance, you don't have to do 200-meter intervals because it's unlikely you'll ever have to run that fast during a marathon. On the other hand, an 800-meter surge at the end of a long run might be long enough (and slow enough) to simulate the sort of speed you could reasonably expect to generate at the finish of a marathon.

Part III
The Racer as Hero

At the party to celebrate the completion of my 1992 marathon training program, I gave out awards to the runners who had proven themselves to be the most heroic. In judging heroism, I didn't necessarily look for outstanding performance, but evidence that athletes had overcome adversity to do the marathon.

Jo Pieper, for example, won the award for greatest heroism in 1992. A 48-year-old high school teacher, a former CIA agent and a mother of three, Jo had seemed to me to be doing the training on a dare. Her son and husband had been in my triathlon training that summer and they had spoken enthusiastically to Jo about doing the marathon program with them. But by her own admission, the diminutive Jo Pieper wasn't "the athlete of the family."

She came to the workouts consistently, but she seemed to be there mostly to socialize rather than train for her first marathon. In fact, there was something about her attitude that led me to suspect she might take herself out of the race itself. Sure enough, as our group was beginning its last run the Thursday before the marathon, she tripped on a crack in the sidewalk, fell, and broke her jaw. Her mouth was wired shut the next morning, and that evening she was scheduled to host a carbohydrate loading party at her home for the fifty runners in the program.

Virtually everyone in the group would have absolved Jo of her commitment to host the carbo-loading party, but she would hear nothing of it. While the rest of us feasted on pasta and carbo-casserole, Jo sifted a blended concoction of fruit and ice cream between the gaps in her wired teeth. And since she wasn't able to communicate above the bustle of the evening, nobody seemed to know exactly what was on her mind with regard to doing the marathon, which was only thirty-six hours away. I personally assumed that under the circumstances she would prefer to skip it.

The next morning I phoned and spoke with her son, John. Jo was indisposed, but evidently still hadn't ruled out doing the marathon. I told John to tell Jo that I would support her in either decision. I didn't expect to see his mother the morning of the race; nor did anyone else in the group. Nonetheless, Jo showed up on marathon morning with the intention of at least starting the race and taking it from there--one section of the course at a time.

And that's exactly how she managed to finish. I saw her at various points and each time she seemed to be gaining strength and confidence. I'll never forget the sight of her at twenty-three miles. She was walking by that point, but striding aggressively with that bandaged chin thrust out and her arms driving her powerfully past the slower walkers. There was definitely a sense of purpose about her that had been missing in the training. Yes, she had done her homework in the training, but I wondered what she must have gone through mentally those last few nights while she summoned the courage simply to begin the marathon.

Afterward, Jo acknowledged in her understated way that she'd had "a few things to consider" before she could bring herself to start the race. One of her major considerations was the possibility of being overcome on the course by the pain she had been experiencing in her jaw. Jo figured she'd be out there for at least seven hours, so there would be plenty of time for the initial excitement of the race to be replaced by the pain she feared. She'd finally decided to bring her pain pills with her in a bag around her waist in case she needed them. But she didn't take any before, during, or after the marathon.

Later, at the awards banquet, I apologized to Jo for having given up on her before the race. I had completely misread the depth of her commitment. Weeks later she expressed her anger to me at the lack of support she had felt from the people in the group, all of whom had wanted and expected her to take the easy way out. But that was not Jo's way of handling adversity, and if we wouldn't support her to finish the marathon in spite of the claustrophobic feeling of having to breathe through a wired jaw, she would do it on her own.

Jo's heroic story is an example of what many recreational racers have overcome to do the marathon. Twenty-six miles is an almost insurmountable barrier to most people, but even the simple act of getting out of bed at five o'clock every Saturday morning to meet the group for a six-thirty workout can be a struggle. For some, it's easier to roll over and go back to sleep, and those are the runners who generally fail to build the confidence to do the marathon because they have not conquered what we call their inner dragons. In this sense, the marathon training is a metaphor for life. Whatever inadequacies, escape mechanisms or insecurities we use to avoid difficult decisions in daily life will certainly become our way of dealing with adversity in the marathon training. Thus, the inner psyche becomes a battle ground for the mythical hero within us.

Everyone has a personal dragon to slay and an uniquely heroic story to tell. In the following chapter on racing, I share the insecure runner's prototypical inner struggle. At different times, I have had to fight different mental battles, sometimes to be victorious and at others to be defeated by unconscious forces within me. But the elements of the heroic struggle and the possibility of victory or defeat were always common themes in my mental preparation.

Chapter Thirteen
The Mental Side of Racing

I've always thought of myself as one of the best runners. If I'd had a different image of myself, say, of being average or even only a good runner, perhaps the mental side of racing wouldn't have been so difficult. As one of the best, however, I could rarely do a race simply for fun. I had to win, and although I could accept being defeated by a better runner, I couldn't stand losing to a peer or, worse, to someone I perceived to be inferior.

As a fifty-year-old masters runner on the comeback trail in 1994, I no longer saw myself as a young man in my prime. I would gaze wistfully at the best of the young runners, knowing I would never again be able to compete with them. But in the small-pond atmosphere of Hawaii I could expect to compete against--and even dominate--the best in my age division. Yet even there I often had to deal with the possibility of being defeated by another 50-year-old.

I had done five races in the first seven months of my 1994 racing comeback. Three of them had been major events on the Hawaii racing calendar, and looking back I could see that the more competitive the event, the greater the pressure I felt to perform. As a physically capable runner, I would have performed well in minor races against mediocre competition. But in the major races against the best runners, I couldn't rely exclusively on innate talent. If I wanted to win, I would be compelled again--as I had in times past--to master the multiple facets of the racing game.

At the beginning of the year, however, I was too arrogant to consider paying my dues. And since I wasn't tough enough or confident enough to deal with the pressure of a major race, I took myself out of contention by overtraining before the Pro-Bowl 5-K in February. Similarly, my performance in the March, 1994 Johnny Faerber 10-K had been impaired by an excruciating side stitch. I knew, however, that my excuse only masked a lack of preparation to run the race I expected of myself.

The fear of not being able to meet my expectations had always been the bane of my competitive experience. Even as a mature runner in

1994, I had fallen into the trap of expecting to be the best instead of simply *aiming* for the top. I could have aimed high without placing undue pressure on myself, but to expect to win added a heavy burden to the already intense pressure of a big race. Still, I persisted in entering major events, spurning smaller races in order to test myself immediately against the best. I consistently placed third in my age division, which impressed my friends but left me discontented. I was acknowledged as being one of the best, but I didn't feel that way at all. I wouldn't be satisfied until I was the best.

Tune-Ups and Major Races: After placing third in still another highly competitive event in April, 1994, I finally decided to run a minor, club event--the Lanikai 8-K on the fifth of June--as a tune-up for the Hard Rock 10-K two weeks later. This is the fourth time I've mentioned this sequence of events--now to illustrate yet another perspective.

I told no one what I planned to do at Lanikai and, as a result, I went into the race feeling minimal pressure. And thus I was free to perform exactly as I had intended. The next week, however, in trying to squeeze in more training before the Hard Rock 10-K, I injured my right hamstring. Needless to say, the injury was unintended, at least on the conscious level. Under normal circumstances, I would never have trained hard the week after a race, even after a minor tune-up. I needed at least a week of light training to ensure proper recovery from a race. Nonetheless, the day after Lanikai, I began a regimen of moderate interval workouts.

I thought I could continue running intervals in harmony with the way I felt. But I was coming off a successful and exhilarating tune-up and I was also less than two weeks from my first goal race of the year. Under the circumstances, I wasn't even paying attention to how I felt. After several days of relentlessly pushing myself in spite of increasing fatigue, the hamstring grabbed me so painfully I was forced to shut down my training, except for easy jogging. This was my first major injury of the year, and like the side stitches during the earlier Faerber 10-K, I knew it wasn't accidental. I suspected that at some as yet unconscious level I had created the injury to take myself out of racing the 1994 Hard Rock 10-K.

On reflection, I realized Hard Rock didn't appeal to me at all. If it weren't for its being the most competitive 10-K in the state, I wouldn't have considered doing it. I disliked the Hard Rock's mega-race atmosphere with thousands of runners clogging an out-and-back course. The race was run on major thoroughfares with only orange cones separating runners from the roaring traffic. The roads were cambered, rutted and dirty. It was a flat course, which made it fast but boring.

I much preferred a race such as the Lanikai 8-K. It, too, was mostly flat, but with several interesting hills, one of which had a magnificent view of Kaneohe Bay set against the windward-facing cliffs of the Koolau Mountain Range. The course followed a bike path around the most tucked-away residential community on the windward side of Oahu. It was a small Mid-Pacific Road Runners Club event, but one I had always enjoyed running.

I also realized that I wasn't ready to put myself on the line against the best in my age division. My inability to acknowledge and deal with this issue had probably been at the root of my hamstring injury. I had seen enough of the best runners to know they were still good enough to beat me. And I was resisting the thought of running Hard Rock only to find I needed another tune-up race and at least a couple of months of training to give myself a realistic shot at the top spot in my division.

Furthermore, my wife Nancy was my most loyal supporter, and she planned to be on the mainland at the time of the Hard Rock 10-K. Since she had always come to my races, I wasn't sure how I would have performed without her support. But I wasn't eager to run a race without her there to share in my experience. If she were willing to put up with the negative aspects of having a husband in heavy training, I felt she should also share in whatever success I might enjoy from the infrequent events which were the culmination of my training.

I was more or less aware of these thoughts at the time, though they are much clearer to me now with the temporary waning of my insatiable ambition. In fact, it wasn't until the night before the Hard Rock 10-K that I decided not to race it. With ambition still dominating my mental focus, I kept hoping the hamstring injury would go away.

But on Saturday evening, with the tenderness lingering on, I finally decided not to jeopardize my long term goals, especially for the unlikely possibility of winning a single event. Nonetheless, I went to the race as a spectator, thinking I might observe my competition and look for ways to beat them later.

Sizing Up the Competition: Ron Peroff was one of the strongest and most consistent runners in the 50-54 age division. I had occasionally raced against him ten years earlier, and since then I'd noticed from perusing race results that he'd remained competitive.

Peroff was a surgeon by profession and often on-call or committed to leaving for a game of tennis after races. He never stayed around to socialize, and our interaction had been generally limited to a handshake and a few words, so I knew little about him personally.

Though we hadn't run in the same race yet in 1994, he must have seen from race results that I was making a comeback. Though I had done little to warrant his concern, if he were normal, he'd probably spent a discomfiting moment or two stewing about the possibility of having to race against me. He may even have seen the list of competitors for the Hard Rock and known I was entered.

I was on the lookout for Peroff as I cruised the Hard Rock 10-K course on my motorcycle. I finally spotted him as he approached the three-mile mark along Ala Moana Boulevard. He appeared to be struggling, as he always did at the mid-point of a race, his chin high and his head well ahead of his body as though he were already leaning for the finishing tape. His unconventional form notwithstanding, Peroff was a tough competitor and a good runner.

At the four-mile mark, I got off my motorcycle and positioned myself where he could see me and I could observe his reaction. When I called out to him he looked up, did a quick double-take, and seemed to cogitate the significance of my not being a factor in the race after all. I could see in his expression a mixture of relief, disappointment and annoyance.

Peroff finished in 39:10, and won the 50-54 age division. I watched the top runners finish the race, including Candy Smiley, who won her age division with a time of 40:02. But I left as soon as possible to attend an early morning church service. As I pulled out of Ala Moana Park on my motorcycle I saw Peroff leaving, too, and I shouted, "Good race, Ron!"

He had won by more than a minute and I doubted whether I could have run as well, injured or not. I still had my work cut out for me, yet I sent out to the universe my silent resolve to beat Peroff head to head in the near future.

A Confidence Booster: My first step was to get back to hard training. The hamstring was improving daily, but I was reluctant to test it immediately with hard intervals. I settled for a series of two-hour runs, monitoring my heart rate and the hamstring, and after several weeks, I felt recovered enough to test myself with another low-key, tune-up race.

I chose one of my favorite Mid-Pacific Road Runners Club events-- the One-Hour Run on the track. In the back of my mind, I had been looking forward to running this event for months. Mid-Pac had previously held the One-Hour Run at various locations in Honolulu, but recently the club's administrators had moved it to a pleasant setting among the eucalyptus trees at Schofield Barracks, high on Oahu's central plane. I had always enjoyed the unique atmosphere of a one-hour run-- the constant visual contact with other runners, each of whom is vying to cover the most distance in exactly sixty minutes.

But since most runners didn't seem to relish the prospect of circling a 400-meter track for an hour, I didn't expect the best runners in my age division to be there. On the other hand, I had a strong hunch that Steve Kingsley--a younger runner of my ability--would compete because the race was being held on his home turf. Steve had beat me in the Tamanaha 15-K, and I had evened the score by out-kicking him at the Lanikai 8-K. The One-Hour Run represented a step up again to the longer 15-K distance, so if Kingsley were to gain another advantage on me, this was his distance and his opportunity.

The longer distance notwithstanding, I felt confident before the race. I had done four long runs during the last two weeks and the hamstring was no longer bothering me. Thinking I wouldn't have to run an all-out effort, I did my usual Tuesday long run, but skipped the one scheduled for Friday in anticipation of the Saturday afternoon event. Before the race, I took a thirty-minute easy warm-up, and noted that Steve Kingsley wasn't warming up at all. With a few minutes to go before the start, I saw him jogging towards the toilet, and when we came to the starting line he stood on the track behind me.

My plan was to run at a pace that would have chopped a couple minutes off my Tamanaha 15-K time. When the gun went off, I started exactly at that quick, relaxed pace and within a few seconds Steve tore past me, surging more than fifty yards ahead during the next lap. At that point, he eased back and seemed to be content with a much slower pace, and I quickly closed the gap. By the fourth lap I had come up on him and another fellow, both of whom were chatting amiably and enjoying a leisurely race.

I went right by them, and they stopped their conversation to concentrate on staying with me. Soon Steve was breathing audibly at my heels and the other fellow, Wayne Neidhardt, came up and challenged for the lead. I was content to settle in behind him, as he was running slightly faster than my intended pace. By twenty-five minutes into the run, however, it was apparent that Wayne was losing his concentration. On alternate laps he would either be on pace or dragging, so rather than continue tripping over his heels, I came up beside him to check his breathing. It hadn't been apparent to me from the rear, but from the side I could tell he was already breathing audibly. I surged ahead immediately, and I was close to lapping both Steve and Wayne thirty minutes later.

The One-Hour Run was a competitive cake-walk, but it told me I was moving up in the divisional pecking order. It took me a week to recover from it, which meant it had been a significant effort, even though I had kept myself away from heavy breathing until the last two laps. The race was a good test of my ability and exactly what I needed to build my confidence.

Focused on a Goal Race: After the One-Hour Run, I set my sights on one of Hawaii's most competitive races, the August 1994 Hawaiian Style 8-K. I liked everything about this event. Eight kilometers was not only well suited to my natural talent, but I had also developed a solid base of 8-K tempo ability with my intervals and racing since the beginning of the year.

Furthermore, as a volunteer race official in recent years, it had been my job to call the two-mile time during the race so I was familiar with the course and the competition. Set deep in Manoa Valley, with dark green cliffs dominating the scenery, it did a loop and a half through quiet residential neighborhoods. The course was hilly, but the steep hills were short and the long hills were gentle, so with my long legs I didn't expect to have trouble with it.

I also liked and respected the race director, Connie Comiso. Connie had been the top woman racer in Hawaii for most of the past seventeen years, and I had often referred to her in talking about Hawaii's best runners. She had recently returned for a visit to the islands after a year on the mainland, and I had taken the opportunity the week before the race to interview her on the topic of her competitive consistency. I wanted to learn how she had managed to perform so well and for so long.

I was not surprised to learn that Connie had always been driven to excel at whatever she did, including running. (My wife liked to point out that she had a well-developed masculine side to her personality--a nice way of saying Connie was as tough as nails.) Her competitiveness ran in the family. Indeed, her father, who was also driven to be the best at everything he did, once demanded to know why she hadn't *won* the Boston Marathon after she proudly told him that she had qualified for and run the race.

During the past seventeen years, Connie had never varied her training schedule. She ran once a day, including three hard workouts a week: a long run of fifteen to twenty miles (her most important run), an interval (speed) workout, and a hill run. Within this basic structure, she varied courses and distances depending on the races she was pointing for, but the basic three hard workouts never changed. Although I would have expected her to vary the structure of her training at different times of the year, it made sense that the most consistent racer in Hawaii was also the most consistent and disciplined runner.

Connie believed that seventy percent of racing was physical training, and ninety percent was in her head. "But that adds up to one-hundred and sixty percent," I said in mock protest. Her answer came back at me like it was shot out of a cannon, "Then make it forty percent physical and sixty percent mental. In a close race, it comes down to who wants it more. I have a high tolerance for pain, and if I can push harder and faster than the next guy, then (she paused momentarily--perhaps searching for a more profound conclusion--laughed and stated the obvious) I'll finish ahead.

"I pick and choose my races according to the time of the year and the course," she added. "But how much effort I put into a race has a lot to do with the carrot, the prize for winning--especially if there is money or a trip involved, as opposed to trophies, plaques or medals."

With the Hawaiian Style 8-K, Connie gave back to the community what she most appreciated in other races. She worked hard as race director, lining up sponsors who were willing to give age-group winners practical and worthwhile prizes. She often said that her Hawaiian Style race awards were "edible, wearable or flyable."

I was tempted to ask her what I would receive for winning my age division in her race, but decided to be surprised. Anyway, for me to talk of prizes a week before the race would have been absurd. I still hadn't come to grips with my expectations.

Tapering and Visualizing: With two weeks to go before the race, I had quit doing my hard workouts and my extra 35-minute hill runs, and shifted to a tapering schedule of moderate interval workouts. I wanted to see how running a series of fast 400-meter intervals would affect my perception of racing tempo and my tolerance for lactic acid.

I intended to run ten 400-meter intervals at a fast pace every other day that week, with ten steady state quarters at a quick-and-easy tempo on the alternate days to recover from the faster workouts (see Figure 12.2 on page 155). Since my 1200-meter intervals had been rapid for me at a pace of 100 to 95 seconds per quarter, I reckoned that anything between 90 and 85 seconds would seem downright fast. Perhaps, I hoped, after a week of fast intervals, my ninety-four-second racing pace would seem relatively slow, and the ninety to eighty-five-second pace might not seem prohibitively fast during a determined, half-mile drive to the finish.

I decided to run the fast intervals during the second to the last week before the race, and then taper my training during the last week with progressively fewer, and much slower, tempo intervals. I was concerned about the possible negative effect of a sudden injection of fast 400-meter intervals--definitely a step up in the volume of my speed-work--and I figured this two-week schedule would at least give me time to back off and recover if I inadvertently threw myself into shock.

On Tuesday evening, I inserted a visualization run on the Hawaiian Style course, knowing from experience it would be one of my most important pre-race activities. I wanted to see the course exactly as I would run it, so I took one of my student runners with me and pointed out the mile marks, the hills, and the gutters that could be used like the banked curves of an indoor track. I saw the places where the road was extremely cambered and where I planned to run on the sidewalk. At every point, I determined my position on the road, looking for the flattest surfaces or places that would offer a competitive advantage.

Later, with the physical layout firmly in mind, I plotted the most likely competitive scenarios. I saw the race developing between me and Ron Peroff. I figured he would go out faster than I, but I would push harder than usual in order to maintain loose contact with him. I wouldn't push the uphills, but after the mid-point, I would use the downhills to my advantage in order to close the gap between us. If I were with him with a quarter mile to go, there was no way I'd let him beat me.

Ten days before the race, my diet of fast 400-meter intervals was going well, but I was feeling out of touch with my racing tempo. Thus, on Thursday morning, I threw in a workout with single intervals of 1200- and 2400-meters, and finished with three 90-second 400s. The workout was a confidence booster because I was able to settle into the longer intervals as though I hadn't missed a week of doing them. And although the fast quarters I had been running didn't seem to have made a positive difference in my performance, they hadn't made a negative difference either. Thus, eight days before the race I felt on track toward an outstanding performance. Thirty-six hours later, however, I made a decision I would regret for the next seven days.

I had been carefully monitoring my leg strength for the past month as I followed my schedule of easy hill runs. I expected that after I stopped running hills before the race, I would begin to feel added power in my quads. Every day during the previous week, as I walked up the stairs to get the mail, I'd asked myself how my quads felt. Most of the time they were slightly inflamed and weak in the muscle tissue just above the knees. Seven days before the race, however, that burning suddenly disappeared and I felt a power in my quads that hadn't been there in years.

"Great!" I thought. If I was feeling this good with a week to go, I could sneak in one more fast workout. I didn't want to peak too soon and feel flat the day of the race. Thus, on Saturday afternoon, I ran a hard interval workout, blasting ten 400s at eighty-five seconds and feeling the exhilaration of the fastest quarters I had done in years.

Unfortunately, after the workout my hamstring became inflamed again. I wasn't expecting that, and the injury threw me for a psychological loop. I wasn't worried about the pain *per se*. I knew from recent experience that it would go away if I rested during the next week. I was more concerned about the meaning of the injury.

Gathering for a Major Effort: The immediate impact of the injury was to keep me from training as intensely as I might have otherwise. I didn't want to baby the hamstring at a point when I should have been running harder. By the Tuesday before the race, however, I was beginning to think it was just as well I wasn't running as I had planned.

I felt so bad I became convinced I had exhausted myself with the fast 400s on the track. Based on experience, I suspected I might need as much as two weeks to bounce back. Of course I didn't have two weeks, so I prayed my energy would return, and to help it along I skipped my Tuesday workout and began carbohydrate loading. With my training mileage at zero for the forty-eight hours between Monday and Wednesday afternoons, however, I soon had the feeling I was over-eating. One imbalance was leading to another.

On Wednesday, during my last low-key interval workout on the grass in Kapiolani Park, I saw Ron Peroff listening to his Walkman and jogging slowly around the bend towards me. My first impulse was to ask him if he would be running on Sunday, but I decided that would reveal my concern. No, I thought, my curiosity would be satisfied soon enough. Meanwhile, this meeting was an opportunity for competitive one-upmanship.

Before Peroff had an opportunity to say anything I called out an enthusiastic greeting. "Hey, Ron!" I said in a loud, clear voice. He raised the Walkman feebly, nodded in my direction and blurted something unintelligible. Peroff had often seemed to me to stagger as he ran so I couldn't be sure whether he was simply leaning too far forward or bowing slightly in my direction. Yet, intuitively I knew I had won a mental point.

My bravado was only skin deep. I wondered why I was running intervals when I felt so tired. Wouldn't I be wiser to "walk the dog" as Peroff was doing on his easy jog? I knew I shouldn't second-guess my training. Yet twenty-four hours later, and only sixty hours before the race, I felt terrible. My energy was shot, my hamstring was still inflamed, and my quads were as achy and weak as ever. I was in big trouble. Kicking myself emotionally, I seriously considered dropping out of the race. Yet I knew dropping out was not an option. I had learned this lesson many times before: no matter how bad I felt--even the day before a big race--miracles often happened.

It had been ten years since I had experienced the pressure of a big race in which I might be a serious contender in my age division, and I had forgotten what the energy-gathering process could be like. Yet I wasn't sure if my mind was unconsciously withholding psychic energy in anticipation of the huge effort I was about to exert, or whether my energy was simply not going to materialize because I had trained too hard five days earlier. This was a mental battle I had fought years before and I shouldn't have let it bother me again. Nonetheless, my confidence couldn't have been lower.

A few times I caught myself fantasizing about the race, and I could feel my heart gear up immediately, as if I were actually running it. I was glad my body was showing signs of readiness, but I also knew the importance of conserving every bit of psychic energy. I had visualized the race until the Sunday before, and then I'd stopped mentally rehearsing it entirely. The last week was not the time to be seeing myself in action.

Thus, I kept assiduously to my usual pre-race discipline of knowing I had a race to run, but not visualizing it at all. I had done my homework in that regard and I trusted that the race would evolve accordingly.

Final Preparation: On Friday, I ate starchy foods at every meal, but against my better judgement I decided to indulge my yearning for a couple buttermilk donuts. Eating them had seemed to give me added energy before other races, though the most recent time I had eaten them I could tell the lard in them had adversely affected my digestion.

That afternoon, I could feel my intestines beginning to rebel, either from the greasy donuts or my compulsive overeating to do something about my flagging energy. I could feel a deep, dull ache in my gut, the precursor of the side stitch that had ruined the Johnny Faerber 10-K earlier in the year. And it wasn't only the greasy donuts I felt, but the cheese and oil I was using to garnish the pasta. I resolved to eat only simple foods on Saturday, hoping I hadn't done irreparable damage to my intestinal track.

The next day--less than twenty-four hours before the race--the ache in my gut persisted and I could feel my anxiety reaching a critical level. Moreover, despite having run a very easy workout the evening before, my quads were weak and achy. I came home from having done some light yard work at church and took a long nap. When I woke up they felt much better, though nowhere near as powerful as they had the week before. I sensed the race slipping away from me so I stayed in bed and read for a while, trying to keep my mind off it. And at three o'clock I went to pick up my racing packet.

One of my former running associates, Ron Pate, was working the packet line. He saw me coming and volunteered immediately that Ron Peroff would be my main competition. My curiosity was finally satisfied, and I noticed I didn't feel a surge of fear in finding out Peroff was in the race. Somehow I had always known he would be. I was anxious, but not about Peroff. Still, to make conversation with Ron Pate and to get a line on Peroff, I asked Ron how hard Peroff usually went out in his races. "Easy," was his quick response. I had to take Ron's opinion with a grain of salt. After all, my "hard" could have been Pate's "easy." Still, this was interesting information. I planned to position myself close behind Peroff at the starting line, and thus I would see for myself how hard he started the race.

Before I left, I thought of scanning the entry-list for the other competitive 50-year-olds, but I hadn't done my homework well enough to know the names of the several other good runners in town. This was another sign of the flakiness I'd felt all week, but I let it go and trusted that, once the race began, I would be able to tell from those around me who my competition was.

The Mental Battle: The Hawaiian Style 8-K was being held on the twenty-first of August, and it would be the last major race of the year for me. Whether I won or lost, I planned to spend the autumn months in uninterrupted base training. But it would be a long fall if I didn't do well against Peroff. Of course, if he beat me and I came in second or third (a likely possibility), no one would think any less of me.

Unless I crashed completely, or there were some ringers in the 50-54 age division, I would probably finish in the top three. That would be good enough for "community relations." But for myself, I wouldn't be satisfied with anything less than a victory. I had trained eight months for this moment. Yet as I headed home that afternoon, I was an emotional mess. Somehow I had to pull myself together, otherwise the training and the visualizations would have been for naught.

I began by cleaning the house. I wanted nothing pending in my life the next morning so I cleaned the kitchen, swept and vacuumed, made the bed and cleaned the bird cage and the fish tank. Then I sat and decided how I wanted to spend the rest of the evening. I planned a simple meal of a couple of bananas and some bread with a little juice. Nancy and I would see a movie as we often did on Saturdays, though this was not part of my usual pre-race routine. I felt oddly confident (or foolish) enough to establish a new one, however. I wouldn't be able to get to sleep early because of the nap I had taken that morning, but I could use the time late that evening setting up the race for myself--not reviewing it visually, but coming to terms with whatever was bothering me about it. Somewhere in my mental preparation I had overlooked something that was causing major mental anguish.

I shielded myself with pastimes until I was finally alone, wide awake, eight hours before the race. My biggest worry--taking precedence over my moderately weak and achy quads--was the persistent ache in my gut. There wasn't much I could do about it except light yoga and deep breathing. But I still couldn't relax my churning, belching intestines. I kept hoping they'd be okay by dawn, but I'd need a long, gentle warmup before the race to deal with any persisting discomfort. Maybe, I told myself, if I started jogging early enough and slowly enough, I could gradually loosen up my gut.

I was concerned that the pain didn't originate in my digestive track, but in my will, which I felt to be centered in my abdomen. Maybe at some poorly understood, esoteric level, my psyche was rebelling at the prospect of what I was about to do. This wasn't going to be an easy effort. Peroff had done a 39:10 10-K only eight weeks before, and at the time I might have been able to run slightly under 40-minutes. Now I had the audacity to challenge for first in the division. Moreover, I intended to win. The shorter racing distance would be in my favor. Still I figured I'd have to cut forty seconds from my Lanikai 8-K time to have a shot at Peroff. Some of that time would come off with improved ability. But I wondered whether I had improved enough.

As I lay tossing and turning, I tried to take confidence from having trained consistently during the past five months. I had injured myself several times, but not so seriously that I'd missed a lot of training. I had maintained a steady regimen of intervals and long runs, I had added hills for power, and several extra recovery runs per week for stamina. I *had* done my homework, but I was afraid I had ruined my performance with bad, last-minute decisions. If so, it wouldn't have been the first time I had been my own worst enemy.

These thoughts came in waves which were difficult to control. I tried every meditation technique I knew, but my mind kept spewing negativity. If I had been truly prepared for this race, I thought, I'd be sleeping like a baby. Something was out of balance and I couldn't put my finger on it. I kept telling myself to relax, but that wasn't working. Finally, as if my mind were a separate entity, I simply commanded it to be quiet. There was no amount of thinking I could do at that point to make me run faster the next morning. My mind had to shut up and accept the fact that my body was going to take it for a ride. I began repeating this idea as a mantra, "My body is taking my mind for a ride."

And soon I dozed off.

I woke up at one o'clock and couldn't get back to sleep. It was a hot and muggy August night, and I was thirsty. I decided to take a chance with my stomach and drank a glass of water. I did some easy stretching and then I broke my routine by going outside for a walk. I headed up the hill, but that was a mistake because I immediately felt a cramp developing in my right calf. I turned and walked back down the hill, feeling the cramp abate but realizing I'd have to be careful with it warming up before the race.

The walk told me what I wanted to know. Though I had felt better occasionally before recent workouts, my energy was good enough to make a go of the race. My quads were still not right, but I had stopped worrying about them. I would perform as well as in my training--in spite of less-than optimum power in my quads. I had done those fast 400s a week ago and I hadn't recovered as I had hoped I would, but there was no use crying over spilled milk. After all, I couldn't be sure at this point whether I would have felt better by training differently anyway. And who knows, I may have done something even more stupid to jeopardize my performance.

Then my perennial worthiness issues came to the fore. I didn't feel worthy of winning the division because of all the mistakes I had made. And my mind kept recounting them. Soon, however, I realized I needed once again to get off my negative position. Yes, the training had gone imperfectly. But hey, I was here with three hours to go and my assessment was that I'd make a good showing. What more did I want? Well, I wanted and expected to win, and I wasn't sure I was willing to pay the price. Ah, at last, *there* was the rub. My body was the vehicle that would have to endure the pain of those last three miles. And I hadn't come to terms with the fear and aversion the physical part of me felt about the coming effort.

The key issue, I realized immediately, was delineating the circumstances under which I would ask myself to really hurt. My training had prepared me to go out at a rapid, even pace, and the physical part of me wasn't willing to go out as fast as I had planned in my mind several weeks before. Thus, I resolved to run the first mile conservatively, and to let Peroff go if he went out fast. Furthermore, if this were to be an all-out effort, I didn't want it to be in vain. In other words, I wouldn't run all-out unless I had a chance to win.

There was no doubt in my mind I'd be within striking distance sometime after the mid-point. At that moment, I would defer to my physical self the decision whether or not to intensify my effort. If my body was still strong, I would go for the win no matter how much effort I needed to exert. I thought up an appropriate mantra to cement this thought in consciousness and finally fell back asleep.

Show Time: My body knows from memory the perfect way of feeling before a race. I have felt it many times and usually I can tell the moment I wake up whether this will be one of those perfect mornings. I was not feeling that way as I got out of bed one hundred minutes before the race.

My energy had not miraculously improved, but by then my energy was a non-issue. I was vaguely concerned about the possibility of stomach pains, but even that seemed far from consciousness. I had dealt with those issues and I had my plan of action. Now I was simply intent on the task at hand. I got dressed and Nancy and I left for the race.

One of the first runners I saw there was Tony Nonan, who had beat me for second place in our age division at the Tamanaha 15-K four months earlier. Seeing him was a coincidence the meaning of which I pondered as I started a gentle jog forty minutes before the race. Now with at least two tough competitors to consider, I had to reaffirm my decision to hold back and run my own race. For if one of them went out fast, I couldn't risk going out with him, dying, and being vulnerable to the other coming up from behind.

I took satisfaction in knowing they were there. These guys were both good runners so the top spots would not be cheap. The winner and even the second place finisher would have to earn their places. I asked myself whether I'd be satisfied with third place. Yes, I could live with that, if they beat me. But I had no intention of letting that happen.

I kept myself out of sight as I warmed up, choosing a course that would have few if any runners on it. I wanted to be alone to focus on the process of bringing myself up to race exertion without exacerbating the leg cramp of the night before or the stomach cramps that--if they weren't handled correctly--could become a serious threat to my performance. Fortunately, neither problem revealed itself as I jogged very slowly during the first twenty minutes.

Then I threw in a forty-second surge and lifted my heart rate from light to steady state exertion--seventy percent of my maximum heart rate. It didn't seem to take much effort to get my heart rate to that level. I had good sustainable energy, and all systems were still on "Go."

It was true I didn't feel as light and quick as I would have liked. But I knew at that moment, from having felt as well while warming up before a dozen interval workouts in the past months, that I would be able to do what I intended.

The Start: I approached the starting line from the front with less than two minutes to go before the gun. I could see Peroff already waiting there and looking at me as I jogged directly toward him. I said a quiet hello to a female runner standing to his left, but walked past Peroff without acknowledging his presence. I had already done that several days before; now it was time to race.

I positioned myself right behind him, but slightly to his left so he could sense my presence. He stood there calmly, and when the starting gun was fired he took off like a rocket. So much for Ron Pate's assessment that Peroff went out easily. I let him go, focused on my spot on the road ahead and settled into that familiar rapid, pressing tempo I'd been practicing for months.

There was no way I would have wanted to stay with Peroff. My pace was as fast as I could handle at that moment, and besides, I wasn't out of the woods yet regarding the side stitch problem. Under the circumstances, a fast early pace would have been suicidal. If Peroff could stay ahead by going out fast, I thought, more power to him. But as he disappeared around the bend at the top of the first hill, I had a strong hunch I'd see him later.

Meanwhile, Tony Nonan was just ahead of me and going out at a rational pace. I wanted to stay in contact with him, but he gradually pulled away on the second half-mile--a long and gradual downhill stretch. I was content to let him go, knowing I was running at least as fast as the 6:20 pace I'd planned. In fact, my first mile was 6:15, and I was delighted that the first critical section of the race had passed, finding me ahead of schedule with my energy intact. Now I had a downhill and level mile stretch in which to reel in people who had gone out too fast. I couldn't see Peroff among the group of runners far ahead, but Nonan was thirty yards in front of me and still pulling away.

I was working as hard as I could, given the stitch in my side that had come on shortly into the second mile, but, although I was pushing hard, it wasn't getting worse. I took confidence in knowing I had run longer, harder efforts before with this particular stitch. I could live with it for a mile or two, and with luck it would go away.

Decision Time: The third mile is the nasty one in this race, with a short steep hill at both ends, and a longer gradual assent in the middle. I was picking off a crowd of younger runners and I could see Nonan cruising about sixty yards ahead, but no longer gaining on me.

My breathing was heavy and audible, but I was feeling as strong as I had hoped I would at this point. The side stitch was still there, but not a major factor. I continued to bide my time on the uphill stretches-- looking ahead occasionally for signs that my competition was beginning to flag. Sure enough, Nonan was coming back and he was bringing Connie Comiso with him. "Wouldn't I love to beat her?" I thought-- especially after our conversation about racing the week before. The pieces were gathering themselves on the chessboard and I was in the best position to see them clearly.

I heard the three-mile time but didn't bother to compute my pace. I was no longer concerned with it. The course levels and straightens at that point and I could see Peroff about seventy yards ahead, with Connie and Nonan gaining on him. Suddenly I realized this was my moment of decision. I didn't need to look at my heart rate monitor to know I was running at ragged edge.

From the sidewalk, my wife yelled that I was looking good, and I cast an affirming glance in her direction. I was running at ragged edge, but I still had energy to burn. Moreover, I knew I could push it even harder without hurting myself unduly. With a sudden sense of urgency I took my effort up a notch.

Bringing Home the Bacon: The stitch was gone, I was running downhill and closing quickly on the three ahead. This was going to be an interesting race and I felt very good about my position. Connie and Nonan had passed Peroff, and I was closing on him fast.

Just past four and a quarter miles I managed to bring my breathing into a semblance of control, though I was still breathing like a horse as I came up on Peroff's outside shoulder. Though he was breathing audibly, too, he wasn't working as hard as I. He looked over at me and immediately surged ahead, and I tucked in behind him while he closed the gap between Connie and Nonan twenty yards ahead.

With three hundred and fifty yards to go, the course takes a ninety- degree right turn and heads up a two-lane street for three hundred yards before turning right again to the finish. As we made the first turn, Peroff was an arm's-length ahead of me and in contact with the others. I cut the turn behind him and as I floated into the middle of the street, my last impression of Peroff was the awkwardness of his position, trying to bull his way between Connie and Nonan, while they appeared to close the gap between them. I took that moment to make a determined move, surging powerfully into the lead and cutting decisively into the path of those behind.

I was living the finish exactly as I had envisioned it twelve days before. I looked back, pleased at the gap I'd opened. I didn't feel myself to be in serious trouble, but the race was at a critical juncture. I had two hundred yards to run with another right hand turn still to negotiate. I had planned to run on the relatively level, central crown of the road, but the race organizers had coned a lane that forced me unexpectedly to run in the cambered right lane.

I was momentarily nonplussed, but quickly realized the coned lane offered a tactical advantage by narrowing the space in which someone could pass me from behind. I pulled up beside a younger runner to narrow it even further, and just before the last turn I surged again. Looking back, all I could see was daylight.

As I cut the last turn I could hear a half-dozen athletes from my training program shouting encouragement to me from the sidewalk. I looked back again and, though I couldn't see the three I was looking for, I kicked into a higher gear anyway, emphatically claiming the last thirty-five meters as my own.

Once over the finish line, I let out a few dry heaves. Considering the violence of the last several minutes, my body was handling the lactic acid well, but it had been an exciting drive to the finish at maximum exertion and I was finally glad I had done those fast quarters in my training.

By the time I had cleared the finisher's chute, my breathing was back to normal, and I paused to shake hands with Connie, Nonan and Peroff. I thanked my wife for her support, and my next impulse was to say a silent prayer of praise for this wonderful victory. Under the circumstances of the past week, it seemed more of a gift than a legacy.

I knew I had done some things correctly, but I gave credit to my higher power for bringing me unscathed through a week of major pressure and resistance. Now I felt as though I had entered into an immensely spacious clearing.

Aftermath: I didn't have words to describe how satisfied I felt with my performance, but my wife supplied one: awesome. That would do. I had run my last mile at a 5:48 pace, thirty-seconds under my average for the race. My time was 31:23--exactly forty seconds faster than my Lanikai 8-K time and precisely as fast as I had figured I needed to run to beat Peroff.

I didn't talk with Peroff after the race. He left immediately, as he usually does. Connie was gracious in acknowledging my kick, and Nonan's first words to me were "What are you taking?" as if some magic potion could have made the difference in my performance. Ironically, I had been taking several highly touted nutritional supplements in the previous months, none of which seemed to have made the least difference in my training or racing.

I didn't mention the herbs and vitamins, but simply told Tony I had decided to do some serious training. He nodded and said he had not been able to train properly before the race because of more compelling work commitments. He had tried to stay with me after I had passed him, but he felt his hamstring tighten up on him so he'd backed off. The hamstring injury, he said, was a chronic problem that occurred whenever he tried to do intervals.

As we chatted, I realized I liked the guy, as I usually do with close competitors. I invited him to run some 1200-meter intervals with me at a hundred to ninety-five second pace. "You should be able to do that," I said. He nodded and we agreed to be in contact after recovering from the race.

The Mental Side of Racing in Perspective: I was surprised by how much recovery I needed after the Hawaiian Style 8-K. I felt some false energy develop on Wednesday, but that was short-lived. It took me a full two weeks before I felt ready to run hard again, given various persistent aches and pains. It had been the second all-out race of my comeback, and it had a much more positive effect on me than the Pro-Bowl 5-K I'd run in February.

Nonetheless, I wasn't anxious to jump immediately into hard training. This was a race to savor, and I enjoyed the recollection of it during most of my private moments. My joy and exhilaration lasted about two weeks. Then my ambition took over again. I knew of at least one other fifty-year-old whom I had yet to beat. But the months of training that lay ahead would be a lot easier to endure knowing my previous five months of hard work had paid off.

I'd realized my potential without having established a prior base of mileage. But it wasn't beating the other runners or gaining transitory glory that gave the story meaning. It was triumphing over my lower, negative and anxious nature. In the final analysis, running the race hadn't been as difficult as the struggle I'd had with myself the week before. Now, I aimed to take my ability to a completely new level.

Chapter Thirteen Synopsis:

- **The Main Issue:** How can I make a mental breakthrough from good races to great races?

- **Concepts:**

    1) Visualization is the activity of seeing a race exactly as you want to run it, including the course, the competition and the way the race is most likely to develop.
    2) A test-effort/tune-up race is one that simulates several aspects of the goal race you intend to run.
    3) A goal race is the central focus of your training. You intend to perform at your best for a goal race because you will be at an adaptive peak and you will have developed a full complement of racing abilities.
    4) A racing goal is a statement of what you are aiming to accomplish during a coming event. Goals give you a way to focus your intention for the race.
    5) Intention refers to your purpose, your plan and the particular meaning the race holds for you.
    6) An expectation is a way of thinking about a coming event that precludes the possibility of other outcomes.
    7) Confidence is the knowledge that you are capable of achieving your goals, based on a realistic assessment of your recent training and your ability.
    8) Being focused is a way of concentrating your physical and mental power on your goals for a coming event.
    9) Gathering is the unconscious storing of your mental and physical energy before a race.
    10) Mental themes are ways of verbally focusing your intention on

the race you want to run.

11) A mental breakthrough is a way of overcoming mental or attitudinal barriers to a best effort.

12) A best effort is a very hard to all-out racing effort that finds you in peak condition, feeling eager to race, and with a full complement of racing abilities.

13) Your racing self-image is the way you think of yourself as a racer and a competitor. Some of the major dichotomies are best runner/worst runner, competent/incompetent, tough/-weak, fast/slow, winner/loser, fully able/unable.

■ Theoretical Tenets:

1) Your self-image can affect your performance as much in racing as it does in any other part of life. It's imperative to have a realistic self-image. Otherwise, you won't be able to focus your intention clearly and cleanly on your racing goals.

2) After your training goals have been accomplished, your intention is the major determining factor in your racing performance. A best effort will occur when your intention is as clear and focused as you can make it.

3) Tune-ups and test efforts can be highly adaptive efforts because they are harder than your usual regimen of hard and easy workouts and, therefore, they more closely simulate the overall effort of the race you want to run.

4) Pre-race themes and routines help to shield you from thinking about a race and, thereby, wasting your psychic energy at a point when you should have already developed a clear intent.

■ Relationships:

1) The more clearly focused you are before a race, the better your chance of accomplishing your goals.

2) The more closely you are prepared to achieve your racing goals, the less likely you'll be to experience pre-race mental anguish.

3) The more closely you accomplish what you intend during training or a tune-up race, the higher your subsequent confidence will soar.

■ **Questions and Answers:**

1) How can I make a mental breakthrough from good races to great races?

First, you must accept the idea that you cannot separate your training from your racing. If you want to run great races, you must run great workouts. This was the subject of part one. Next, you must build a full complement of racing abilities. Knowing how to set up your training to build specific abilities was the subject of part two.

Next, you've got to resolve the following issues: how do you want to feel and how hard do you want to run? If you want to feel eager to race, then you've got to be fully recovered from recent training and well rested on a specific day. This is the subject of part five.

In this part, I explored the issue of one's willingness to run an all-out effort. No matter how hard you plan to run, you must be *willing* to run that hard. Sometimes it helps to make agreements with yourself, setting the conditions under which you will actually push yourself to a certain limit. To say that an all-out race isn't easy is an understatement in the extreme. It can be outrageously difficult, so you had better be mentally prepared.

You don't need to have run all-out in training to be able to run all-out in a race. In fact, ironically, if you do too much all-out training or racing, you may end up adamantly resisting the prospect of racing all-out when the time comes to do so in a goal race. On the other hand, you'll forget the pain of all-out racing if you give it enough time between all-out efforts. So unless you are very mentally tough, don't expect to run all-out every week.

2)   How can I develop a clear intention?

Here the issues are: what do you want to accomplish? What is your plan for reaching your goals? And what importance or meaning does this race have for you?

Obviously your goals must be consistent with your self-image and your ability. If they aren't, you'll probably suffer mental turmoil before the race. You may even find a way to take yourself out of it with an accident or an injury. Similarly, your plan has to be designed to reach your goals. You can't just step into a race without having visualized it and thought about it.

Finally, the race has to have some meaning and importance, otherwise why would you put so much effort into it? Sometimes the meaning of a race is not entirely apparent until the event itself. Nonetheless, you should know why you are running the race and how important it is for you to accomplish your goals.

Part IV
Adaptation

The first track event I ever ran was a 2:14 half-mile, which was the equivalent of running about a 5:03 mile. I was a junior in high school and completely unassuming about my ability. Within ten weeks of my first race I brought my times down to 2:02 in the half and 4:37 in the mile. These were excellent high school times for Hawaii in 1961, and local track buffs marveled at my potential. Even I began to wonder how fast I would eventually run.

My hero at the time was Herb Elliot, the world record holder in the mile. In reading Elliot's book, *The Golden Mile,* it was apparent to me that he was extremely tough. He did arduous workouts and he never lost a mile race, no matter how strong the challenge. I dreamed of running under four minutes for the mile as Elliot had, but I wondered whether I had the talent to run four minutes, or the mental toughness to push myself that hard in training.

During the following years, I brought my mile times down to 4:28 as a senior, to 4:19 as a UH freshman, to 4:12 as a transfer student and, ultimately, to 4:06 as a UO junior. My times improved because each year I upped the ante in my training, adding long ·runs, hills and intervals. But my increased training load was no more difficult to bear as a college junior as it had been my first year in high school. I was doing more in college, but the overall effort wasn't harder.

Similarly, as my mile times improved, the effort it took to run them remained the same. Each year, my best performance was an all-out effort--extremely uncomfortable and as fast as I could run. Ostensibly, nothing had changed about the races except my times. Yet there had to have been something else at play. Certainly, my training had affected my performances, but only indirectly. Training affects capacity for exertion, and capacity responds to the metabolic forces of adaptation.

If adaptation is a noticeable, long term increase in capacity for exertion, there was no question I had adapted to my training. Though I couldn't see the effects of adaptation on a day to day basis, over a period of weeks or months something would happen to my capacity that enabled me to do more in my training, and to lower my mile times, too.

Along the way to my fastest mile, one of my most important steps was to add twice-a-day workouts to my training regimen. In retrospect, I see that learning to run "double workouts" helped me establish a base of eighty-mile training weeks, which was a key to my fastest mile. Yet even the effort it took to run twice a day was manageable. In fact, the toughest part of running double workouts was in deciding initially to do them.

In this part, I begin by telling how my experience of running double workouts at UO affected my decision to run them again during my 1994 comeback. My goal each time was to take my ability to a higher level. And in 1994, I aimed to measure my adaptive progress.

Chapter Fourteen
Double Workouts

The University of Oregon during the 1960s was one of the most competitive running environments in the nation. I didn't know if I could make the track team there, but the last of Oregon's recent crop of four-minute milers was graduating when I arrived in the spring of 1964, and I would have a shot at being one of the best milers during the following school year. I was willing to put in the work, but I wasn't sure what it would take to be one of the best. I was concerned about the simplest issues.

I had heard about Eugene's heavy rainfall, for instance, and I was worried about having to run in it. I asked the top senior miler, Archie San Romani Jr., what the best runners did when it rained. He said they put on rain gear and went out for their run. Obviously, Archie gave no quarter when it came to rain. He took me to the army surplus store in Eugene, where he pointed to a hooded, rubberized raincoat hanging on a rack. It was olive drab and it weighed a ton, but with a light sleeveless sweat shirt underneath, plus mittens and long winter underwear, I would be warm, if not totally dry in the wettest weather.

While we were shopping, Archie gave me some advice. He said the best runners at Oregon all ran twice a day. The message was clear: if I wanted to be one of the best, I should run what he called "double workouts." I was afraid he was going to suggest that. I had already given double workouts a try. One foggy morning that spring, I had risen early for a morning jog. It was freezing cold, the streets were deserted, and I didn't have a clue how long or how hard to run. As I jogged along a muddy path through a graveyard near the school, my mind went wild with reasons why I should be back in bed instead of pursuing this insane and disagreeable activity. That had been my only previous attempt at twice-a-days.

I returned to school in the fall, having qualified for a track scholarship that spring by running a 4:12 mile. Being on the team brought me directly under Bowerman's tutelage, and I discovered immediately that he had scheduled me for double workouts. All the other runners had similar schedules, but some ran only once a day, and they advised me to skip my morning runs. In their opinion, running easy workouts twice a day made the three weekly hard workouts too difficult to perform. I noticed, however, that the best runners not only did their double workouts, they seemed to thrive on them, while I still hadn't summoned the courage or the wherewithal to begin.

I was used to sleeping until the last moment and then grabbing a quick breakfast in the dorm cafeteria before my first class. It would be rough rolling out of bed before six-thirty in order to be back in time for breakfast. Moreover, a claustrophobic feeling came over me at the prospect of running fourteen times a week instead of only seven. Naturally, I wondered whether I could hold up, but fear of the unknown bothered me the most.

Support for Doubles: Ultimately, I decided to put my trust in Bowerman's schedule. All I needed was a way to begin. Since I wasn't tough enough to start the workouts on my own, I asked around until I found another runner who also needed support to start a double workout regimen.

Cedric Wedemire lived in an adjacent dorm, and with our common interest in running I had been attracted to him immediately. He was a little guy with powerful legs and a quick smile, but he was deadly serious about running. His ambition--like mine--was to be one of the best runners at Oregon, but we both knew we would have to do it with hard work and relatively meager talent. We made a pact that fall to run together every morning on a hilly, four-mile route through Hendricks Park. Our regimen is indelibly imprinted on my mind.

I slept at the other end of the hall from the room where I studied and kept my clothes. The "sleeping porch" was just large enough for two double-decker bunks. It was also unheated, and in the winter the windows would be coated inside and out with ice. Dangling above my head from the springs of the upper bunk, my alarm clock hung by its cord--a constant reminder that I couldn't afford the luxury of sleeping in. When it went off at six twenty-five, I would reluctantly shove the covers aside, step into the hallway and shuffle painfully to my room. It was only forty feet away, but after the abuse of training the day before--often at a very fast pace and on steep hills--my feet and legs would be so stiff and sore I could manage only four-inch steps. It felt as though putting any weight on the balls of my feet would tear my achilles tendons from my heels.

By the time I was lacing my second shoe, I would hear Cedric coming through the dorm's main entrance four stories below my window. Since I had given him permission to roust me out of bed should my perseverance begin to flag, he had become dogged in his determination to get us through our morning regimen. The front door would slam shut and a moment later another door would crash open and I'd hear Cedric's shoes clopping two steps at a time up the stairwell. I shuddered at the thought of my dorm mates trying to sleep through this early morning din. But Cedric was oblivious to the commotion, as he was also to the physical agony I was still experiencing in my legs as we headed out to greet the morning with a run.

Being young and unwilling to admit to pain or weakness, I struggled uncomplainingly at Cedric's shoulder, but slightly behind so as not to rile him into taking off at an even crisper pace. It would take twelve minutes or so for my legs to warm up. Meanwhile, the icy wind from passing cars was so uncomfortable--considering the recent cocoon-like warmth of my bed--that I often ran for the cover of the nearest hedge row. Being from Canada, Cedric was unfazed by the relatively mild cold of Oregon. He wouldn't even look around as I disappeared and he never seemed to have missed me when I caught up.

Soon we were jogging on the deserted one-lane road though the forest of Hendricks Park. In the early fall, dawn revealed a myriad of soft autumn hues, and at the highest point of the hill, sunlight burst white and brilliant through the evergreens. By that point, my legs were usually feeling loose and warm, and we would jog along at a pleasant pace, often chatting about our classes, girls or running. When we got back to the campus, Cedric would stop at his dorm and I would continue on to mine. I was the only person on the street, and I was training. Though not yet twenty-one, I had often known the satisfaction of accomplishing projects by small and constant increments. Doing a single morning jog seemed trivial, but doing them day after day gave me a feeling of quiet confidence. I knew I was working harder than my competition, and with each run I was moving closer to my goal of being one of the best.

As fall turned to winter, the golden mornings turned to cold and forbidding night. Yet my satisfaction with the morning run never waned. I would sometimes gaze out my window at the east end of town and trace my route through Hendricks Park, standing high on the hill that cradled Eugene like a long and solid arm. It was so far away, and yet every morning I ran that distant ridge from here to there and back. Four miles at a glance seemed like a long way, but jogging it was amazingly easy. Now, from the perspective of thirty years, I don't recall the workout ever having been a burden.

One morning in the middle of the winter term, I found myself taking off on the run alone. Cedric had been complaining for several weeks of a sore foot--to the point of limping during recent workouts. I stopped at his dorm on my way and found him waiting in the lobby looking forlorn in his pajamas. He said he had a stress fracture and was unable to continue on our morning runs. He was apologetic about leaving me to do the run by myself, but I told him not to be.

I empathized with Cedric's misery, knowing how much he wanted to be a part of the team. But I had mixed feelings about training with him. I would miss his company, but by then I no longer needed his support. It was a calloused point of view, but I was relieved to no longer have to keep his pace. Cedric rarely trained as hard as I, and thus he wasn't as sore at the start of our morning runs. I preferred to do the run on my own so I could keep my own pace.

Cedric would remain at Oregon for another year, but he would never realize his dream of making the track team. Most of the other runners, myself included, thought he wasn't tough enough to handle the training. Cedric was very tough, but mental toughness is a relative term, as even I would soon discover.

Carrying on With Minimal Support: I had no trouble maintaining my schedule through the rest of my junior year. I did double workouts even when I was racing the same day because Kenny Moore, who was my best friend on the team, always asked me before a track meet whether I had run that morning. We kept one another on schedule as neither of us wanted to admit to having missed a double workout. They were easy enough to do, and they never seemed to bother my training or racing performances. I was now totally into the discipline of double workouts, feeling they added as much to my confidence as they did to my capacity.

I had a successful junior year on the track team, running a 4:06 mile and helping Oregon win the Northern Division and the PAC-8 Track and Field Championships. When I returned to school that fall for my senior year, I had high hopes of making the team again, and of running a four-minute mile. There would be new and talented runners vying for places on the team that year, however, and I expected to have a tough time competing for the three spots on the traveling squad. Roscoe Devine and Dave Wilborn were among the newcomers, and I had discovered--by beating them in a half-mile time trial early in the fall--that I was in excellent condition. Nonetheless, I worried about being able to maintain my edge through the following spring. During cross country season, I was consistently third man on the team behind Mortenson and Moore. But my training didn't seem to be as well grounded as it had been the year before. My mileage wasn't as high because we were racing more in cross country. I was also bothered that my double workouts were sporadic and uneven.

Early in the fall, Bowerman had organized a jogging program for a group of sedentary men in the community. It was a pioneering program, about which he would write a seminal book that helped initiate the jogging movement in America. Bowerman used his runners from the cross country team to lead and support the joggers through their early morning regimen. For a small stipend, I walked and jogged around the Hayward Field track with groups of five or ten men several mornings a week. But I did this workout in lieu of my usual run around Hendricks Park, and though the jogging program may have been right for the men I was leading, it was much too light for me. Mentally, I measured my training against the year before, and I wondered how I could compete with the newest runners on the team when I wasn't training as hard as I had been then.

I didn't have the presence of mind or the strength of will to get up earlier to run. And though I could have quit Bowerman's jogging program, I needed the money and I felt obliged to help. Since I couldn't see a way out of my dilemma I did nothing to restore my confidence, and it decayed as surely as it had grown the year before.

A Long Winter: I stayed with Kenny Moore and his parents over the Christmas break that year. We had planned to train together, but I recall struggling to keep up with him at the end of a long run one afternoon. It was windy, dark and rainy, and I wasn't enjoying the run because my energy was low and the pace was much too fast for me.

It snowed heavily the next day and I went out in it to do my morning jog. My habit at the time was to break the run in two parts, with mass at the local Catholic church in between. On my way back to Kenny's in the freezing, snowy weather I pulled the tendon on the front of my hip. It was so sore I couldn't jog and I must have looked hobbled and distressed because a woman driving by asked me if I needed a ride.

I needed more than that. In ensuing weeks, the injury lingered on at the severe level and soon I found myself going the way of other runners I had known at Oregon, who fell behind and faded away because of debilitating injuries. Training for a four-minute mile had been a driving focus in my life for five years. And although I still thought of myself as a runner, I could no longer run competitively.

I was devastated--especially when Bowerman pulled my track scholarship that spring term. I felt like the hired gun who was fired because he had gotten too slow to hold his own in a fight. And yet, I eventually discovered that separating myself from the track team was the best thing that could have happened to me.

When I returned to school as a graduate student in the fall, the injury was healed, I had new goals, and I went back to running the hills of Hendricks Park with all the pleasure I'd experienced on those morning runs with Cedric during my junior year.

More Recent Attempts at Doubles: The only other time I was able to run double workouts with the consistency of my junior year in college was during the fall of 1982. At the time, I was emulating one of my heroes, Doctor Jim Gallup, who at fifty was one of the best runners in Hawaii. Gallup had a simple training regimen that included running eighty-four miles a week, back and forth to work. Of course, he did other workouts, too, but I was convinced that his twice-a-day, seven-mile commuter runs were the mainstay of his success.

When I developed a groin injury in the fall of 1982 and was forced to run only short slow workouts, I took the opportunity to run ninety miles a week by simply running five or six miles every morning and evening. I jogged slowly on those runs, avoiding further injury and often feeling tired from the mileage. But when the injury finally healed and I reduced my mileage in January of 1983, my running energy soared. During the following year, I was able to train and race with tremendous power.

I continued racing through mid-1986, often running twice a day, but never with the commitment necessary to maintain consistent double workouts. I often ran too hard for regular and adequate recovery, so I would end up skipping some recovery runs. By mid-1986 my ambition was finally dissipated, and I decided to take an extended layoff from competitive running.

A Perfect Easy Run: During the ensuing eight years, between 1986 and 1994, I maintained basic fitness by running an easy workout three times a week from my home on Maunalani Heights--one of the ridges that dominate the Honolulu skyline. I started the run with a mile-long, gradual descent into Kaimuki, one of the oldest communities in the city, and the place where I had been raised as a babe and a youngster.

I crossed the Kaimuki business district at a point where it was only a block wide and continued on a tree-lined, undulating course through a neighborhood of homes built mostly in the thirties. Doubling back through the business district, I passed the library where I had borrowed my first book, and I finished the run by climbing scenic Sierra Drive with its panoramic views of the city.

For the eight years prior to 1994, this had been my only run. All I had wanted from it was an opportunity to get some exercise and reflect on the day's events. Nonetheless, I loved the run, with its long hills and short flats, its interesting streets and homes. Above all, running past places so familiar to me added a dimension of continuity to my life, of remembering what it was like in Kaimuki even in the late forties. I had never wanted to live anywhere else and I felt the same about the run.

It was a perfect, easy run. I would start slowly on the downhill, pick it up through the rolling middle portion, and if my energy was good, I would work a little harder on the mile-long up-hill stretch to home. I rarely timed the run, but I knew it took about thirty-five minutes. I also knew if I ever started training hard again, I'd make it the cornerstone of a double-workout regimen.

Flagging Health and Fitness: For years, whenever people asked me why I wasn't racing, I'd beg off by saying, somewhat facetiously, that training and racing required too much hard work. Of course, I missed the thrill of racing, but I was content to bide my time, enjoying the freedom of not having to apply myself to an arduous training schedule, while waiting for my desire to return.

As the years passed, I was careful to maintain my racing weight, but I could tell my fitness was dwindling. Not only were my easy runs getting tougher to do with the power I'd had years before, but what bothered me the most from a health and fitness standpoint was the problem I was having with my heart. In the early eighties, I'd had a bout of arrhythmias--pounding and irregular beating--which was disconcerting enough for me to seek medical attention. The cardiologist who diagnosed my symptoms told me that if I were not in training as a runner, he would be concerned.

Since the doctor wasn't concerned about my heart, I wasn't either, and the problem soon abated. During the ensuing years, however, and especially after I had stopped competitive training, the arrythmia problem began recurring on a mild and occasional basis. During the early nineties, though, the pounding and irregular beating had gotten progressively worse. By late 1993, I was experiencing an "arrythmia attack" for about ninety minutes after every meal.

Since the symptoms seemed related to my eating, my hunch was I was eating too much for the amount of exercise I was getting. So as an experiment during Christmas of 1993, I started doing my easy Kaimuki run once a day instead of three times a week. The daily exercise reduced the arrythmia problem immediately. As a result, I started doing some longer workouts with the runners I was coaching, and the arrhythmias disappeared completely.

Double Workouts in Perspective: My workouts evolved with my ambition during the first half of 1994, and in April I suddenly realized I had a competitive image to maintain. The bug of ambition had finally bitten me and I unexpectedly developed the necessary drive for serious training.

I trained once a day until June, but I decided at that point to add several extra workouts each week, using my Kaimuki hill run to boost my leg strength. Since I was only running two hard workouts per week, I had time and energy to insert easy hill runs into my weekly schedule.

Initially, my plan had been to run these workouts twice a day. But I found myself rationalizing my way out of doing some of them, especially just before or after a hard workout. I was averaging eight to ten workouts a week, but my attitude was definitely not in keeping with the spirit of constancy essential to doubles training.

I promised myself to run my final race in August and to shift the context of my training to include double workouts during the final four months of the year. By the first of September, I was ready to begin.

Chapter Fourteen Synopsis:

- **The Main Issue:** What role does a "double-workout" regimen play in becoming a better runner? What will it take for me to raise the training ante to a completely new level?

■ **Concepts:**

1) A double workout regimen is one in which you run twice a day during a training period.

2) Constancy refers to the level of commitment necessary to run a double workout regimen. You need to be absolutely faithful to your training regimen.

■ **Theoretical Tenets:**

1) Double workouts contribute to your base of stamina by adding mostly light exertion running to your training regimen.

2) Your training base consists of time on the road. Each workout is like a separate exertion platform, which holds up a highly adapted level of ability.

■ **Questions and Answers:**

1) What role does a "double-workout" regimen play in becoming a better runner?

The major factors affecting your running ability are frequency, duration and intensity. Workout frequency is a major adaptive stimulus because frequent training forces your body to recover quickly. And the quicker you can recover, the more quality training you can eventually do.

2) What role does the support of a training partner play in starting or continuing a double workout regimen?

You may need some social support to take your training to another level. The toughest part is to find someone with whom you are compatible. Your natural abilities should match, you should be in the same general condition, and you should enjoy one another's company. Moreover, you should be clear that you are out there to support one another, not compete against one another. Save your races for the races.

Chapter Fifteen
A New Training Base

After my Hawaiian Style 8-K victory in August, I was able to see myself as the dominant fifty-year-old runner in Hawaii during 1995. But to actualize that vision, I'd have to sacrifice my 10-K racing ability to gain a broader base of stamina. From that base, I planned to build exceptional speed and endurance the following year.

I had three objectives as I began my base-building regimen. I wanted to run three hard workouts a week--one more than I had been running. I wanted to run twice a day, which would raise my mileage from fifty to seventy per week. And I wanted to maintain the regimen, without injury, for sixteen weeks until the end of the year. At that time, I'd decide whether to maintain my mileage. Meanwhile, my goal was to survive what I expected to be a difficult initial period.

I wouldn't have a running partner to support me because I wasn't willing to keep a set time schedule. I preferred to run at odd hours, whenever I woke up in the morning or whenever I had finished my work for the day, and I knew my personal discipline was sufficient to establish the new regimen. Anyway, my main concern wasn't getting started, but creating balance. My training regimen had to be hard enough to stimulate improvement, but not so difficult that it became intolerable.

I had no illusions about how slow I would have to run to balance the initial jump in mileage with my limited capacity for exertion. I didn't plan to ease into the schedule by increasing my mileage gradually or by giving myself a break with fewer miles every other week. I could survive the increase to seventy miles a week by running slower than I had at fifty. Nonetheless, I expected the new regimen to kick me in the proverbial butt. There would be times when I'd be so tired that skipping workouts would seem like the best option.

Nonetheless, if I had correctly estimated my capacity, I'd have passable energy to maintain the new schedule. But having sufficient energy didn't give me room for error. I'd have to hold myself back, not only during the hard workouts, but during the recovery runs as well. Otherwise, I could easily find myself with inadequate energy, or worse, being unable to do what I had scheduled.

Context for Recovery: As I finished my first few recovery runs, I knew I'd never survive the new regimen if I continued doing them in thirty-six minutes. I still felt relatively fresh from the two-week recovery period I had taken after the Hawaiian Style 8-K, but as I added mileage to my training during the first week of September, I felt myself heading into deep fatigue.

I was in the habit of attacking my Kaimuki run. From now on, however, I'd have to run it with the least amount of effort. I was concerned about becoming injured or exhausted during the first month, especially knowing my penchant for biting off more than I could chew. Each time I started down the hill, therefore, I asked myself how slowly I would have to run to recover for my next hard workout.

Starting downhill allowed me to coast at twelve minutes a mile with my heart rate in the mid-nineties. At thirteen minutes, I was at the bottom of the hill, still cruising at a very slow pace. My heart rate was 100 bpm--50% of my maximum and only mild exertion. But 100 bpm was also *double* my resting heart rate, which meant I was doing more than I would have been staying home and doing nothing.

As I jogged the rolling middle portion of the run, my heart rate gradually rose to 110 bpm, still mild exertion. During my first few workouts, the pace had seemed distressingly slow. But, I was so tired after the first week, I soon became content to amble along at twelve minutes per mile. I simply didn't want to run faster. Usually, however, I was warmed up and feeling stronger by the time I returned to the bottom of the hill, so I could push a little harder during the last twelve minutes, with my heart rate approaching 125 bpm.

I was surprised initially at my times for the recovery run. It was taking me forty-three minutes to run what had taken thirty-six. Yet these weren't my usual circumstances. I was into my first few weeks of base training, I had run two hard workouts in the last seventy-two hours, and considering that only ten months before I had been averaging a mere eleven miles a week, I was downright pleased even to be attempting the present jump in mileage. Nonetheless, my pace was so slow I was having trouble imagining how it could ever have a positive impact on my capacity to win a major 10-K.

Intensity is by far the most important adaptive stimulus in competitive running. Yet most of my weekly running was nowhere near the specific level of exertion necessary to run a rapid pace for ten kilometers. I kept reminding myself, however, that high-mileage training at a slow pace could be a powerful training stimulus, too.

I wouldn't see results immediately, but I anticipated new energy eventually to show up during my recovery runs. When it did, I could run them a little faster. Until then, I had to be patient and keep the faith.

The Hard Workouts: In addition to my recovery runs, I scheduled myself for three hard workouts a week: an interval workout to build my tempo ability, a hill run to develop my muscle power, and a long run to augment my stamina.

The Interval Workout: As I reflected on my previous training regimen, I realized I hadn't built a prior base of steady state, tempo running. My ambition had been to race well immediately so I soon fell into running a workout of five or six 1200-meter intervals at or near my anaerobic threshold. This workout had been a powerful, but limited adaptive stimulus.

During the five-month training period between April and August, my interval times hadn't improved significantly unless I pushed the pace down with a harder effort. And although I raced well, the interval workout never became easy enough for me to add intervals or intensity without endangering myself with injury or exhaustion. In other words, having reached an adaptive plateau with 1200-meter intervals, I was stuck with keeping the workout as it was, or changing it drastically to stimulate improvement in another way.

The purpose of my new interval workout was to build a broad base of quick, steady state running. I planned to run a 20-K race in early February, which gave me something to focus on as I did the intervals. But since I hadn't done eight 1600-meter (mile) intervals since my sophomore year in college, I could feel myself reaching back in memory to a time when I had done them at five minutes per mile.

My exertion then was very similar to what I·was currently experiencing. I would cruise along at a seven-minute pace, churning out the miles without hearing my breathing. It was a tough, but satisfying workout from which I'd be tired for the better part of forty-eight hours.

The Hill Run: I designed my hill workout to build leg strength, especially in my quads, hamstring and gluteal muscles. My stride wasn't as long and powerful as it had been when I was younger, partly because I hadn't practiced a long and powerful stride in recent years, and partly because I simply wasn't as strong as I had been as a young man.

Traditionally, I had lifted weights to increase my muscle strength for running. But I had read an article recently in *Running Research News* that got me thinking about novel ways to augment my muscle power. The gist was that the standard weight lifting exercises, such as leg extensions, are not specific to running.[15] The article described three resistance exercises, one of which was similar to walking stairs two at a time. The article got me thinking about a workout I had envisioned years before.

In the early eighties, I had taken a hike to the top of Koko Crater-- an extinct volcano that rises twelve hundred feet like an inverted ice cream cone near the Honolulu suburb of Hawaii Kai. I had hiked up the mountain on a defunct tram track that led straight to a huge bunker left over from the Second World War. The railroad ties were far enough apart to walk them as though I were taking a flight of stairs two at a time. And what a flight of stairs. Thoroughly wiped out by the climb, I was unable to work or run effectively for the following several days. I had no energy or desire to do more than mope around and take long naps.

For some time thereafter, I'd wondered about the possible effect of training on that tram track. Judging by the effect it had had on me, even getting in shape for it would represent a significant increase in my capacity. During the following year, I'd done a series of stair workouts and managed to gain some proficiency at walking stairs two at a time. But I'd never summoned the courage necessary to make Koko Crater a regular part of my training.

During my subsequent eight-year layoff, I thought a lot about the workout. Maybe it would have no effect at all on my ability to run 10-K, but to train on Koko Crater certainly seemed a worthy challenge, and the possibility of getting significantly stronger was definitely worth the experiment. Of course, if I hadn't been in shape a decade earlier, I wasn't in shape to do the workout as I began my base-building regimen in September, 1994. But I knew a way to build my power on another extinct volcano with another challenging flight of stairs.

During the Second World War, the military had installed gun emplacements at the peak of Diamond Head to protect the Waikiki coast

---

[15] *Running Research News,* Volume 10, Number 1, January-February 1994, page 1, and 4-8. For Subscription information, write *Running Research News,* PO Box 27041, Lansing, MI 48909.

against sea invasion by the Japanese. A trail from the center of the crater gave access to the gun emplacements at the peak. In the late seventies, the state government had developed the trail as a tourist attraction, with hundreds of visitors making the trek every day to the scenic lookout at the top of Diamond Head.

In early September, after testing my injured legs with a couple of moderate hill workouts on Paula Drive, I started doing a 2-hour run from my home to the top of Diamond Head and back (see Figure 16.1 on page 209). The workout had lots of gently rolling areas with two major hills thrown in for variety. But my main reason for doing the workout was to build my leg strength on Diamond Head's infamous flight of ninety-nine stairs.

The steep and narrow staircase was the first thing unsuspecting tourists saw upon exiting a long dark tunnel, and the sight of it always evoked gasps of dismay and disbelief. But I looked forward to walking the stairs two at a time, thereby forcing my legs through a wide range of motion, which would, hopefully, build my ability to sustain a more powerful stride.

The Long Run: My weekly schedule also included a long run with the joggers in my 1994 marathon training program. I was running with them on Monday and Wednesday evenings, but these workouts were generally short and slow enough for me to get away with running them as easy to moderate recovery runs. I decided, however, to run their two-hour Saturday workout as a "junk mileage," hard run.

I ran with one of my middle ability groups, reckoning their twelve-minute mile pace would be about all I could handle. My experience soon proved this hunch correct. I could barely do a slow, two-hour workout on Saturday and still recover by Monday morning for my 1600-meter intervals on the track. Nonetheless, my intention was to establish a base of time on the road rather than brag about my pace or mileage.

By mid-October, I still didn't have a plan for adding mileage or intensity to my long runs because I still couldn't feel myself adapting to my overall regimen. However, I could see ahead to mid-November when my marathoners were scheduled for a three and a-half-hour run, and I wondered whether I'd be able, by then, to run it with them.

Base Building In Perspective: I had few expectations for my new training regimen. Of course, I wanted certain things to come of it, but-- as with most training regimens--this one was mostly experimental.

I wasn't certain the Diamond Head stairs would increase my leg strength. Nor was I sure that setting aside threshold intervals for a longer slower variety would develop my capacity to run a faster 10-K the following year. Nor did I know whether my body was capable of handling three hard workouts a week as it had when I was younger.

Nonetheless, I was committed to following through on the regimen as a means of achieving my competitive goals. My workouts established a minimum of eighty minutes a day on the road, divided into morning and evening workouts. And I didn't care how slow I went at this point in the training, as long as I survived. I had to start somewhere, and I considered my base to be the time I spent running, not the intensity.

The first six weeks were as rough as I had anticipated. My hard workouts seemed to jump up at me before I was ready for them, but often I was amazed at the way I would recover at the last minute. An anticipation of danger added to the flow of adrenalin as I dressed for a hard workout. Actually, it usually felt like my adrenalin was *seeping,* not flowing. But with the amount of training I was doing, I was glad for even a limited experience of energy.

By the end of the first six weeks, I was confident of completing the sixteen week training period because I usually felt ready for the hard workouts. I didn't feel the sort of readiness necessary for high-quality training, but quality wasn't my primary goal. I wanted to establish a base from which I could run faster later, and to do so I had to survive the sixteen week training period without injuring myself.

Chapter Fifteen Synopsis:

- **The Main Issue:** How can I build a new training base, from which I can take my ability to a significantly higher level?

- **Concepts:**

    1) A training base consists of the frequency and the duration of your weekly workouts. The more time you spend in training, the broader your training base.
    2) A training period refers to the time frame in which you will maintain a certain workout regimen. Training periods are measured in weeks or months.
    3) A workout regimen is the training stimulus that precipitates a

training cycle.

4) A training cycle is your metabolic response to a workout regimen. There are three phases to the cycle: shock, adaptation and exhaustion, each measured in weeks or months.

5) An adaptive plateau occurs at a point in a training cycle when your capacity is no longer responding to a training stimulus.

6) A training stimulus is a new or added workout regimen to which you want to adapt.

■ **Theoretical Tenets:**

1) The training process is unavoidably cyclic, meaning you cannot continue to adapt or improve in an uninterrupted straight line. Sooner or later your ability will plateau or decline.

2) Once you have reached an adaptive plateau, the only way you can take your ability to a higher level is to restructure your training regimen, and thereby begin a new adaptive cycle.

3) The logic of adaptive training demands that you maintain your training effort within adaptive limits. Thus if you add effort in one form (distance), you must subtract it in another form (speed) to stay within your capacity.

4) Your capacity for exertion responds to a new training stimulus by going through three adaptive stages: shock, adaptation and exhaustion. Adaptation increases your capacity, while shock and exhaustion decrease it.

■ **Relationships:**

1) The more frequently you train, the more quickly you have to recover from your workouts and the larger your capacity must grow to accommodate the added workouts.

2) The more you add to your training in frequency and duration, the more you must subtract in speed or intensity, at least until you have passed through the initial shock caused by the added effort.

■ Questions and Answers:

1) How much can I add to my training in the way of workout frequency and duration?

   There are no rules or pat answers to this question. However, there are some general principles. First, you can only do so much training within the context of a hard or easy workout. If you plan to do three hard workouts a week and double workouts, too, then you are limited by what you can do and still recover adequately for each workout. So the question is how much can you add in the way of mileage, while still being able to recover.

   One answer is to estimate the new training regimen you think you can handle, based on your present regimen and your level of adaptation to it. If you are running fifty miles a week, for instance, and you feel well adapted to it (as I was at this point in my training), then you ought to be able to add, say, 20 miles per week. Next the question is how to add it: in increments or in one fell swoop.

   The traditional advice has been to add by small weekly increments, such as five or ten percent per week. This is certainly one way to minimize the shock of added training mileage. However, this method may require that you change workouts from week to week, which is not the way runners tend to operate.

   On the other hand, if you increase your mileage in one fell swoop you're almost sure to experience severe shock in reaction to the sudden increase in mileage. You must be willing to compensate for added mileage with decreased intensity, otherwise you may not survive (see below).

   Perhaps the best approach to creating a new training regimen is to combine the "incremental" and the "one fell-swoop" approaches. For instance, in this chapter I described how I added frequency and duration in one fell swoop, while adding

incrementally to my hard workouts. Thus, my mileage was
roughly 70 per week from the outset, but I added one flight
of stairs per week to my hard hill workout.

2)   How can I build a new training base without becoming sick,
     injured or exhausted?

The most important thing about adding to a training base is
being able to survive initially. If you exceed your capacity
for exertion by biting off more than you can chew, you could
become sick, injured or exhausted. Thus, you've got to
balance increases in frequency and duration with decreases in
tempo and intensity. In other words, slow down.

If you take the attitude that your training base is simply time
on the road, then it doesn't matter how fast you run initially,
as long as you survive. This may be a radically different
attitude from the one that governed your recent peak training,
especially if it required race specific tempo training or speed
work.

Nonetheless, slowing down is exactly what you have to do to
survive a drastic increase in mileage. You may eventually
lose some of your peak abilities (tempo, speed and endurance), but you can refocus your training on peak abilities once
you've built a larger base of stamina.

3)   Why do I need a broad base of stamina?

Stamina equals energy. The more stamina you have the more
energy you have to run fast or long. So if your racing ability
has plateaued, it may be time to stop building race specific
abilities and concentrate on stamina so you'll have more
energy for faster running later.

Think of your training as divided into major periods. In the
first period you'll build your stamina and in the second you'll
build race-specific abilities. Since you can retain your
stamina/energy for weeks or even months once you have built

it, you can cut back considerably on mileage while you focus on building tempo, speed and endurance from the extra energy you'll have from running fewer miles.

Each time you return to building stamina, you won't start from scratch, but you'll be somewhat stronger than you were the last time you raised your mileage. In this way your training proceeds in periods, while your ability improves in cycles.

Chapter Sixteen
Minimizing Shock

In September 1994, I was operating on a vague recollection of what it had been like the last time I tried to build a training base years before. In a sense, my lack of recent experience was an advantage because I had few preconceived notions. I approached the sixteen-week training period as a beginner, albeit an experienced one.

I was running easy workouts twice a day and hard workouts three times a week. And though I had prior experience with all the workouts on my schedule, I had never done them in this particular mix. I felt like an inept juggler, holding more objects aloft than I was used to. I didn't know exactly how my training would affect me, but I could survive by being conservative and methodical, and by taking time after every workout to assess the way I felt.

And it wasn't long before I was feeling terrible. I was in shock from the new things I was doing, especially the double workouts, the longer intervals, and the stairs. Shock goes with the territory of introducing novel training activities, and I expected it to take three forms: an increased number of stress symptoms, less energy, and greater risk of injury. My intention was to minimize the impact of shock on these three aspects of my physical being.

Shock and Stress: When I first started training distance runners for a living in 1979, I realized almost immediately that I didn't know much about the physiology of training. I recall a workout in which my training partner and I imagined we could see the inner workings of our calf muscles. What was going on down there? Neither of us had a clue.

The next day, I purchased a book by David Costill on the physiology of training. It was a short volume, but it whetted my appetite for more. For a while, I read every book I could on the subject of exercise physiology, even trying to understand advanced biochemistry from the latest university textbooks. I soon discovered I didn't have the educational background to understand difficult biochemical concepts on my own.

Fortunately, however, my volunteer work with the Mid-Pacific

Road Runners Club brought me into contact with several Ph.D.'s who were able to answer my questions. One of my associates at the time was Dr. Stan Karansky, an M.D. with a private practice in Honolulu. Though Stan was nearing retirement age, he was new to running and approaching it with child-like zeal. I recall pumping him for knowledge from the medical perspective as we jogged around Kapiolani Park.

Stan's main contribution to my understanding of the training process was the idea of a stress threshold. We both agreed that running was stressful, but Stan believed everyone had a limit to the amount of stress they could tolerate without manifesting a myriad of stress symptoms (see below). He called this limit a stress threshold, and in hearing him talk about it, I immediately recalled my boyhood encounters with excessive stress.

List of Stress Symptoms

Loss of interest	Nervousness
Depression	Drop in performance
Irritability	Insomnia
Loss of appetite	Can't stop eating
Blood in urine	Swollen glands
Constipation	Diarrhea
Absence of menstruation	Nausea
Cold/sore throat	Running nose
Rise in resting heart rate	Tight, sore muscles

As a kid I played very hard at football and other games requiring fast running. Sometimes after a particularly active day, I'd have an attack of diarrhea. I remember making a vague connection between too much play and diarrhea, but I saw it as "getting sick" rather than a symptom of too much exercise. Besides, since my mother bought the illness idea, too, I got to stay home from school, get some needed rest, and read a good book. My conversations with Stan Karansky confirmed that my body had been reacting to some very stressful physical activity.

More recently, I had noticed as an adult in training that I could get away with a very hard race or workout when I was feeling *eager,* but a very hard/*ready* workout would set off a period of irritability, non-communicativeness, insomnia, and stiffness in my leg muscles. I also noticed my stress threshold was a moving target, much like the adaptive limit I described in chapter six. In fact, I would violate my stress threshold whenever I ran harder than my adaptive limit. Typically, I'd try to run a hard workout when I wasn't adequately recovered. I might get away with a hard/lazy workout at reduced pace and mileage. But if I tried to achieve my usual hard/ready performance, I'd be "stressed out" for several days.

Similarly, every time I did something *new* in training, I would run the risk of putting myself in shock. I called it biting off more than I could chew. And a classic example was the first couple of Diamond Head workouts I did in September, 1994. As I described in the last chapter, I was doing the workout to build my muscle power by walking flights of ninety-nine stairs near the peak of the crater rim. I had tried to break into the new regimen by doing a couple of easier hill workouts prior to my first Diamond Head run (see page 99). But even a 900-foot assent to the top of Maunalani Heights didn't prepare me for the novel stress of doing Diamond Head's ninety-nine stairs.

Walking a steep flight of stairs two-at-a-time forced me to raise my thighs to the horizontal position and lift my 150-pound body weight as I stepped up. This was tough work and my heart rate rose from 115 to 150 bpm or more during each forty-five-second interval (see Figure 16.1). I did five flights the first time I did the workout, and afterwards I could barely make it home. My quads seemed to be most affected, but my hamstring and gluteal muscles--the prime movers during running--had to have been affected, too. I was reduced to taking tiny steps that belied my six-foot three-inch frame. And during the next three or four days I had great difficulty getting up from chairs or walking up the stairs at home to get my mail.

I also had an attack of diarrhea after the first two Diamond Head workouts, and during the first few hours after both runs my urine turned purple with blood. These symptoms were gone after the third workout, but I was still so wiped out I needed morning and afternoon naps to relieve my weariness. I was definitely in shock, but I wasn't about to back off on the stairs.

My only concession was to cut out part of the final hill I had planned to do. To have jogged an additional mile to the top of Paula Drive would have made the workout much too hard, and I knew it as I headed back from Diamond Head on my first workout. It was all I could do to finish at my home, half way up Maunalani Heights. Even on the shorter way home I found myself scheming to avoid certain hills. But by avoiding one I'd hit another, dismayed at the prospect of having to negotiate it.

Figure 16.1:   Diamond Head Hills and Stairs.

**Heart Rate Ranges
In Beats Per Minute:**

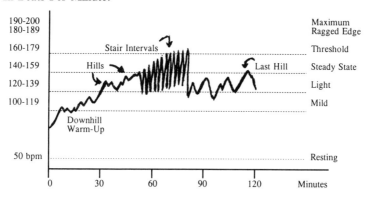

Most of this two-hour hill workout was run at light exertion with brief forays into steady state on hills and stairs. The stair intervals created a novel structuring of effort, and, with the combined effects of the other workouts I was doing at the time, this ended up being a very stressful workout.

Starting with five flights was too ambitious. But I could hark back ten years to when I was doing ten or more flights, and I couldn't accept that a "measly" five was too much. Nonetheless, I could have reduced my stress load considerably by starting with two or three flights of stairs instead of five. By contrast, I broke into my new regimen of eight 1600-meter intervals in a more sensible manner.

Minimizing Shock: In September, I had decided to do eight 1600-meter intervals instead of the six 1200-meter intervals I'd been doing. My many previous experiences with intervals had taught me to respect the possibility of sudden injury. And since I knew the new workout would be significantly longer than the old one, I decided to segue into it gradually. The first week, I ran ten 800-meter intervals at steady state, mostly because the distance and the quick, relaxed pace seemed compatible with the way I felt at the time. I was still injured from the recent Hawaiian Style 8-K.

After this first interval workout, I projected myself ahead four weeks and planned to increase the number of 800s by two per week until I was doing sixteen (with a 200-meter jog between them). At that point, I planned to change the workout to eight 1600-meter intervals at steady state.

Steady state was a significantly lower level of exertion than I had been running my intervals during 1994, but I had to balance the physical demands of running eight miles of intervals as opposed to the four-and-a-half I had been running for the 1200-meter workout. Backing off to steady state seemed to have the right compensating effect.

Running at steady state was also easier to cope with mentally. Though the new workout was longer and tougher than the 1200-meter workout had been, I was able to relax at steady state rather than having to press the pace. Nonetheless, I was barely able to maintain eight mile-intervals, so I planned to keep my heart rate at steady state during the next several months.

If I were to adapt to this regimen, my times would eventually drop below seven minutes per mile. But pushing them down with threshold level running would have made the workout too hard for adaptation, and it would have also violated my stress threshold.

Shock and Injury: In early September, I had three nagging and persistent injuries, each of which required my attention. My right calf--where it connected to my achilles tendon--still hurt from the Hawaiian Style 8-K on 21 August. The pain definitely put a ceiling on my training pace, but it was improving slowly and I wasn't worried about it because I didn't think I was training fast enough to exacerbate it.

In addition, the bursa of my left achilles hurt after every hard workout. This was a chronic problem that had affected my running for the past fifteen years. It would cause me to limp in the hours immediately after a hard run, but I had been able to control the problem by wearing new shoes and by taking a couple of aspirin with my first meal after hard workouts. Fortunately, the bursitis was no worse than usual during the first several weeks of the new regimen so I was able to continue.

Of much greater concern was the discomfort in the tendon just under the front of my right hip bone. It had been tight and tender at odd moments during workouts, and I noticed definite twinges of pain whenever I massaged and stretched the area between workouts. This was a potentially debilitating injury--the same one that had taken me out of running during my senior year at Oregon. Yet I'd had no recent experience with it, so I couldn't predict its onset nor discern its cause.

I dealt with the injury by slowing down immediately whenever I felt its symptoms, and by experimenting with different pairs of shoes to see which ones might be causing or alleviating the problem. I was anxious before every hard workout that the hip would suddenly degenerate into a serious injury and cause me to curtail my training.

Since I couldn't fulfill the purpose of my base-building regimen if I became seriously injured, my first priority was to remain injury-free. I was willing to run. slowly enough to maintain sufficient energy, but there were inherent features of the hard workouts--such as the volume and intensity of the intervals--that increased the risk of injury. Thus, I approached each hard workout with a healthy measure of trepidation.

Nothing is certain in this game, especially for an old warhorse with imperfectly healed battle wounds. At least, I knew most of the pitfalls from experience. For example, I had used the machines at a local shoe store to build a varus wedge into a shoe I used during interval workouts. I thought the wedge might reduce the bursitis in my left achilles, but the first time I tried the shoe during my interval workout, I felt a twinge on the medial portion of my left calf.

I immediately connected the calf pain with the new varus wedge. But could I get through the workout without a major injury? I slowed down and the pain went away. As I started the fifth interval, however, I could feel a mild twinge in the same area. Recalling times when I would have continued running, even through a growing pain, my mind raced ahead to the most likely scenarios, including the possibility of injuring myself and having to back off on training for several weeks while I recovered.

Unwilling to deal with that eventuality, I aborted the workout immediately with four more intervals to run. That afternoon I fixed the shoe, returned to the track and completed the workout with no recurrence of the injury. I ended up missing my afternoon recovery run, but that was a small price for remaining injury-free.

Shock and Energy: Having enough energy to survive my new
regimen was also a major concern. I'd had good energy during my

previous training period, which consisted of fifty miles a week. So I counted on having an energy reserve to cushion the shock of the new, seventy miles a week regimen. But would I also have enough energy for living and working normally? I could recall times past when I'd been unable to function effectively during the day, and I wanted to avoid that experience as much as possible.

Nevertheless, my added mileage soon threw me into an uneasy lassitude. I often found myself sighing heavily at the prospect of getting up and walking across a room. I tried every trick I knew to keep my energy up. Fortunately, I had a flexible work schedule that provided time for napping several times a week. I also rehydrated immediately after every run, added carbohydrate powder and electrolyte concentrate to my water, and ate my fill of pasta and homemade cookies immediately after hard workouts. Even after all that, I could expect a window of at least twelve hours between every hard workout when I'd be dragging.

I was also irritable and non-communicative with my wife during my down times between hard workouts. At other times I'd have better control of myself with Nancy, at least to the extent of being civil. But I was riding a fine line between the good husband I aspired to be and the jerk both she and I abhorred. This wasn't a new problem. In fact, I had resolved early in the year to shield Nancy from my stress-induced cantankerousness. The new regimen was definitely testing that resolve.

Nancy and I suffered this phase of the adaptive process for six weeks, hoping for relief while harboring the fear we might never get it. I knew what it felt like to adapt to a training regimen from many years of preparing for major races. As I trained, I could expect my workout performances to gradually improve with seemingly little or no increase in effort.

Similarly, I could look forward to recovering quicker from my hard workouts, and to feeling they took progressively less out of me. Gradually, I would have fewer stress symptoms: less irritability, shorter bouts of insomnia, less inflammation and muscle stiffness. This was the way I was finally beginning to feel in mid-October.

Shock in Perspective: It had been a tough six weeks since I'd begun my base-building regimen. As I completed my hill workout in the sixth week, however, I felt a glimmer of hope. For the first time, I finished it feeling strong.

Having energy for a single hill workout certainly didn't establish a trend, but having completed eleven flights of stairs on Diamond Head, I expected--as usual--to be shot for several days, and to be moping around in a dazed and weary state, needing frequent naps in order to do my work.

Indeed, I had almost skipped the workout because I didn't want to be blown away during the next several days on a trip to Kona to support my athletes for the Ironman Triathlon. I did the workout anyway and I was surprised to feel okay during the trip. I even did a two-hour run in Kona forty-eight hours after the hill workout, and although I started it feeling tired, my energy developed and I finished strong.

That made two hard workouts in a row of feeling strong at the finish--still not a trend, but definitely cause to think I was seeing light at the end of the adaptive tunnel. Still I wondered whether these recoveries were an anomaly or whether I was finally breaking out of the shock-induced lethargy that had enveloped me since the beginning of September.

Chapter Sixteen Synopsis:

■ **Main Issue:** What is shock and how can I survive it whenever I add effort to my training?

■ **Concepts:**

1) Shock is a long-term change in your capacity for exertion that reduces available energy and increases the risk of injury.

2) Stress is the physiological reaction to any life activity.

3) A stress symptom is a sign of having exceeded your stress threshold.

4) Your stress threshold is the amount of stress you can tolerate, beyond which you manifest increased numbers of stress symptoms.

5) "Biting off more than you can chew" refers to doing more in a workout or training regimen than you are adapted to or ready for.

6) Progressive adaptation refers to the process of adapting to effort in one form while you maintain your ability with little or no effort in another form.

■ **Theoretical Tenets:**

1) Any time you add something new to your training, your body reacts by going into shock.
2) There is a limit to the amount of stress you can tolerate without manifesting stress symptoms.
3) You must put yourself into shock in order to bring about an adaptive response.
4) At the beginning of a new training regimen, the minimum effort necessary to do a workout is the right effort to avoid becoming unable to do it.

■ **Principles:**

1) Cumulative stress: Stress is cumulative, i.e., stress in different forms (physical, mental, emotional) adds up physiologically. Thus you must take all forms into account when considering your total stress load.
2) Progressive Effort: In order to adapt, you must stress yourself progressively with effort. Progressive effort doesn't mean harder effort, but novel effort.
3) The Logic of Progressive Effort: When you add effort in one form you must subtract it in another form to stay within your adaptive limit.

■ **Relationships:**

1) The more stressful an activity, the greater the chance that you will experience stress symptoms from it.
2) The harder a novel training effort, the greater the shock and the greater the risk of becoming unable to continue training.

■ **Questions and Answers:**

1) Why is it that I can train and not improve?

There are no training guarantees. Thus you may be training, but you may be losing or simply maintaining your ability. Remember, your capacity responds to metabolic forces beyond your direct control. Wanting adaptation to occur will not make it happen unless your body is physiologically predisposed to it.

It helps to make the distinction between training periods and training cycles. Periods refer to workout regimens; cycles refer to adaptive responses. You've got to pay attention to both, making adjustments in your training to bring about desired changes in your capacity. If you lay on a new training regimen, for instance, it should be hard enough and novel enough to shock your system into an adaptive response, but not so hard that you can't survive the shock of doing it.

2)   How can I survive the shock of adding effort to my training?

First you should be aware of the ways shock can affect you: your energy will decline, your risk of injury will grow, and the number of stress symptoms you experience will increase.

Next, you've got to run easy enough to maintain sufficient energy for training and living; easy enough to keep from getting seriously injured; and easy enough to keep from becoming ill, which is ultimately what too much stress can do. If you are burning out or getting sick and injured on a regular basis then you have bitten off more than you can chew and you must cut back on effort when you try again to establish the training regimen.

It helps to add effort incrementally so you spread out the period of shock. This is especially true when you are introducing a new hard workout. Instead of running the new workout as you envision it in your fully able state, plan to build up to it incrementally by adding miles, intervals or pace each week until you are at the level you want to hold for the rest of the training period.

If you can survive several weeks without getting sick, injured or exhausted, then you can probably maintain your regimen until shock subsides and adaptation begins.

Chapter Seventeen
Measuring Adaptation

For most of my adult life, both as a runner and a coach, I have pursued the Holy Grail of adaptation. Having experienced it many times, I didn't doubt its reality. Yet adaptation was beguilingly difficult to measure.

In theory, as long as my workout efforts stayed the same and my performances improved, I must have adapted to the training that produced the faster times. Measuring performance was the easy part of this equation. All I needed was a stop watch and a willingness to repeat certain workouts. But measuring effort had always been a bugaboo.

Though I had previously devised several scales for measuring effort, they were too imprecise to accurately measure adaptation. Furthermore, I was perennially distracted from a controlled approach to adaptation by the thrill of quickness and the spur of competition. As a result, my training had been a two-edged sword. Sometimes it made me faster, but sometimes it made me slower. On the comeback trail in 1994, I was still looking for a reliable way to tell whether my training was having its intended effect.

The key, in my opinion, was to be able to accurately measure exertion during my workouts. There is a strong correlation between heart rate and performance, but the hand-to-throat method of measuring heart rate had proven inconvenient and imprecise. Thus, I was intrigued by the possibility of using one of the heart rate monitors on the market since I had last competed in the mid-eighties. In late 1993, I started looking for a monitor to use with my computer.

The POLAR VANTAGE XL®, with a computer program available for entering and processing heart rate data, turned out to be the perfect model. I could set the monitor to record my heart rate automatically at sixty-second intervals, and I could record my time and heart rate at any other point of a run by simply pressing a button. I could also store information from a maximum of eight workouts before I had to enter it into my computer. I could then use the POLAR® software to generate useful graphics which told me visually how well I had maintained my exertion within certain target ranges.

More importantly, I could use other computer generated information to reveal adaptive trends, for by correlating accurate heart rate data with my workout times I could infer what was happening to my capacity.

Capacity for Exertion: In trying to understand adaptation, I imagined having a capacity for exertion--like the engine that powers an automobile. Obviously, fast cars have big engines, which is why expanding one's capacity is so important to the game of running.

In my view, training was a process of playing with effort to expand capacity. In this process, effort was no more dynamic than capacity itself. Thus, my experience indicated that workouts were adaptive only when they were coordinated with discernable metabolic changes going on within me.

As I began my four-month base-building regimen, I expected my capacity to fluctuate from day to day according to a short term recovery cycle (see page 45). The recovery cycle could radically affect my performances depending on the way I felt: sluggish, tired, lazy, ready, or eager. Before I learned to recognize the signs of adaptation, I used to fool myself into thinking I had improved when, in fact, I had only recovered to the point of feeling eager. Yes, my performance was significantly better than during previous hard/ready workouts, but rest and recovery had caused these changes, not necessarily adaptation.

Adaptation affected capacity according to a different cycle, which I measured on a separate scale: unable, ineffective, passable, effective, and fully able (see Figure 17.1). Ideally, anytime I added a new workout to my training regimen, I'd be "passably" able to do it. And by the end of the training period, I would have become "fully able" to do it. But not necessarily. As I repeated a workout over a period of, say, ten weeks, I could expect it to affect my capacity in phases: shock, adaptation and exhaustion. If I weren't careful, shock or exhaustion--which are on the negative side of the adaptive coin--could make me become unable to continue doing a workout.

Thus, from either the short or the intermediate perspective, adaptation depended on my ability to manage my training efforts. During the first six weeks of the current training period, for instance, I had completed forty-one recovery runs on my hilly Kaimuki course. In my diary, I noted feeling sluggish for five of those runs, tired for twenty and lazy for sixteen. In other words, sixty-four percent of the time I had little or no energy (tired or sluggish, as opposed to lazy). In responding to the way I felt, I generally started very slowly, and I would only work a little harder as I warmed up about twenty or thirty minutes into the run.

I rarely felt like pushing the pace because shock had reduced my capacity for exertion. Until shock had run its course, there was no use trying to perform as well as I had in recent months. A harder effort would only increase the strength of the shock reaction. My first priority was to minimize the effects of shock by running the slowest pace consistent with the purpose of the workout.

Only after adaptation had set in and further training had occurred could I expect to build to peak capacity. And since there had to be a valley after every peak, I could eventually expect my performances to plateau at a level somewhat lower than my peak. Meanwhile, I would have to be patient, riding out the periods of decline to enjoy the periods of growth.

Figure 17.1: Three Phases of the Training Cycle.

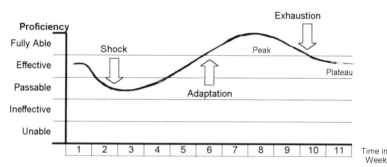

You can measure your training proficiency on a scale from unable to fully able. Any training activity changes ability on this scale according to three adaptive phases: shock, adaptation and exhaustion. If there are no changes in the effort of the activity during, say, a ten-week training period, ability will eventually level off lower than its peak--in this case at an "effective" level.

First Signs of Adaptation: In mid-October, I was still anxious to sense improvement from the base building regimen I had begun six weeks earlier. Since I was running twice a day, I got to assess my energy every twelve hours, recording the way I had felt on a five-level scale in my diary.

Later, I transferred this information to my computer, and by mid-October it was apparent I was feeling tired or sluggish on my recovery runs on an increasingly frequent basis. In fact, during the three two-week periods since the beginning of September, I had been sluggish or tired during 54%, 60%, and 68% of my recovery runs, respectively (see Figure 17.2).

Figure 17.2: Workout Energy During Recovery Runs.

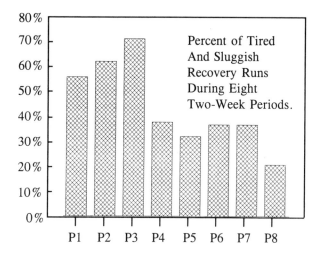

The bars indicate the recovery runs in which I felt tired or sluggish during eight two-week periods. Clearly, I ran increasingly more recovery runs at a tired or sluggish level during the first six weeks. Soon after, however, I began feeling tired or sluggish on progressively fewer recovery runs.

I wasn't particularly surprised by these results, considering that during the same six-week period I had also doubled the distance of my intervals and added six flights of stairs to my weekly hill workout. I was usually recovering in time for my hard workouts, so I probably hadn't overestimated my capacity, but I wasn't sure whether my energy would return. Then, after six weeks, I suddenly began feeling better.

Figure 17.2 shows a remarkable shift in my energy between my third and fourth two-week periods. And from then on, the percent of recovery runs in which I felt sluggish or tired would continue dropping from thirty-five to nineteen percent, even though I would continue my training unabated.

Something had happened to my capacity in mid-October to increase my workout energy. I recall hitting the bottom of the long first hill of my recovery run one evening, and as I turned a corner and headed up a slight hill, my energy suddenly clicked in and for the first time in weeks I was able to lift my knees and quicken my pace. I was at a loss to explain this shift in energy from a physiological point of view. But I knew my patience and hard work were finally being rewarded.

Moreover, with ten weeks to go in my base-building period, I was confident that adaptation would eventually reveal a new level of racing ability. Meanwhile, I was delighted with my new-found energy because it would also have a positive effect on my workout performances. As a coach and student of the game, I intended to measure that effect.

Closing In On Adaptation: Since I always ran the same recovery run, never varying the 3.74-mile course, it was an excellent vehicle for comparing my performances. I hadn't expected my times to drop by leaps and bounds, but by mid-November, they were definitely coming down. From an average of almost forty-two minutes during September, they had dropped to forty minutes in late October.

And with the exception of a two-week period in November when I was in shock from having run an 18-miler I wasn't prepared for, this downward trend would continue until late December, when I averaged less than thirty-eight minutes on my recovery runs. The troubling part of this downward trend in times was an upward trend in average heart rate. In other words, my times were probably coming down at least in part because I was working harder on my recovery runs, not necessarily because I was adapting.

It wouldn't have been the first time I had pushed my times down with effort instead of waiting for adaptation to increase my capacity. Previously when this had happened, I had often gotten injured or come down with a major illness that disrupted my training for several weeks.

But in mid-November, I was still injury-free and I hadn't had a cold in years. Furthermore, since my recovery runs still felt easy and I was still recovering in time for my hard workouts, I didn't think I was in imminent danger of exhausting myself.

Perhaps I was running faster because of the daily changes (just described) in my workout energy. Since I was feeling better on my recovery runs, of course my times would drop accordingly. I confirmed this hunch in late December, when I graphed the distribution of times for all of my recovery runs during the four-month training period (see Figure 17.3).

As I expected, the times on my recovery runs made a bell-shaped curve (not shown in Figure 17.3) with most of them falling between thirty-eight and forty-one minutes. Far more interesting to me, however, was the way my times were distributed according to the way I felt when I ran them (the curved lines in Figure 17.3). The better I felt during a workout, the faster I ran. When I was sluggish, for example, my recovery runs took between forty-two and forty-six minutes, but when I was ready, they took between thirty-four and thirty-eight minutes.

Figure 17.3: Distribution of Times for Recovery Runs During a Sixteen-Week Training Period.

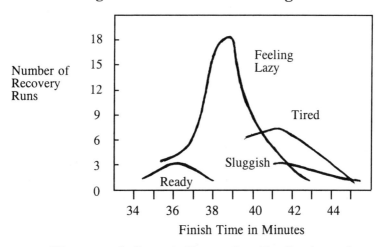

The curved lines indicate the distribution of finish times by workout energy (sluggish, tired, lazy and ready). The better I felt, the faster I ran. For example, when I felt ready, I usually

ran the workout in 36 or 37 minutes, but when I
felt lazy, I ran it mostly in 38 or 39 minutes.

Thus, at least some of the drop in times between September and late
December had to be a reflection of the shift in my energy from mostly
tired and sluggish to mostly lazy and ready.

Controlling for Workout Energy: There was also a corresponding shift in my average heart rate for each run. The better I felt
the harder I ran, as reflected by my average heart rate during the
workout.

There was nothing wrong, I decided, with running harder, as long
as I felt better and didn't overtrain. But were my times coming down
only because I was working harder or because I was also adapting? I
wondered whether my times would show a downward trend if I
controlled my data for the way I felt during each workout.

Working on my computer in late December, I studied the fifty-eight
recovery runs in which I had been feeling lazy. First, I sorted them
according to my average heart rate during the workout. (I had set my
monitor to record my heart rate at sixty-second intervals during each
recovery run, and the POLAR® program enabled me to compute an
average heart rate for each workout.) The averages ranged from 101 to
117 beats per minute, with most of the workouts falling into the average
heart rate bins between 108 and 110 bpm. Then I sorted the workouts
in these bins by date, expecting to see downward trends in my times
between September and December.

And downward trends were exactly what I discovered. Between
early September and early December, for example, I had done eight
easy/lazy recovery runs at an average heart rate of 109 beats per minute
(see Figure 17.4). And my times for these workouts had dropped from
forty-three to thirty-eight minutes. Since I only compared workouts in
which I felt lazy, I concluded that the downward trend in times was not
caused by short term changes in my workout energy, but by longer term
changes in my capacity.

A Measure of Skepticism: For the first time in my running
career, I seemed to be measuring adaptation objectively. But I was still
skeptical. I knew just enough about statistics to think I might be
overlooking something. I could see a downward trend in times, but I

didn't know if it was statistically significant. Nor did I know whether
I had a sufficiently large sample to validate my findings.

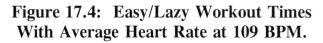

**Figure 17.4: Easy/Lazy Workout Times
With Average Heart Rate at 109 BPM.**

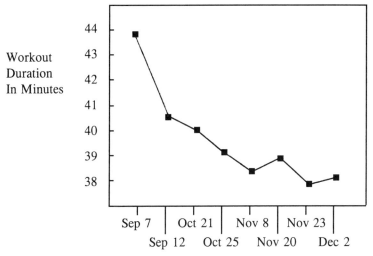

**I ran eight recovery runs in which I felt lazy and
also averaged 109 beats per minute for the whole
workout. The times show a downward trend
from 40 to 38 minutes during a three month
period.**

I was also bothered by using data that depended on a subjective
reading of my workout energy (such as lazy). In fact, during September,
I'd had trouble distinguishing between tired and lazy. My energy
seemed uniformly low for most of my recovery runs at the time, and I
was having trouble fitting my new base-building experience into previous
standards for measuring my workout energy. Thus, the radical drop in
times between September 7 and 12 could be misleading. Perhaps I had
fooled myself into thinking I was lazy on the seventh when I was really
tired, which would explain the slower time.

Nonetheless, I had expected adaptation to reveal itself during the
training period with greater energy and faster recoveries, and with faster
performances at the same heart rate. And I reckoned this would be true
not only for my recovery runs, but for my interval workouts, as well.

I had followed a careful protocol for my 1600-meter interval workouts on the UH track. Each week, I started with a mile warm-up jog, and I included the same 200-meter rest jog between intervals. Thus, like the recovery run, the interval workout was an excellent vehicle for measuring adaptation. I'll pursue this subject in the next chapter.

Chapter Seventeen Synopsis:

- **The Main Issue:** How can I use a heart rate monitor to measure adaptation in my training?

- **Concepts:**

    1) Adaptation is the second phase of a three-part, cyclic process that includes shock, adaptation and exhaustion.
    2) An adaptive trend is a noticeable positive change in your capacity which increases workout energy, reduces stress symptoms or improves racing ability.
    3) Performance potential refers to your inherent, unrevealed proficiency to do a race or workout. Your capacity changes on the following scale: unable, ineffective, passable, effective, and fully able.
    4) An adaptive plateau is a temporary state of balance between your training and your capacity for exertion. Your ability will be better than it was before you began the new regimen, but it will be lower than its recent peak. Thus, you'll usually feel like you can train or race effectively, but you probably won't feel fully able.

- **Theoretical Tenets:**

    1) Adaptation occurs as you repeat a series of workouts during a period of weeks or months.
    2) Your potential to perform a workout is revealed as you adapt to it during a training cycle.
    3) Adaptation can reveal itself with faster performances at the same average heart rate and the same level of recovery.
    4) The more effectively you can do a workout, the better adapted you are to the stress it produces.

■ **Relationships:**

1) The greater the shock, the greater the potential for adaptation, but the greater the risk of utter debilitation, which renders you unable to continue training.
2) The more your workout efforts are in harmony with short term changes in workout energy, the less they will be affected by shock and exhaustion.

■ **Principles:**

1) Metabolic forces govern adaptive cycles. You cannot affect these forces directly, but only indirectly with training effort.
2) Repeating Workouts: Adaptation occurs in response to a constant training stimulus over a period of weeks or months. You don't have to repeat a workout exactly every week, but the adaptive stimuli should be similar. Otherwise you'll keep yourself in constant shock with the novelty of your training efforts.

■ **Questions and Answers:**

1) How can I measure adaptation in my training?

You've got to accurately measure three aspects of training over a period of several months: performances, average level of exertion, and workout energy. In order to see adaptive movement, you have to hold two of these aspects steady, while looking for a positive change in the third.

For instance, adaptation reveals itself when your:

A. Workout energy improves at the same effort and the same performance level;
B. Performances improve at the same heart rate and the same level of workout energy.
C. Heart rate drops at the same performance level and the same level of workout energy.

2) What's happening when I can't seem to measure adaptive progress in my training?

It could be that you are stuck on an adaptive plateau.

Remember, it's difficult to initiate adaptive movement unless you put yourself in shock. You have to take your training to another level by adding some form of effort to it, whether frequency, duration or intensity.

And since shock is the opposite of adaptation, you have to be willing to lose your ability while you're in shock, in order to gain it later as you begin to adapt to the stress of the new training regimen.

Chapter Eighteen
Intervals and Adaptation

When I was on the football team in high school, I found wind sprints and sustained action drills in practices to be brutally violent. But when I went out for track, I soon discovered that interval training for the mile and half-mile was equally violent.

In those days, I did what my coaches told me to do. When they said to run faster I ran faster, and somehow the training had worked. I revelled in my personal records and delighted in new-found strength. While on my own during the seventies and early eighties, however, I discovered that the training process didn't always make me stronger. Sometimes it made me weaker and, thereby, ruined my racing performances.

I remember how perplexed and embarrassed I would feel, having trained for months expecting to run a great race, only to crash and burn. My training had been as I remembered it earlier in my career. But obviously the game wasn't as simple as I thought. And if I were to master it on my own as an adult, I would have to reconsider my assumptions about intervals, especially about the effort needed to improve with them. I assumed, for example, that intervals had to be run at a progressively harder effort from week to week.

This was the way I had been taught, especially in high school and at UH: to push my interval times down with progressively harder efforts. Typically, I would run a moderate workout the first week of a training period, but I'd be blasting as hard as possible on the last week. My interval times improved, of course, but I couldn't tell whether adaptation or increased effort was the driving force. In such cases, I assumed my interval times had dropped partly due to increased effort and partly due to adaptation. But not necessarily, as my racing performances sometimes showed. I had great difficulty reconciling all those very hard workouts with such poor racing performances.

Finally, I decided I'd been working harder than I needed. Wouldn't it be easier to train just hard enough for adaptation? My times wouldn't drop as dramatically, but the purpose of training, I decided, was to race well, not to run spectacular workouts. In reflecting on the training I had done before my best races, it was apparent I had trained *consistently* for many weeks, not tremendously for a few.

Following this line of reasoning, I assumed from then on that adaptive progress occurred when I found the narrow range between too much and too little effort. I called this range "right effort." And much of my work at the time was to identify its qualities. Foremost among them was consistency.

Right Effort: In teaching classes about adaptation, I often conveyed its meaning with an analogy. Adaptation is like baking a cake. One has to combine the dry and liquid ingredients into a consistent mixture, otherwise the cake will be either too dry or too moist.

In a similar sense, adaptation depends on carefully measured efforts and recoveries. If I were scheduled to do a certain hard workout from week to week, I would have to be consistently ready to do it--not lazy one week and eager the next. Nor could I run a moderate workout one week and a very hard one the next. Right energy and right effort are no more nor less than scheduled.

But finding right effort is easier said than done. And if I were to run too hard during the initial stages of a new regimen, I could easily injure or exhaust myself. Thus, I would begin a new series of workouts aiming for the easy side of right effort, paying attention to the apparent difficulty of the workout, my experience of fatigue during and after it, the time I needed to recover from it, the severity of inflammation I experienced, and the incidence of other stress symptoms. My observations would tell me how hard the workout was as a whole. And from experience I knew it couldn't be excessively hard or I probably wouldn't race well.

There had been many times when I'd found right effort in this way. Just as often, however, I would attack a new workout as though there were no tomorrow. And if I didn't injure myself with the first workout, I'd have to back off on effort the next few times I did it, knowing that the dissonance of my reaction was not compatible with right effort. I was looking for harmony in my response to the workout, and if I were patient enough to find and hold it for six or eight weeks, my times would improve with little added effort. On the other hand, whenever I lost my adaptive focus and became obsessed with pushing for faster times, I often became injured or exhausted.

As a fifty-year-old, I was no longer willing to waste time injuring or exhausting myself. Having begun yet another comeback in 1994, I resolved to improve my performances by adaptation, not harder effort. And with a heart rate monitor and a computer, I finally had the tools to home in on right effort scientifically, instead of relying solely on my intuition.

Repeating Workouts: The key to revealing adaptation was repeating certain workouts so I could compare my heart rate with my performances. Fortunately, I enjoyed duplicating workouts according to the dictates of a specific structure of exertion, such as eight 1600-meter intervals at steady state. All I had to do to adapt was repeat the workout.

Ideally, I could overlay on my computer screen the heart rate graph of one interval workout and it would appear exactly the same as the next. In the real world, however, my capacity was never exactly the same from week to week, and thus the heart rate graphs for my interval workouts in late 1994 were never exactly the same. I was constantly having to adjust my exertion to my energy in order to create right effort. This was never a boring process, but one of the supreme challenges in my running.

Nonetheless, by late September I had met the challenge by establishing a "right effort" workout consisting of eight 1600-meter intervals. I planned to continue running the workout once a week until the end of December, so I had a lot of time to see improvement from it.

Right Effort Intervals: Each Monday, I was up at the crack of dawn to join the walkers on the UH track. While they walked and chatted amiably in the outside lanes, I jogged a warm-up mile, focusing intently on what I was about to do. I carried my heart rate monitor in one hand and a stopwatch in the other to keep careful tabs on my performance. But during the first several weeks, I didn't know exactly what my heart rate or my times should be during the intervals.

As I jumped into my first interval, I would project myself ahead to the end of the workout. I wanted it to be a hard workout and I wanted my intervals to feel quick and relaxed, meaning steady state. From prior testing, I knew my steady state range was approximately 140 to 160 beats per minute (bpm). And based on my experience of doing 800-meter intervals during the previous several weeks, I also knew my target range would be a narrower 155 to 160 bpm.

Yet right effort wasn't necessarily in that range. Sometimes it seemed better to start below 155 bpm while I continued warming up (see Figure 18.1). Typically, my legs were stiff and heavy at the start. In fact, during the first few weeks, I never had the energy to run faster than eight minutes per mile on the first interval. At my slow starting pace, my heart rate would be a light 130 beats per minute.

Figure 18.1: A "Right Effort" Range During a 1600-Meter Interval Workout.

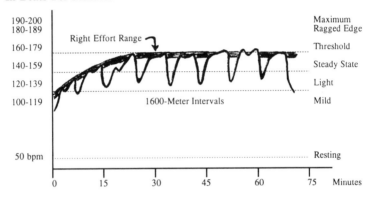

I began this workout with a slow mile jog (not shown) before the first interval. The dark, horizontal band is a range of effort approximately five beats per minute wide. Being in this range felt "right" as I warmed up during the first three intervals. Near the end of the workout, I felt eager to run harder, but held myself back to my target range. This enabled me to keep the overall workout effort manageable so I could recover in time for my next hard workout.

Usually, by the third or fourth interval I was holding 155 to 160 bpm, but once I needed five intervals to reach that level. Occasionally, I was able to jump right up to 155 bpm on the second interval. It all depended on how I felt. Sometimes I was on the lazy side of ready, sometimes I was simply ready, and sometimes I was on the eager side of ready. The better I felt, the sooner I warmed up and the sooner I was able to approach the 155 to 160 bpm range. Meanwhile, I would simply focus on a quick relaxed pace, and as I warmed up my stride would lengthen and quicken automatically.

Sometimes I would lock into right effort as if I had put myself on cruise control and no longer needed to adjust my accelerator. I would glance at my monitor and see 157 or 158 bpm--lap after lap. And my times for each interval would be equally steady--often staying within a second of, say, seven minutes from one interval to the next, even though I never checked my pace during an interval but only at the end.

At the end of the workout--as I became either somewhat fatigued or thoroughly warmed up--I would sometimes lose my focus and press my heart rate above 160 bpm during the last couple of intervals. This was not as hard as I could have run, but it was definitely a notch above steady state.

When I graphed my heart rate for the whole workout, my exertion typically formed a rising curve from interval to interval as I found my target range and, then, continued pressing into my lower threshold range. At first, I had rationalized pushing faster near the end of the workout because I usually felt better at that point and, therefore, I thought my target range was rising. But I soon noticed that when I worked myself up to 165 bpm or more after the fifth interval, I would have trouble recovering in time for my next hard workout.

Similarly, when I pressed my times down at the beginning of the workout, I'd be flagging on the last few intervals, and also taking longer than I wanted to recover from the workout. It was better, I decided, to take my time getting up to my target range than to press too early and become overly fatigued. Running eight 1600-meter intervals at 155 to 160 beats per minute was tough enough, without making it unnecessarily tough.

After each workout, I would stand at my motorcycle with an electrolyte replacement drink as my reward, thinking of what it had taken to get out of bed that morning to do the workout. I often tried to talk myself out of doing the intervals, battling the threat of injury, heat and humidity, heavy wind and rain, lack of sleep, flagging energy, or an impending cold. And every time I did the workout anyway I came away from it a stronger, tougher and more confident runner.

Furthermore, my interval times were gradually coming down. In late September and early October, while still in shock from my new regimen, I was averaging 7:15 for the eight intervals in the workout. By mid-October, however, I was running close to 7:03, and a month later I had chopped my times to 6:54.   On December 5, I ran my fastest interval workout of the training period, averaging 6:49.8 per interval.

As my times improved, my average heart rate for the interval workout began to rise.[16]   Naturally, I wondered whether my times were coming down because of adaptation or increased effort.   The October 24 and November 7 workouts were the hardest, with average heart rates of 151 and 152 bpm, respectively.   On the alternate weeks--October 18, October 24, and November 15--my average heart rate was a more moderate 145 bpm.

Each time I came back to an average heart rate close to 145 bpm, my times came down a little lower than they had been previously at that heart rate (see Figure 18.2).   I was excited when I juxtaposed this downward trend in times with my average heart rate for the workouts because it showed a clear indication of adaptation.

Figure 18.2: Average Pace and Heart Rate For 1600-Meter Intervals

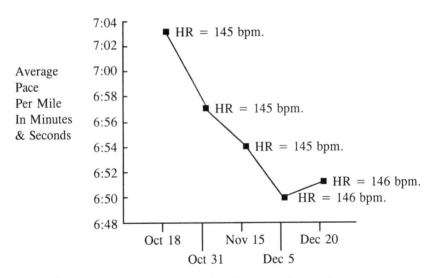

My average interval pace for three workouts between

---

[16] Average heart rate includes the minute-to-minute readings for my tempo intervals and rest jogs, but not the warm-up jog before the first interval.

**18 October and 15 November improved by nine
seconds per mile.** Since my average heart rate was
constant for these workouts at 145 bpm, I concluded
I was adapting during this part of the training period.
On 5 and 20 December, my times were faster than
they had been at 145 bpm, but my average heart rate
had risen to 146 bpm so I couldn't be sure that I was
still adapting. Since my heart rate was steady for the
last two workouts and my average pace slowed, I may
have been coming to the end of my adaptive period.

Adaptation in Perspective: I had begun the new interval workout
in September, intending initially to gauge my ability to sustain quick,
relaxed running. I started with eight 800-meter intervals, and as I added
intervals to the workout during September, it became apparent that I had
more than sufficient ability to do it. Thus, on September 26, I doubled
the distance of the intervals to 1600 meters.

During the next several weeks, my energy was low and I suffered
from the aches and pains common during a period of shock. I was very
careful with my effort at this point, knowing that too much stress during
a period of shock could easily ruin my ability. My previous successes
with shock had indicated that the *minimum* effort necessary to do a
workout was the right effort to avoid becoming unable to do it.

Later, as shock subsided and adaptation set in, a growing sense of
energy and well-being enveloped me. My times began to drop from
week to week, but I didn't seem to be working harder than I had been
earlier. The aches and pains had subsided and my legs felt lighter and
more alive. In the midst of this adaptive period, I was sometimes
tempted to blast the intervals, especially on days when my energy was
close to eager. From experience, I knew this would be a major pitfall
because running significantly harder would reverse adaptive processes
sooner than if I were to maintain right effort.

By early December I was definitely feeling effective, but I was
never fully able to hammer my workouts with impunity. In fact, I
expected exhaustion might set in before I became fully able to do the
workout. At that point, my ability would peak and soon begin to
dwindle. If I were to back off slightly on my effort, my ability would
plateau at a level somewhat below its peak.

But if I tried to fight exhaustion by pushing to maintain or improve my times, I would suffer a radical loss in my capacity--maybe to the point of getting injured. Since I wanted to avoid this worst case scenario, I would have to continue holding right effort.

Chapter Eighteen Synopsis:

■ **The Main Issue:** How do I know when I'm exerting the right effort for any workout in my training regimen?

■ **Concepts:**

1) Right effort is between too much and too little effort. Right effort is also the amount of effort that minimizes shock, maximizes adaptation and avoids severe exhaustion.
2) Right exertion is that level of exertion which is in harmony with your changing feelings of energy during a workout.
3) Right energy is having adequate energy to do a specific workout. The harder the workout, the more energy you'll need on the workout energy scale: sluggish, tired, lazy, ready, eager.
4) Consistency refers to the right amount of effort and the right amount of energy.
5) A target range is the level of exertion that will result in building a race-specific ability.

■ **Theoretical Tenets:**

1) Right exertion changes according to the amount of running energy you feel at any moment during a workout.
2) Target ranges are generally narrow, say, five heart beats per minute wide. Your target range will usually rise during a workout as you warm up and your capacity expands.
3) Once you have warmed up, your target range should plateau along with your pace.
4) If you are not able to recover regularly and adequately from a workout, then your target range is too high, or you are running too long within it.

■ **Relationships:**

1) The better you feel at the beginning of a workout, the sooner you'll warm up and the sooner you'll be able to enter your race-specific, target range.

2) The harder you train during an adaptive period, the sooner you can expect to plateau or become exhausted.

■ **Principle of Consistency:** You cannot adapt unless your training is consistent. Your workout effort must be in harmony with your workout energy, and your exertion must feel right in relation to your running energy.

■ **Questions and Answers:**

1) How do I know when I'm exerting the right effort for any workout in my training regimen?

   All or most of the following characteristics must be present:

   A. Your exertion feels right in relation to your running energy.
   B. You are able to recover within your scheduled recovery period.
   C. You survive whatever stress symptoms arise without having to cut back on your training.
   D. You eventually show adaptive progress.
   E. You feel increasingly more effective as you repeat the workout from week to week.
   F. Once your ability plateaus, your performances level off and you continue running effectively.
   G. You don't attempt to force your performances down with increasingly harder workout efforts.

2) How can I measure adaptation in my interval training?

   In terms of equipment, you'll need a sophisticated heart rate monitor that allows you to average your heart rate during the intervals and the whole workout so you can compare your exertion from week to week. You'll also need a stop watch, preferably one that records into memory your times for the intervals. And you'll need a measured course, like a track, to do the intervals on.

Next, you've got to repeat the same workout at the same level of exertion and the same level of recovery. If your interval times improve under those circumstances, then you are adapting. But you've got to be sure that you're keeping your exertion and your recovery the same. Repeating the workout means that it has the same number and length of intervals, and the same recovery period between intervals. If you time everything that happens during a workout, then you can compare workouts to make sure they are the same.

Your workout energy should also be the same from week to week. If it varies from, say, ready to lazy, you'll get different performance results because your capacity for exertion will be different. Thus you should run the same workouts with the same effort and energy leading up to the interval workout so you are regularly ready to run the workout, not ready one week and lazy or eager the next.

Finally, you should be using a narrow target range so your average heart rate is the same from week to week. If you keep your heart rate within a range of five beats per minute during the intervals, you should be able to keep your overall average for the whole workout (including rest intervals) to the same number from week to week.

Consistency is imperative. Without the same effort and energy, your interval times are meaningless for measuring adaptation--like comparing apples and oranges.

3)	What if I am being consistent and my times are not improving?

It could be that you are not adapting. Maybe you are already well adapted to the interval workout. Or maybe you are still in shock and haven't started adapting yet.

If you have been repeating the workout for weeks or months, you might be able to shock your body into adaptation by running a shorter, faster version of it, which nonetheless maintains your overall workout effort at, say, a hard level.

The main thing is to experiment. If you've been repeating the workout without measurable results, it's probably time for a change.

Chapter Nineteen
Avoiding Exhaustion

I didn't know in 1978 what line of work I would pursue when I left high school teaching. During my first year without a job, I lived on savings, traveled, and got married. One day, I was perusing a friend's bookshelf when I noticed the seminal book by Hans Selye, *The Stress of Life*. I borrowed the book, not realizing it would lead me into a new career of coaching adult distance runners.

I had coached for seven years on the high school level, but I was burned out and didn't see myself coaching in the future. Being idea-driven, I needed a new perspective on the training process before I could jump into coaching as a career. Selye's book gave me an idea I could pursue with vigor. He called it the "General Adaptation Syndrome"[17] and it explained in a nutshell my entire experience of running.

After reading Selye, I saw that endurance training was essentially an attempt to adapt to the stress of racing effort. To help my students understand this idea, whenever I gave a seminar I began by describing an experiment from Selye's book.[18] I called it the "rat experiment," and my purpose was to get new students to think about the meaning of adaptation from the scientific perspective.

"Suppose you are a team of scientists," I would tell a group. "You've got a hundred white rats in your laboratory, and every day you bring them out of their cages and let them swim around in icy water to study how they adapt to the cold. Soon, some of the rats begin to die, and during the next seven days, a total of twenty rats succumb to the icy water. In the following weeks, however, the surviving rats seem to thrive with no ill effects."

In continuing with the case study, I explain that eventually something unexpected happens. I would give my students time to digest this

---

[17] *The Stress of Life* (revised edition), Hans Selye, M.D., McGraw-Hill Book Company, New York, 1956, 1976, page 79.

[18] *Ibid*, pages 112-13.

piece of information, and after a thoughtful moment, someone would venture, correctly, that perhaps all the rats had died in the cold water.

A Theory of Adaptation: Next, I would have my students develop a theory to explain what happened to the rats' resistance to the cold. They would usually come to the same conclusion that Selye had come to, that our physical resistance to a stressor moves through three stages: shock, adaptation and exhaustion. This general adaptation syndrome was Selye's major contribution to science. And its implications for distance running are as useful as they are for life itself.

Selye said that everyone has a finite amount of adaptive energy, which we may use in adapting to virtually any of the things we want to do in life. Anytime we do something new, he said, our body goes into shock. But if we have sufficient adaptive energy, we can survive this period of shock and enter a stage of increasing resistance to the stress of the activity. Eventually, however, we run out of adaptive energy and become exhausted. Our resistance runs down and, unless we take a rest, we can develop any one of a number of stress related diseases. Of course, the ultimate exhaustion is death.

Applied to running, this means that all of us are limited in our capacity to adapt to the stress of endurance racing. Since we cannot adapt indefinitely, sooner or later we must become exhausted. This is a bitter pill to swallow for a group of runners who thought they were taking a class on how to run faster. Some persist in holding on to old beliefs, such as "only the strong survive." I counter with a different belief, "Only the most intelligent survive the vagaries of hard training by learning how to cope with the ebb and flow of energy."

Every time we try to establish a training regimen, we are faced with the prospect of immediate shock, possible adaptation and eventual exhaustion. There is no escaping one phase in preference for another. The only viable options we have as runners are: minimize the effects of shock, prolong adaptation, and avoid extreme exhaustion. The first step in this process is to acknowledge the reality of the three adaptive phases, including the inevitability of exhaustion.

Exhaustion Sets In: In my own running, I had seen the effects of exhaustion many times. Usually, I would first experience a slight drop in energy--no more than a minor shift in recovery levels (see Figure 19.1). With less energy, however, my times would be a little slower than in previous sessions. And if I tried to press my times back down to recent levels, I would soon discover I had even less energy during subsequent workouts.

If I were unable to stop the ensuing cycle of harder efforts and less energy, I would soon run completely out of energy, and even a total layoff would not restore it inside of ten days or two weeks. In addition, I would suffer a marked increase in stress symptoms, including muscle soreness, insomnia and irritability. I would sometimes blame such symptoms on the other stressors in my life, while overlooking the enormously stressful contribution of competitive running. And if I continued to push myself, I'd come down with a major cold or the flu, which would force me finally to take a rest. Selye's book made me realize the folly of trying to overcome metabolic forces.

Figure 19.1: Exhaustion Constricts Capacity For Exertion.

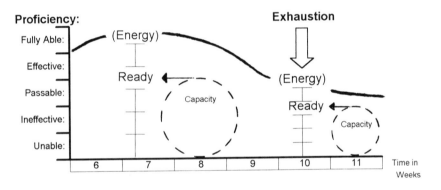

The workout energy scale is elastic vis a vis cyclic changes in ability. Thus, exhaustion (the downward arrow) constricts capacity in week ten by restructuring the way a runner feels during the workout. Ready is still ready, but there is less energy available to do a workout at the ready level than during week seven. Capacity is thereby limited in this example to the passable level, and I might be able to do, say, only six intervals rather than eight during a hard/ready workout.

Instead of fighting my metabolism, I had to coordinate my efforts in harmony with it. If I was getting tired of running a regimen of long, slow distances, maybe it was time to quit. This was exactly how I was beginning to feel about my training at the end of 1994. During the previous sixteen weeks, I had averaged seventy-two miles a week, including a schedule of three hard workouts a week.

By December, I was getting tired of repeating these workouts. I needed a change of scenery and a change of pace. In short, I was experiencing the first signs of exhaustion. I could keep doing the workouts, but I saw no sense in that. It would be better to restructure my training to stimulate a new cycle of adaptation. And my first step was to evaluate where I was with each workout.

The Hill Workout: My hill workout usually took about 105 minutes. Less than forty minutes of that was actually spent running uphill. In this sense, I considered it to be a "light-weight" hill workout. But it was all I could handle given my first priority of running for 105 minutes during the workout.

The highest quality exertion wasn't even running; it was walking the flight of ninety-nine stairs at the top of Diamond Head. As I described in chapter sixteen, my initial goal had been to build from five to twelve flights of stairs before attempting what I remembered to be a much tougher walk on a defunct tram track that rose more than a thousand feet, from sea level to the top of another extinct volcano called Koko Crater.

By mid-November, I was overdue on my intention to walk Koko Crater. I could still recall the extreme duress walking it had caused me years before, and I didn't want to subject myself to so much stress again without adequate preparation. However, I had procrastinated long enough. On the morning of November 12, I drove to the base of Koko Crater, anticipating a tough workout but discovering a piece of cake.

I walked the railroad ties in intervals of one hundred steps, and it took me ten intervals to make it to the top. But these intervals were not the same as the ones on Diamond Head. Even though I was taking twice as many steps per interval on Koko Crater, the first four or five hundred steps rose at such a moderate incline that I didn't need to stop. Even on the steepest sections, my heart rate only got up to 140 bpm--ten to twenty bpm less than on the Diamond Head stairs, which were much steeper than the ties on Koko Crater.

When I reached the summit of Koko Crater, I was both disappointed and relieved. The workout I thought would be so tough wasn't even as tough as my Diamond Head run with a dozen flights of stairs. In fact, the toughest thing about the Koko Crater workout was coming down the mountain. Since the railroad ties were spread two feet apart, I had to step as though I were taking two steps down instead of one as I did on Diamond Head. Since the Koko Crater workout was easier than the Diamond Head run, I recovered quickly and had no stress symptoms afterwards.

In comparing the two workouts, I decided I preferred the Diamond Head run. I liked the convenience of running from home rather than commuting to Hawaii Kai to do Koko Crater. I also enjoyed the variety of the terrain on Diamond Head. And, truth be told, I relished the interaction with tourists along the way. The average person was completely taken aback by the prospect of having to climb the ninety-nine stairs. Many took the stairs in segments, stopping every thirty or forty steps to get their heavy breathing back to normal. And while they struggled to the top I was usually able to complete a couple of flights-- walking briskly up two stairs at a time at steady state, then turning and jogging briskly down.

Occasionally someone would gasp, "How many?" At first I thought they were asking me how many flights I was doing. What they really wanted to know was how many steps to the top. "Ninety-nine," I learned to say, finally realizing that the average person didn't have a clue what I was doing there or the sort of condition I was in, even as a fifty year-old, to be able to walk ten to fifteen flights of stairs in a single workout. Thus, having tourists there helped keep my effort in perspective because I tended to forget what sort of shape I was in, often comparing my present regimen with the hills I had done as a younger man.

But I could only revel in their reactions for so long. Eventually, I began to worry about the effect the workout was having on me. The hip injury which had been bothering me earlier in the training was worse by mid-December. I had aggravated it one evening while practicing a new stretching routine. It twinged when I made lateral leg movements, and, though I didn't experience the injury directly while running or walking stairs, it seemed to be worse after the Diamond Head workout. So as much as I enjoyed doing Diamond Head, I was running it on borrowed time. Finally, on December 22, I ran my last Diamond Head hill run.

It was difficult to put my Diamond Head workout into "scientific" perspective. I hadn't kept accurate heart rate records, but there was no question I was stronger from having done the hills and stairs. Otherwise, I wouldn't have been able to do Koko Crater without blowing myself away, as I had years before. The reason I had started doing the stairs was to build the strength in the large muscles on the front and back of my upper legs. For months they had seemed weak and achy, but by mid-December they weren't bothering me at all. I was walking stairs as I had when I was younger--with strength and resiliency.

But would the hills and stairs make me better able to run ten kilometers? I couldn't say with certainty. Nonetheless, it had been an enjoyable, challenging workout. With the challenge wearing thin, however, it was time to look for new ways to build my leg power.

The Long Run: I had always heard that stamina was the most difficult ability to rebuild after a long layoff, and my experience of doing two-hour runs earlier in the year had confirmed what I'd heard. On November 12, I ran the first eighteen-miler of my comeback in 3:09 with my marathoners. I held myself back from the start and through the middle miles, but when one of my runners came by with five miles to go I picked up the pace and ran in with him, never breathing hard or suffering extreme fatigue.

That evening, however, I had my slowest recovery run of the sixteen-week period--fifty-one minutes to do 3.74 miles. Not even "sluggish" could describe how badly I felt. My legs were wobbly and I had so little energy I had to walk in places up the mile-long hill to my home. Clearly, I was in shock from having increased my time on the road from two to three hours. I needed two weeks to summon the nerve to do another eighteen-miler. This time I didn't carbohydrate load sufficiently before the run so I was lazy at the start, and I had to limit the workout to thirteen miles instead of the eighteen I had planned to do.

I was careful to eat some pasta and drink some cola before my next long run a week later. This time I managed eighteen miles in 2:46, which was twenty-three minutes faster than I had run three weeks earlier. I skipped my easy run twelve hours later and ate my fill of carbohydrates to speed my recovery. I was tired on my next run, doing it in forty-two minutes, but at least the run was bearable.

Maybe, I thought, I'm getting a handle on this long run business. But no such luck. Although I had ample energy at the start of my next long run a week later, I went out too fast and had to cut the workout to sixteen miles, struggling to finish in 2:38. I ran two more long runs before the end of the training period, and both were difficult efforts. I was beginning to wonder whether I was trying to do too much, running seventy miles a week and eighteen-mile long runs, too. I'd had a couple of good long runs, but the others had been so difficult that I didn't care if I ever did another.

As much as I resisted the thought of being on the road for close to three hours, however, I felt the need to do eighteen-milers. I had a spurt of extra energy when I recovered from them, and it also helped my confidence to know I could run that far without crashing. On the other hand, whenever I did crash, I would be apprehensive about doing the next one. I hated the feeling of biting off more than I could chew, either because I was inadequately prepared or because I had gone out too fast. Nonetheless, after a week or so, I would forget the pain I had suffered and psych myself up to do another eighteen-miler.

Though I was willing to run the distance, I could tell that it wouldn't take much to exhaust my mental and physical resources. Finally, I decided to settle for an intermediate distance I could manage on a consistent basis.

The Interval Workout: Something happened with my interval workout on December 12. I tried to do it, but my heart wasn't in it. For the first time in sixteen weeks, I aborted the workout at six intervals instead of finishing with my usual eight.

The Honolulu Marathon had been run the day before, and although I hadn't run, I had been under unusual work stress the previous week, organizing bus tours of the marathon course for hundreds of Japanese runners. At the same time, I was coming down with a cold, so I backed off on my training, running once a day instead of twice.

Although the cold never materialized, when I went out to do my intervals the following week, I didn't want to be there. In the past, when I'd tried to make excuses for not doing a workout my commitment had always seen me through. But this was an entirely different feeling: devoid of ambition, drive and energy.

The following week, though my energy was revived, my spirit was still at half-mast. I was burned out on 1600-meter intervals, my times seemed to be plateauing and my mind was no longer focused on the base-building regimen I had sustained for the past fifteen weeks. I was thinking about the 10-K race I wanted to do in early January, and what I needed to do to prepare for it. In short, I no longer wanted to carry on with the base-building regime.

I was becoming exhausted. And the best way to avoid serious exhaustion was to restructure my training. I needed a way to stimulate adaptive processes without exacerbating whatever I was feeling at that point. Since it was probably a function of the distances I had been running, I decided to cut my mileage on my hard workouts and run them faster. Thus on December 26, I changed my interval distance from 1600- to 1200-meters, and I also increased my target range from steady state to threshold.

The first time I ran the new workout I averaged 151 beats per minute[19] and the next two times I ran it I averaged 155 bpm. This represented an increase in my average heart rate from the 145-148 bpm I had averaged during my recent 1600-meter workouts. My new target range was 165 to 175 beats per minute, which was mid-threshold for me, and ten beats per minute faster than the old target range had been. The shift from steady state to threshold exertion brought my pace down from 6:54 to 6:29 per mile.

The previous July, I had averaged 6:30 and 156 bpm for five 1200-meter intervals. Now, six months later, I was averaging 6:25 and 155 bpm for eight 1200s. And the January 1200-meter workout was still only hard, not very hard, as it might have been with eight 1200s in July, 1994. Thus, my training results indicated I was getting stronger.

Exhaustion in Perspective: During the previous twelve weeks, I had improved my average interval times by more than eight seconds per mile. Since my average heart rate for the interval workout had remained fairly constant, I was convinced I was stronger than I had been the previous September.

But would these improved interval times translate into a faster 10-K? I was probably in better shape to run a half marathon than a 10-K, simply because my intervals had prepared me to run at a quick, relaxed tempo rather than a rapid, pressing tempo. Nonetheless, since my preferred racing distance was closer to ten kilometers, I decided to test myself with the Pearl Harbor 10-K on the seventh of January, 1995.

Though I'd officiated at the race many times, I had never run it,

---

[19] My average heart rate for a workout includes the eighty-second rest-intervals, but not the mile warm-up.

usually preferring to train or do other races at that time of year. This year, however, I was drawn to the race for the very reasons that used to turn me away from it: the competition was usually good and it was a flat, out-and-back course along the bike path next to Pearl Harbor. There were scenic views of the water and Ford Island, but much of the territory was semi-industrial. I would have no trouble concentrating on the race.

Five days before the event, I did a 1200-meter interval workout, but I skipped my next hard workout and my recovery runs during the last sixty hours, eating well and resting to give myself a chance for a good effort. And I was feeling eager the morning of the race. The competition included the aforementioned Ron Peroff, one of the top runners in my age division. I was delighted to see him in the registration line, knowing he would give me incentive to push myself.

Peroff went out faster than I was willing to go, but he didn't run away and hide as he had the last time we'd raced the previous August. At the turnaround, he was only forty yards ahead and I knew I could catch him if I pushed the second half. I had developed a stitch during the second mile, which was still bothering me during mile four. Yet in spite of the unpleasantness in my gut, I was able to catch Peroff at five miles, win my age division, and finish with moderate strength in 40:02.

It was a good race, considering my energy and my competitive results. I was satisfied, though not particularly thrilled by it. I didn't have the competitive drive to catch several younger runners at the finish, and my legs were very heavy immediately afterwards. Still, I hadn't raced in more than four months, and in that period I had never sustained a training heart rate above 165 beats per minute. Since I'd averaged 178 bpm in the race, I couldn't say I had prepared for the specific exertion of a 10-K. I was eager and energetic enough to race well, but there was definitely something missing that faster training may have given me.

Nonetheless, my performance indicated I hadn't lost much of my 10-K ability. When I used Jack Daniels' performances tables to compare the Hawaiian Style 8-K the previous August with the Pearl Harbor 10-K, it turned out I had run only about twenty seconds slower on the 10-K. That was certainly a tolerable performance loss, considering my average heart rate was two beats per minute slower on the 10-K and I hadn't raced nearly as hard during the last mile as I had the previous August.

Thus, I was convinced I had accomplished my purpose with my base-building regimen. In spite of not having trained for the 10-K, I had evidently gained sufficient stamina to compensate for losses in 10-K tempo and endurance. And potentially I was now in a position--with a broader mileage base--to bring my 10-K times down with a more appropriate training regimen in the months ahead.

Chapter Nineteen Synopsis:

- **The Main Issue:** How can I avoid extreme exhaustion at the end of a training cycle?

- **Concept:** Exhaustion is a noticeable, long term change in your capacity that reduces racing ability.

- **Theoretical Tenets:**

    1) We are all limited in our ability to adapt to the stress of endurance training.
    2) Since we cannot adapt forever, sooner or later we must become exhausted.
    3) Every time we establish a new training regimen, we are faced with the prospect of immediate shock, possible adaptation, and eventual exhaustion.
    4) Our only viable options are to minimize the effects of shock, prolong adaptation and avoid extreme exhaustion.

- **Relationships:**

    1) The harder you train while you are exhausted, the more exhausted you will become.
    2) The more exhausted you are, the harder it becomes to maintain or exceed your training performances.
    3) The more exhausted you are, the more stress symptoms you'll experience, and the greater your risk of injury and illness.

- **Questions and Answers:**

    1) How can I avoid extreme exhaustion at the end of a training cycle?

You've got to take a rest. After all, you're exhausted. Ironically, however, the most common reaction to exhaustion is increased effort. If your focus is on your deteriorating performances, you'll want to maintain them with harder effort. But this is exactly what your body doesn't need.

Rest means backing off on effort, which is psychologically difficult to do when you have a big race coming up. The tendency is to redouble your efforts the closer you get to the race. However, this is like shooting yourself in the foot. The harder you press against exhaustion, the harder it presses back at you.

Part V
Theory and Practice

As a coach and runner, I've always found it useful to have a training theory. My theory derives its tenets from exercise physiology, but it's not *about* physiology. Rather, it explains the relationships between the fundamental structures of endurance training, describing them in terms immediately accessible to any runner through self-observation.

For example, when I talk to runners about their sensations of effort and energy, I'm using ideas they can understand from their experience. When I talk about adaptation, I'm indicating ways they themselves can measure their progress. And when I talk about running satisfying races, I speak to their ultimate performance concerns. Any training theory must address these concerns in an effective manner. For the training process seems simple, yet it is dynamic and complex. Thus, a good theory should point the way to effective decision-making on a day-to-day--even a minute-to-minute--basis.

I needed a good training theory as I came to the end of my base training period in December 1994. More than mundane training decisions, I was faced with developing a new training schedule. What new workouts would I employ to race effectively in the spring? How could I avoid injury and exhaustion while taking my new base ability to an even higher level? These were important questions because I had burned out on the workouts I'd been doing since September. If I kept doing them, my racing ability would probably plateau and I would go nowhere.

On the other hand, my theory suggested I could continue improving if I were willing to restructure my workouts to stimulate a new adaptive cycle. Unfortunately, this process would upset the delicate balance I had established during the past sixteen weeks. If I changed my workouts now, I would undoubtedly throw myself once again into shock because I would not be used to the speed and duration of my new workouts. Thus, I'd be forced to strike a balance between my new workouts and my old capacity.

For example, I had been running my mile intervals at a quick tempo, and now I planned to run at a rapid tempo so I could prepare for 10-K races in the spring. How could I run the intervals faster without exhausting myself? Fortunately, an internal logic governs the training process: when you add effort in one form, you must subtract it in another. I could thereby balance faster intervals with a shorter workout.

Indeed, running eight 1200-meter intervals was easier than the eight 1600-meter intervals had been. It was still a hard workout, and I was still just able to recover from it in sixty hours, but evidently cutting the main portion of the workout from sixty-five to fifty minutes made up for the faster intervals.

Figure V.1: Sharpening from 1600s to 1200s

**Heart Rate Ranges as
Percent of Maximum:**

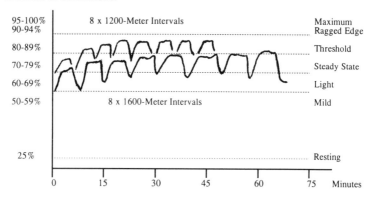

Both interval workouts shown above were designed to build tempo ability. The longer 1600-meter intervals built my ability for the half marathon, while the shorter, faster 1200-meter intervals were supposed to build my tempo for the 10-K. I did the longer intervals during my base-building program, and "sharpened" by running the shorter intervals at a higher level of exertion.

After my base-building period I was able to run two additional 1200-meter threshold intervals in a hard workout. In other words, I was stronger after my base-building period than I was before it.

With these changes in my Monday interval workout, I had launched a new training period. I was running fourteen workouts a week, and theoretically each workout was a base from which I could peak for the races I'd scheduled between March and June. However, with the exception of my Monday morning interval workout and my long hill workout (which would become a shorter quarter-mile interval workout), I wasn't willing to cut the mileage of any of the other workouts on my schedule.

I was especially reluctant to reduce the frequency of my double workout regimen. I had worked hard in the past four months to establish double workouts. They were at the heart of my ability to run seventy miles a week and I wasn't about to forsake that ability in early January. I kept thinking about my hero, Jim Gallup, and how at my age he had been able to race effectively at eighty to a hundred miles a week. If Jim could manage a hundred, I thought, I should be able to manage seventy. Without facing up to the truth of my circumstances, however, I knew there was something wrong with my logic.

If I wanted to exert myself at a higher level, I had to cut my mileage so I could garner the energy for faster training. Jim Gallup had raced well on eighty to a hundred miles a week, but he had previously built his mileage to a hundred and twenty miles a week. In other words--incredible as it may seem--Jim was sharpening at eighty to a hundred miles a week.

It wasn't necessarily true that I could race effectively at seventy miles a week, because seventy was my base, analogous to Jim's hundred and twenty. Furthermore, though I was able to run seventy per week effectively, I wasn't feeling fully able to run that much. In fact, as I described in the last chapter, I was still on the edge between getting by and getting injured. My energy was better than in early October, but it wasn't what it needed to be to train faster without breakdown.

Nonetheless, I wasn't willing to reduce my weekly mileage because I was afraid of losing my base abilities before my goal races. I had two months to train before the 1995 Johnny Faerber 10-K and six months until the Hard Rock 10-K. I had blown both races in 1994, and I wanted to vindicate myself in 1995. Yet I didn't know exactly when I could back off on my weekly mileage and still retain the adaptive effect of my base training. Both my theory and my prior training experience indicated I could hold a peak for a month or two. But could I hold it for *six* months in my *first* year of coming back to training as a *fifty* year-old?

Without mapping out my training with a written schedule, I decided to maintain my mileage for a month before cutting back during the last five weeks before the Faerber 10-K. After that race, I would build my mileage again through April before cutting it in May for the Hard Rock 10-K in June. In this way I hoped to sharpen my race ability twice. But I was really looking for a way to postpone the decision to cut my weekly mileage. For although I had cut the distance of two hard workouts, I'd also added distance to my long run and maintained my double workouts. Thus, in early January, my mileage base was still intact.

I felt secure with this approach because I assumed that my two hard interval workouts would provide my main adaptive focus. As long as they were shorter than before, I could run them faster without hurting myself or jeopardizing my program. However in early January I was bringing into play another factor which would soon prove to be injurious. And my training theory notwithstanding, I wasn't quick enough to adjust to these new circumstances.

Chapter Twenty
Peaking for a Goal Race

I had a fortuitous meeting on a vacation trip to the San Francisco Bay area during the summer of 1993. My wife and I were enjoying the ferry ride from Sausalito to Angel Island when I saw one of those gaunt-looking characters who--dressed in shorts and a Boston Marathon T-shirt--could only have been a runner. His name was Rick Batty, and we had a lot in common. Not only were we heading for the same picnic, but we soon discovered our intense mutual interest in running.

Several days later, I visited Rick at his home near Sausalito. We took a trail run in the Mount Tamalpais area and spent the afternoon talking about running. I had recently started writing a book on training and I was delighted to share ideas with someone who could give me another perspective. Rick had years of experience in the game and he also had strong opinions which he was willing to share. But the most valuable thing I brought away from our conversation was a source of information on running I had previously overlooked.

Rick was high on a quarterly publication called *Running Research News* (RRN). On his recommendation, I soon hunted down and read all the back issues, beginning with the first, which was published in 1985. *RRN* was billed as, "Your guide to training and sports nutrition. The only running newsletter actually written by exercise physiologists." The writers kept abreast of the latest research articles in exercise physiology, explaining and interpreting new findings for their readers. I saw immediately that *RRN* would be a lodestone of inspiration for my personal experiments in running and coaching.

I had always found it difficult to sustain a fresh perspective on the training process, tending to repeat the workouts and procedures that had worked for me before, while losing sight of the experimental aspect of training that makes it fun. So I was excited to find a publication that spoke directly to my interest in how to perform better in the sport of recreational racing. By November 1993, I was already including new ideas from *RRN* in my plans for the 10-K training program I would direct beginning in January 1994. I was also reaching a point in my own life where a racing comeback was looking possible. And being motivated primarily by ideas, I saw *Running Research News* as playing an important role in that comeback.

The September-October 1993 issue of *RRN* contained an article on the way biking affects running. The gist was that high intensity interval training on a stationary exercise bike had a strong positive effect on five and ten kilometer racing performances.[20] I could definitely relate to these results. I recalled that when I first got into running during high school, it had seemed to me that my outstanding leg strength was an outgrowth of my years of biking as a kid. I also recalled that in the mid-eighties, Jim Gallup had tried to talk me into using an exercise bike, claiming that high intensity intervals had made a big difference in his racing performances.

In fact, I was convinced that the weakness I'd experienced in my quads was related to my years of inactivity on the bike and in the hills. My quads were feeling much stronger after several months of doing stairs on Diamond Head, but by the end of 1994 I was ready to add some biking to my training so I could continue building muscle power in my upper legs. At that point, I carefully reread several articles on biking in *RRN* to understand the common and critical elements necessary to build my capacity on the bike.

I envisioned a regimen of easy workouts on the exercise bike in my basement, planning to do three per week in lieu of my usual Kaimuki recovery runs in those time slots. Each bike workout would last thirty-five minutes--approximately the same duration as my 3.74-mile recovery runs, and on that basis I decided to count a bike workout as three and a half running miles. I began with an easy workout the last week in December. During the first twenty minutes, I took my heart rate up in stages from mild to steady state. Then, between twenty and thirty minutes, I cranked up the tension on the wheel and blitzed five one-minute intervals at audible breathing before finishing with an easy cool-down during the last five minutes.

When I got off the bike, my quads were heavy and unresponsive. I'd expected them to feel that way, knowing how biking affects my triathletes going into the run portion of a triathlon. But I didn't expect to have such a terrible time on my long run forty-eight hours later. It

---

[20] *Running Research News,* Volume 9, Number 5, September-October 1993, pages 1-4. For information on how to subscribe, write PO Box 27041, Lansing, MI 48909.

seemed as though I didn't have enough muscle power to take my normal stride, and I struggled through the second hour of the workout, jogging at a distressingly slow pace. I was surprised that a simple thirty-five minute bike activity could have had such an adverse effect, even after forty-eight hours. I did another bike workout a day later, and one in the middle of the following week, but with the Pearl Harbor 10-K coming up that Sunday, I skipped my Monday and Friday bike workouts because I didn't want to risk being in shock for the race.

I was approaching the Pearl Harbor 10-K as a test effort. But wanting to feel eager for the race, I did only one hard workout that week and I took Friday and Saturday off from running. My mileage total for the week was 27.5--forty miles lower than my average weekly total since September. As a result I felt very energetic at the start of the race. Immediately after the race, however, I did a fifteen-minute cool-down jog and my quads felt as heavy and unresponsive as they had immediately after my recent bike workouts. If both activities could radically diminish my muscle power, I had to be on to something by using the bike for 10-K training. This was an exciting discovery, one which galvanized me to assault my capacity with the bike regimen.

According to the *RRN* articles, the training effect on the bike was maximized by intensity. Therefore, beginning the Tuesday after the race, I began pushing the intervals in a standing position. I did five bike workouts during the second and third weeks in January, and, during the intervals, my heart rate rose to 170 bpm, with heavy breathing and extreme intensity. In fact, I was so uncomfortable I wondered whether I had reached my maximum biking heart rate. The intervals were only a minute long, but I couldn't imagine going longer or harder.

These all-out intervals made the bike workouts harder than the easy recovery runs they were suppose to supplant (see Figure 20.1). In fact, the overall effort was so difficult I had to log the bike workouts in my training diary as "moderate" instead of "easy." I rationalized working at that level by thinking I could recover quicker from a moderate bike than I could from a moderate run. Still, I knew I was risking break-down.

The bike intervals were burdensome, if not downright oppressive. If it weren't for my compulsive urge to maximize my potential for the coming races, I would never have done the intervals at an all-out level. At this point, however, I was unable to think rationally about how the biking might affect me.

Figure 20.1: An Exercise-Bike Workout And a Recovery Run.

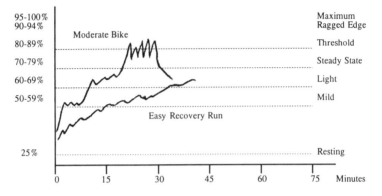

Heart Rate Ranges as
Percent of Maximum:

The bike activity (top curve) includes five heavy breathing, one-minute intervals. The intervals made the workout "moderate" in contrast to the "easy" recovery run (bottom curve). Although my heart rate indicates I was working in my threshold range for the bike intervals, my breathing and sense of discomfort indicated that I was close to maximum exertion, which opened the possibility for me that the target ranges (at the right) are compressed for the bike as compared to the run.

Breakdown: On January 20, at the end of the second week of my new biking regimen, I went to Kauai for a weekend of meetings with the coaches in my triathlon program. We stayed at the Hanalei Bay resort hotel, and with beautiful seaside golf courses to explore and several running buddies pressing me to keep them company, I extended the duration of my usual easy workouts.

At the end of one 60-minute run, I felt a slight cramping of my right calf muscle. Thirty-six hours later I was back on Oahu, doing a moderate hill workout with the runners in my 10-K training when I noticed a pain on the medial side of my right knee cap. I suspected the pain was caused by the extra miles I had run over the weekend, but the right shoe I was wearing felt compressed along the medial side so I suspected it might also be contributing to the knee problem.

Nonetheless, I had run in compressed shoes before and I had never had a serious knee injury in my career. Thus, I also suspected the knee problem might be caused by something I had never done before, such as using the exercise bike. Those five sixty-second bike intervals were arduous, and I was having trouble keeping my right leg straight in the standing position because the bike was too small for me. Working my leg in a bowed position could easily have weakened the knee so that the compressed shoes were too much for it to handle. Still, I wasn't sure what was causing the injury, nor did I know how badly I was injured.

The next morning, I started my scheduled interval workout on the track, thinking the knee pain might go away as I warmed up. But it persisted at the achy level and I had to cut the workout short. Twenty-four hours later, the knee was much better so I did the bike workout in the sitting position. By the afternoon the knee was swollen, and the pain was worse than it had been the day before, which meant it was sensitive to the biking. The ambitious part of me wanted to continue the bike regimen, but I decided to stop until the injury healed completely and I could figure out a gentler way of introducing the activity. Meanwhile, my top priority was to get rid of the injury so I could get back to hard running as soon as possible.

I did only easy workouts for sixty hours and by then the knee pain had disappeared, so I decided to run my scheduled quarter-mile interval workout on the grass in Kapiolani Park. I was definitely taking a chance on reinjuring the knee, but I didn't think I would. I had changed my shoes, quit the biking, and gotten back to my regular hard-easy schedule. Nonetheless, this was the third time I would do this interval workout, and, unfortunately, I was no longer keenly focused on my original intention of running the quarters at steady state.

As my quarter times came down during the workout, my heart rate crept up to about 165 bpm, which was low-level threshold for me. My energy was wonderful so I could rationalize this breach of faith, but I was making a big mistake. On the ninth interval my right calf--the one in which I'd felt a slight cramp the week before--tightened up on me, and I was forced to cut the workout after the tenth interval.

The next morning, on my recovery run, both the calf and knee were aching. At this point, with six weeks to go before the Faerber 10-K, I knew my training program was in serious jeopardy. Obviously I had done more than I could handle, and in such cases I knew to look within.

Contextual Factors: Something had to be the matter with the way I was thinking about my training and racing. I had no experience with the bike workout, so perhaps I could excuse myself for underestimating my capacity in that regard. Nonetheless, I could tell when I was getting compulsive about my training, and my compulsiveness was pointing at deeper, contextual issues.

For instance, I was anxious about racing soon. With the exception of the recent low-key 10-K at Pearl Harbor, I hadn't competed in five months, so the thought of putting myself on the line was frightening. Most of the races I planned to do in the spring were major events on the Hawaii road racing calendar, and especially so in my mind. I enjoyed racing, but I hated the pressure I usually felt before a major race. And in early January the pressure was already building.

With racing, there was always the possibility of an embarrassing disaster, and I'd experienced my share of those. Yet there was something else about a major race that caused me to lose my psychological balance. It wasn't the nearness of a major competitive event, but my unrealistically high expectations. I had put a lot of effort into my recent base training, and I expected a lot out of it. Yet I was worried about having taken too much time to build a base. And with "so little time to train" before my first race, I didn't think I could reap the benefit of all those miles without a drastic shift in emphasis, meaning faster running.

At that point, I still had nine weeks before the race, and my 10-K tempo ability would almost certainly have increased from week to week, assuming I ran my quarter intervals at the right effort. But with my focus on pace instead of right effort, I was doomed from the get-go. My mistake was in thinking that harder, faster intervals would make the adaptive curve rise at a steeper, quicker rate (see Figure 20.2). Theoretically, I couldn't adapt more quickly than my metabolism allowed. But, emotionally, I was too caught up in my ambition to pay attention to a training principle, no matter how important.

In becoming injured, I had rediscovered the human side of training. I found it difficult operating within an adaptive context. As long as this was true, the training process would continue being as much an art form as a science for me. Even though experimental science was uncovering new training methods, I still had to apply them in my running. But contextual factors often influenced my decision-making at the outset.

Knowing this was true for me, I had been concerned about a misplaced emphasis when I began my base building program the previous

September.   This was why I had chosen not to do the Honolulu
Marathon in mid-December 1994.   With a marathon to prepare for, I
might have tried to do too much.   Now, my racing season was upon me
and something had to be out of whack or I wouldn't have injured myself.
Clearly I was focused more on the end result than the journey, because
during the next several weeks I kept exacerbating the calf problem.   The
pain went away on four separate occasions, and each time--thinking the
injury was healed--I had tried to do a scheduled race or workout only to
have the pain recur.

Figure 20.2:   An Optimum Adaptive Curve.

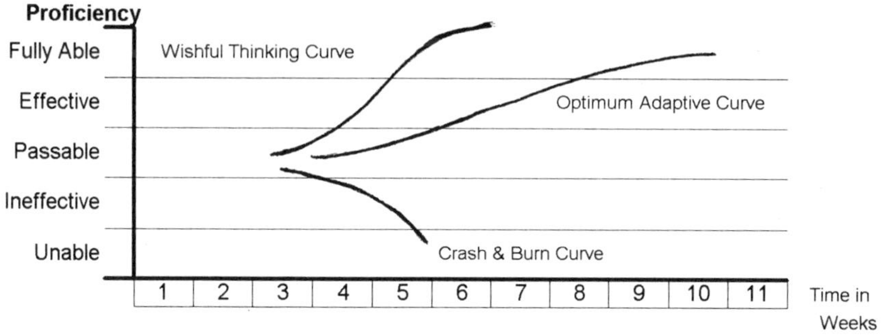

In mid-January, I wanted to race faster than I
thought I could with the time I had to train--about
nine weeks.   Thus, I tried to cheat the optimum
adaptive curve by running and biking harder and
faster than scheduled.   This was wishful thinking on
my part because too much effort doesn't hasten
adaptive processes.   At best it only changes the
purpose of the workout (from, say, tempo to speed).
However, since I didn't make my speed workouts
short enough to compensate for increased exertion, I
threw myself into injury and was unable to continue
hard training.

In the midst of this craziness, I happened to read an article in *Sports
Illustrated* about a gathering of former world record holders in the mile.
Fifteen of them had met in England on the fortieth anniversary of the
first four-minute mile, and the writer had done a marvelous job of

sketching the personalities of the various runners, some of whom had been my early running heroes. When I read that so-and-so was making a comeback after having a chronic calf injury I suddenly realized that *I* was that runner, unless I could control my compulsive urge to overtrain.

Finally, on February 13, I realized my capacity wouldn't support the training I was demanding of it. My anxiety, my ambition, and my deep-seated feeling that I could "never do enough" had caused me to do more than I should. Now it was probably too late to prepare effectively for the 1995 Faerber 10-K. Nonetheless, it was never too late to take control of myself and my running.

Finding a Way Out: My goal wasn't to correct my psychology, but to get rid of the calf injury. In reflecting on my behavior, I could see a pattern. First the pain would disappear, then I would try to get back on schedule with a moderate to hard workout and the calf would painfully tighten up. A few times I had managed to complete the first workout without pain, but I couldn't get through the second. This was exasperating, but knowing the pattern at least I could see a way out.

First, I decided to throw out the old schedule because it wasn't working. From now on, I would play with the calf intuitively from day to day until the injury went away. During my first morning run it was feeling tender, but for the next three days I was able to do my usual easy recovery runs, morning and evening, without pain. Then on Thursday, the 16th of February, I did ten easy 400-meter intervals at the UH track. The fastest quarter was a relaxed, seven-minutes per mile pace, and my heart rate stayed below 150 bpm (mid-steady state). I did my usual recovery run the next morning, and that afternoon I returned to the track on my motorcycle and repeated the interval workout without pain.

I was encouraged by these results because--even though I was holding my pace in check--I had finally run two successive up-tempo workouts without pain. I ran for seventy-five minutes the following morning with the slowest runners in my training program and I took the evening off to be sure I wasn't overdoing it. The following morning-- three weeks before the Faerber 10-K--I ran an easy recovery run to test the calf, and there was still no pain. That evening, I ran from my home to the UH track, where I did ten 400s again, but this time with an average heart rate ten beats per minute faster than the previous two 400-interval workouts. Then I ran back to my home on the hill. This was a seventy-five minute, moderate workout and definitely a step up in duration and intensity. Yet again I survived without pain.

At this point, I was feeling good about my progress, but I knew the real test would come the next day. Could I survive another moderate, ten-quarter workout on the grass in Kapiolani Park? I had arranged to run with Gerry Lindgren--one of the coaches in my 10-K training. Coincidentally, Gerry and I were recovering from exactly the same calf injury. For several weeks we had been comparing notes as to what was working or not working. During our conversations, I had grown close to Gerry, trying to understand the particular mental context that was driving him. This was the same Gerry Lindgren who had won the 10,000 meters in a track meet between the United States and the Soviet Union in 1964. With that victory, Gerry had become a national hero, and he soon owned national records at three and six miles as well.

Now in his late forties, Gerry seemed unable to forget what it had been like for him to run "forever" at a five-minute pace. I had seen him struggle recently to run quarter-mile intervals at that pace, but he still had that clipped, efficient stride and an amazing ability to cover ground at a good pace in spite of his diminutive size. Having been a contemporary of Gerry's, every time I looked at him I saw one of the best runners in the world. However, he still saw himself as he had been in junior high school: a puny runt with no talent. As a result, Gerry had convinced himself that the only way he could compete with the best runners was to train extremely hard. He still liked to recount for anyone who would listen how he had run four times a day, covering fifty miles--day after day--as though it were nothing.

It had been decades since Gerry had run that kind of mileage. Meanwhile, he had aged, gained and lost weight, trained fast without a base, gotten injured again and again, and rarely since the seventies had he performed to his potential in a race. In fact, even in his prime, his best performances had occurred more or less by accident. Yes, he had always done his homework, but whenever he had raced well or set a record, it was usually because an injury or an illness had forced him to back off in the weeks before a competitive race. Gerry had run some great races, but he had also been sick for the 1964 Olympics, where the game was to be in top form on a specific day.

Our stories were different, but at a deeper contextual level, Gerry and I were cut from the same cloth. Even in my early fifties, by most standards I could still run like the wind, yet I felt inferior and inadequate, too. I could trace these feelings to early childhood experiences, but knowing their antecedents didn't relieve my compulsive need to assuage those feelings with hard work--as though *doing* more could make me *be* more than I felt I was. Ironically, I was a much better athlete than Gerry Lindgren. On the surface, at least, I was bigger, stronger, and faster. As a youth, I had won quick and easy success in running, which had contributed greatly to my self-esteem.

Perhaps if I had been like Gerry and remained physically small, I may have felt the need to train much harder than I did. But early success in running came easily for me, and I managed to compensate for my inadequacies as a person with an almost schizophrenic arrogance. Based on my high school experience, I considered myself to be one of the best runners in Hawaii, and, by default, I later became one of the top runners on the University of Oregon track team. But when I became a UO senior, there were several younger runners coming up whom I considered to be better athletes. At that point, like Gerry Lindgren, I decided to train as hard as I could. But I wasn't able to sustain my training as long as Gerry without breaking down.

In the eighties, I found myself in an even more competitive environment than college. I was older then and definitely not one of the best runners. Yet I still thought of myself that way, and I was still dealing with my feelings of inadequacy with super hard training. At that point in life, I was unwilling to accept outside coaching, and I also found it difficult to accept my own still tentative ideas about adaptive training. As a result, my easy workouts often seemed too easy and my hard workouts were rarely hard enough. I did have enough knowledge to know when I was on the wrong track, however, and sometimes I even had enough self-control to keep from breaking down. But just as often I ended up overtraining and being disappointed with my racing performances.

Now I was into another comeback, and my recent training for the Faerber 10-K seemed to have developed along the same self-destructive lines as years before. In fact, I was feeling so discouraged about my prospects for performing well in the race that I wanted to pack it in and aim for the April 1995 Tamanaha 15-K instead. I wanted to feel prepared and confident when I put myself on the line for a race, and Tamanaha would give me four more weeks to train--a tempting prospect.

Unfortunately, my heart wasn't in the Tamanaha 15-K. The Faerber 10-K in March 1994 had been the first race I had run as a fifty year-old, and I couldn't forget how I had blown it with inadequate training, unrealistic expectations and a painful side-ache. Now I was coming full circle on my first comeback year. I wanted completion and I wanted vindication.

Confidence Boosters: My central focus was still to get rid of the injury so I could run the race. Never mind about training. There was no time for that. Even the present 10 x 440-interval workout on the grass with Gerry Lindgren was more about survival than getting in shape. I had been in the midst of a three-week period of injury only a week before, and I'd been "training" now for only four days.

My confidence was growing, but I wasn't out of the proverbial woods. I felt ready for a hard workout during the run, but I held back to the same moderate effort I'd run the night before on the UH track. My times came down from 98 to 91 seconds per quarter-mile, but my heart rate never got above 158 bpm. Meanwhile, Gerry was blitzing ragged edge quarters in the low eighties. I held my breath for both of us, and somehow we survived.

A week later, I was approaching crunch time before the race, but I hadn't done a hard workout in four weeks. I still wasn't sure I could do a hard workout without reinjuring the calf, but I wasn't about to step into the race without having done at least one hard workout. On Monday, February 27, therefore, I hit the UH track for a mixed purpose interval workout, covering four 1200s for tempo, a 2400 for endurance, and three 400s for speed. I was feeling eager to run the workout, and although I could feel the stress on my calf muscle, I survived.

Something was happening to my energy at this point in my training. With all the rest I had given myself while getting over the injury, I was feeling very energetic and very powerful. On Wednesday afternoon, ten days before the Faerber 10-K, I did a moderate/eager interval workout on the grass in Kapiolani Park with my runners. For the past five weeks, I had slogged along with the joggers, watching the top runners from a distance, unable to run with them because of the injury. Today for the first time I was decisively in the lead. It seemed as though my upper legs were charged with electricity, whisking me forward with a power I hadn't felt in years.

This workout was exhilarating, but not without a touch of irony. Notwithstanding my newly earned sense of energy and confidence, the previous evening I had been reflecting on the disruption of the past five weeks and how good it felt to finally be able to train hard again.

Suddenly I realized I didn't want to risk another injury with the Johnny Faerber 10-K--an injury that could conceivably put me out of hard training for another month.

Even if I ran the race without reinjuring myself, it would be at least another three weeks until I could get back to hard training (assuming I rested for the next ten days and for another ten days after the race). On the spur of the moment, I decided to skip the Faerber 10-K and train instead for Tamanaha.

Another Fortuitous Meeting: The day after I decided not to run the Faerber 10-K, my wife and I had a guest for dinner. Shakti Narayani, originally Pat Scott-Henry when she was raising three children as a single mother in Berkeley, California, during the fifties and sixties, was Nancy's "other" mother.

Nancy had been one of a half dozen kids in their childhood neighborhood to whom Pat had been a close friend and confidante. When her kids were grown, Pat went back to school, earned a masters in psychology, put out her shingle and practiced counseling for years. Upon retirement in the early eighties and for the next ten years, she'd sequestered herself in a religious community, learning a new discipline from her Guru, mata Amritanandamayi, an East Indian Mahatma.

Nancy had had no contact with Narayani during those years, but recently she had started corresponding with Narayani and had even visited her in Santa Fe, New Mexico. Now Narayani was visiting us in Hawaii, and I was delighted to have her to our home for my fifty-first birthday dinner. Willowy, world-wise and thoughtful, she was a good listener and someone from whom I was eager to get some feedback on my writing. After dinner, I read the "Double Workouts" chapter of part four to her as a way of starting a conversation.

Narayani immediately zeroed in on the "patterns of behavior" I had mentioned as leading to my injuries. "It's all part of having a reactive mind," she said. Then, as if she knew about my inner struggle with the Faerber 10-K, she said, "If you want to be successful, you must relax your expectations and accept your ability as you find it now, as well as for your next race." This was a shocking revelation--simple, yet right on the mark. In a flash I realized how I'd been playing the spoil-sport by deciding not to race the Faerber 10-K. I hadn't liked the way my training had gone since January, and since I didn't think I could race well under the circumstances, I simply refused to race.

But how could I be sure I wouldn't perform well? My expectations were only in my thinking. What if I stopped expecting to perform a certain way and simply went out and did my best? It might not be what I expected, but it would at least be my best. If I injured myself, I'd deal with that at the time. But I realized I had no intention of injuring myself. Therefore, I had no reason not to run.

Peaking in Perspective: The next afternoon, it was pouring rain, yet I was able to run 32:33 on a moderate/ready recovery run, the fastest time I'd done on my 3.74-mile Kaimuki course in years. I felt a slight cramping of my calf during the run--a reaction from the intervals of the day before. But a day later I ran yet another personal record (PR)--30:51--a moderate/eager effort with no residual discomfort in the calf.

I was achieving these times not because I was pushing myself particularly hard, but because I was feeling exceptionally strong. I could recall reading stories about famous runners doing PRs on training courses as they came to a peak, and I could recall from my own training years before the feeling of being fully able to do a workout. With nine days to go before the 1995 Faerber 10-K, I knew I was ready.

Chapter Twenty Synopsis:

- **The Main Issue:** How can I peak for a goal race? Why do I self-destruct before a goal race?

- **Concepts:**

    1) Peaking is the process of becoming fully able to do a race or workout. Peaking is a way of feeling about your workouts, which can be measured as unable, ineffective, passable, effective, and fully able. As you peak, you feel stronger, more confident, and more aggressive about your racing ability.
    2) Sharpening is the activity of restructuring your workouts from long-and-slow to short-and-fast.
    3) The optimum adaptive curve is the fastest rate at which your body can adapt to a workout or a training regimen.
    4) A crash and burn curve is the path your training takes when you train harder than optimum.

5) Compulsion is the psychological tendency to be locked into a course of action, without being able to choose another course.

6) Mental context refers to the framework of thoughts and attitudes that determines a course of action, and precludes other actions which are outside of that context.

7) In training, mental balance refers to the stability necessary to maintain a mental context that encompasses a theory of progressive adaptation. To be out of balance is to be focused compulsively on one essential aspect of training to the exclusion of another.

■ **Theoretical Tenets:**

1) A mental context limits you to actions within that context. Actions outside that framework are impossible, unless you are able to expand your mental context to include those actions.

2) It's impossible to run by feeling when you are focused on ambition, fear and effort.

3) You cannot be psychologically balanced unless your thinking encompasses a theory of progressive adaptation. Most athletes slip in and out of being balanced.

4) Expectations tend to limit your mental context by excluding other possibilities. If you want to be successful, you must drop your expectations and be willing to accept your ability as you find it.

5) Adding effort to a workout doesn't hasten adaptation. Rather, it either changes the nature of the workout, which can throw you into shock, or it exceeds your adaptive limit, which leads to breakdown.

6) Sharpening enhances your ability to run at a faster pace than is possible with base training only.

■ **Relationships:**

1) The harder you do a workout from week to week, the sooner you change the ability-building purpose of the workout.

2) The more mentally balanced you are, the easier it is to maintain your confidence and to train within your adaptive limits.

3) The more you allow narrow thinking to dominate your behavior, the greater the risk of compulsive overtraining and consequent breakdown.

■ **Principle:** You cannot adapt more quickly than your metabolism allows.

■ **Questions and Answers:**

1) What is peaking?

Peak ability is maximum ability and the highest form of readiness. Once you are fully able to do a race or workout, there is nowhere else to go. You can only hope to peak when you are not yet fully able.

Peaking restructures the way you feel so you have the energy to use an ability more effectively than before. Greater ability means you can run longer or faster at the same effort because you now have more energy than you did earlier in the training period.

Peaking doesn't mean running progressively harder workouts before a goal race. That sort of "peaking" leads to overtraining. Since peaking is a form of adaptation, you cannot bring your ability to a peak by training progressively harder, especially if you exceed your adaptive limit.

Finally, peaking isn't the same as sharpening. Sharpening is the activity of restructuring your workouts from long-and-slow to short-and-fast. Of course, you can peak as a result of having adapted to a sharpened training regimen.

The ultimate form of peaking is being fully able to use all five racing abilities during a race. But you can also peak by building a single ability to a peak, even though you may be deficient in the other abilities.

2) How can I bring myself to an adaptive peak?

The simplest way to peak is to repeat your workouts with right effort. If you are training within adaptive limits, you'll peak as you adapt. You don't have to train harder.

Progressively harder training presumes that you need to work harder each week to constantly stimulate further adaptation. This isn't necessarily true, especially when your current training regimen is still providing sufficient adaptive stimulus for continued adaptation. If you are not yet fully adapted to your current training regimen, you can throw yourself into shock or exhaustion by laying on too much effort.

Remember, the effort of a workout is sufficient to stimulate adaptation. The only time that it makes sense to do a workout harder from week to week is early in a training period when you are shifting out of shock and into adaptation. If you've been trying to minimize the effects of shock by training on the easy side of, say, hard, you can afford to add some effort as you search for the right workout effort.

But once you are doing a hard workout, what's the sense in making it very hard? Especially when, by training harder, you might overtrain and become exhausted. More speed or intensity does not produce more or quicker adaptation. At best, it only changes the structure of the workout with little effect on your metabolism. At worst, it will create a new workout and throw you into shock, thereby decreasing your capacity for exertion, which is the opposite of peaking.

3)   But how can I *maintain* my ability if I'm training easier?

Your body will maintain its ability long after you quit doing the workouts that built the ability. This is the principle that enables you to build one ability upon another, sequentially.

Remember, you build your ability in periods: from base building to sharpening, and from sharpening to racing. During the sharpening period, your weekly mileage may be lower, and you may be doing fewer long runs. But you still retain the stamina to run long and slow, if you have to.

4) If I plan to race all-out, don't I have to train that hard, at least occasionally?

No. All-out training doesn't prepare you for all-out racing. Adaptive training builds ability; all-out training wears you down.

You can always run an all-out race. You don't have to practice it in training. Practice races get you in the ball park with very hard efforts. But all-out efforts can be extremely difficult, which is why pre-race mental preparation is so important.

5) How do I know when I'm peaking?

Notice the way you feel during a workout. As you adapt you'll feel increasingly strong, confident, energetic and aggressive. When you feel fully able you'll have more energy available to do a race or workout.

If resting helps you to peak, then feeling well rested can be a sign of being at a peak. Resting doesn't necessarily mean no running. It can mean running shorter, easier workouts which enable you to recover more fully than you did during your previous training.

6) Why do I self-destruct by overtraining before a goal race?

You are playing a difficult psychological game. To play it well, you have to master your tendency to slip out of psychological balance. Everyone has this tendency. Moreover, in the game of competitive endurance athletics, most runners slip in and out of balance. Thus, there is nothing wrong with you individually because you do, too.

And although the problem appears to be overtraining, it really begins with the way you think about your training and racing.

You'll never train correctly unless you can think correctly. That's why it's important to understand the training process as it is, rather than the way you wish it would be.

The theory of progressive adaptation advocated in this book is an accurate representation of the training process. But it is so comprehensive that it demands an equally inclusive mental context. Unfortunately, your thinking cannot encompass these training tenets when you come from your narrow, self-concerned and insecure way of thinking. That sort of thinking will be dominated by effort-related concerns, often to the exclusion of energy-related concerns.

Thus, the first step out is to take a look at what's driving you. For your thinking determines your mental stability as well as your behavior. If you want to be successful in running, you've got to examine your thinking as much as your training.

Chapter Twenty-One
A Strange Victory

My wife Nancy has a way of testing my mood with a few easy questions as we leave home the morning of a race. The Faerber 10-K was no exception to her pre-race routine, and my responses, though patient, were weak and spiritless. She left me to myself for the rest of the ten minute ride to Kapiolani Park, and as we drove, I reflected on my voice, surprised how zombie-like I'd sounded--as if I were resigned to a fate I couldn't predict.

I wasn't feeling confident, but I was definitely focused. There were a number of things I wanted to achieve with the race. I wanted to run even or slightly negative 5-K splits, though I knew the long hills would disrupt my pacing from mile to mile. I wanted to make a good competitive showing, though I had no idea who would be in the race. Most importantly, I wanted to finish without reinjuring my calf. I had no idea how the stress of an all-out race would affect my recently healed injury, but I reckoned from my recent training I could run very hard without hurting it again. So I'd decided to hold myself to a very hard effort.

Finally, I wanted to run under forty minutes, though my training gave me little reason to believe I could. I'd run only two hard workouts in the past seven weeks so I was hardly in a position to predict a time for myself. I felt competitively shaky, but since I had no expectations I felt an inner calm that had been totally missing the last time I'd run this race a year before. I'd done my homework, reaching back to September with double workouts and seventy mile weeks. The only question was whether my base would translate into a competitive ten kilometers today. I didn't know. Everything depended on my energy, and I couldn't wait to see how it would develop.

When we got to the park, I immediately took a walk under the banyan trees that line Monsarrat Avenue next to the Honolulu Zoo. It was still dark and I had more than an hour before the race, but I could tell without breaking into a jog that my energy was good--maybe even very good. It was a cool morning, but still and muggy. And by the time I returned to the car, large rain drops were splattering their warning of a deluge about to hit. I dug into the trunk of Nancy's car for an umbrella and we walked briskly to the Waikiki Bandstand as the storm broke.

There were several hundred male runners seeking shelter in the dimly lit confines of the bandstand. My crew of eight who were also racing that morning found some space in the percussion section to do our stretching, and by the time we were through the rain had stopped, so we headed out to warm up around the zoo. Two of my slower runners were jogging with us so I made sure the pace was slow enough for them, which made it very slow for me. After we'd jogged for twenty-five minutes, Doug Folsom, my fastest runner, and I separated ourselves from the others and started a series of quick and easy pick-ups on Kalakaua Avenue. On the first pick-up I noticed something about my legs I hadn't noticed while we were jogging slowly.

There was a power and quickness to my stride I hadn't felt in ten years. I was very pleasantly surprised. After months of slogging along with medicine balls for feet, in a flash I was running light as a feather with my feet zinging away from the pavement like golf balls off a tee. I flashed back to the quick, spinning turn-over of the exercise bike, though I hadn't been on it in weeks. And as Doug and I surged again, I saw flashbacks of the stairs I'd done on Diamond Head, along with flashes of my recent interval training. Somehow, in spite of injuring myself, I had arrived at this moment in peak condition. My spirits were soaring.

A throng of several hundred runners had already gathered for the start as Doug and I squeezed into the second row and waited for the starting cannon. I couldn't wait to be running, if only to reconfirm the eager-to-race way my legs had been feeling moments before. We were standing on the right side of the narrow park road and, at the start, a crowd of runners surged by us on our left. I lowered my gaze and narrowed my focus to the area just in front of me. As eager as I felt, this wasn't the time to be racing other runners. I was going out at a rapid tempo, but not too quickly. And the combination of power, tempo and energy in my legs gave portent of a great race in the making.

Several minutes into the race, when I was confident I could hold the pace without crashing, I looked up at the male bodies still shuffling for position around me. I saw a few familiar faces--guys I would have expected to see coming back to me later in the race. I was especially surprised to slip past Wayne Neidhardt before the mile. We had raced several times in the last year and he was always near me at the finish. He had even beaten me by several seconds at the Pearl Harbor 10-K in January. Yet I could tell by his effort as I went by that I wouldn't see him again today. He wasn't struggling, but I could already hear his breathing, and since I couldn't hear mine, I had to tentatively conclude that I was having a better day. My time at the mile was 6:32--not particularly fast, except that the last quarter mile was run on a steep hill, which had to have slowed me down. I wouldn't know how fast I was really running until I'd averaged my first mile time with the second, which was mostly a gradual downhill.

I pressed the timer button on my heart rate monitor as I went through the second mile at Fort Ruger Park. I would compute my mid-race splits later. Meanwhile, as I headed out on the two-mile loop that would bring me back to Fort Ruger Park, I could see my nemesis, Ron Peroff, only five yards ahead. Ron never went out slowly, so catching him at two miles had to mean I was having a good race. I did a quick assessment of my energy and my exertion. I was feeling very strong and my heart rate and breathing were still under control. I came up on Peroff's shoulder, got a sense that he was already struggling, and went by, stifling my glee. It was too early in the race for exultation. Especially since at that moment a gray-haired and balding fellow I'd never seen before surged past me.

He was wearing a pair of shorts emblazoned with the Canadian national emblem and I immediately dubbed him "Canada." I fell in behind him and checked him out. He had a long and powerful stride, but he was heavier than I by fifteen or twenty pounds, and on that basis alone I decided I could beat him. As we headed down 22nd Avenue next to the cemetery, Canada slowed his pace and I came up on his shoulder to take the lead. He looked over at me and immediately surged ahead, which was fine with me. I didn't mind following as long as we continued at a rapid tempo. I settled in about three yards behind Canada so he could wonder who this guy behind him was who had a woman on every street corner cheering for him.

At three miles, I was surprised to see Gerry Lindgren running at a slow pace just ahead. As I went by, he said something about reinjuring his calf. As I described in the previous chapter, we had both had the same injury in January, and we'd both reaggravated it several times in the process of trying to train through it. When we finally recovered, we had done several interval workouts together on the grass in Kapiolani

Park. As far as I was concerned, Gerry was a maniac. He had pushed his quarter intervals into the low eighties from the start, breathing like a freight train, though he claimed to be running at an easy, relaxed pace. Evidently, Gerry had weakened the calf to the point where it was hurting him now. Too bad, I thought.

As I went by the five-kilometer mark, I could hear Nancy and several women runners in my training program yelling their encouragement. Candy Smiley was there, too, doing a quick calculation. "Brian, you've got a fast time," she shouted. I heard my 5-K time, but since I hadn't thought about specific timing possibilities before the race, the numbers had no meaning. Nonetheless, I could tell I was having a great race by the way I felt. My racing flats were still smacking the pavement with the same rapid tempo I'd started with. My breathing was audible but under my control. Canada was only a few yards ahead and we were running the downhill stretch along scenic Elepaio Street through the posh residential area of Waialae Kahala.

I was still feeling confident as we turned onto Kahala Avenue with its canopy of graceful palm trees. At that point, the course heads up a steep quarter-mile hill before breaking into the sunlight at Ruger Park. As we started up the hill, Canada, who was running to my left and slightly ahead, lowered his gaze, increased his effort and began pulling away from me. This was great, I thought. I could tell he was forcing his pace, and though I'd have to work hard to catch him, I had no doubt that his effort to get away from me now would take more out of him than it would be worth later. At this point in the race, he still had enough distance left to open a commanding lead. Yet from a tactical point of view, I refused to stay with him. I didn't want to overstress my calf muscle on the hill. And, in my estimation, it was still too early to be racing head to head on this course.

We were running what's known in the Honolulu Marathon as heartbreak hill. It starts before the end of mile twenty-four, but it doesn't end with the steep assent to Fort Ruger Park. There is a mile-long, gradual assent from there to the Diamond Head lighthouse which is really the heartbreaker in the marathon. For many runners, that twenty-fifth mile in the morning heat never seems to end. And though it wasn't a marathon we were running, the fifth mile of this particular 10-K was demanding enough without adding the stress of a breakaway surge. Canada could work as hard as he wanted on this section. I planned to make my move on the steep downhill past the lighthouse and onto the flats leading into Kapiolani Park.

The race was developing as I'd planned at the lighthouse, a mile and a quarter from the finish. Canada was thirty yards ahead and I was feeling strong and confident. Suddenly I noticed another graybeard just ahead of me. Where had *this* guy come from, I wondered. He was clearly in the over-fifty age group, but I'd never seen him before. Two ringers in the same race. No wonder I had felt so helpless that morning--unable to foresee my competitive circumstances. The Johnny Faerber 10-K was living up to its reputation for smoking the top runners out of the woodwork. I came up on the new graybeard and he immediately increased his pace to stay with me. We were running inches apart and I could tell from his breathing that he was working as hard as I. But I was sure I could beat him because it was he, not I, who'd been fading moments earlier.

We were barreling downhill, past the imposing lava rock walls on our left that conceal luxury homes from public view on the ocean side of Diamond Head Road. The area had a rustic, wilderness feeling about it with the barren cliffs of Diamond Head towering above us in the early morning sunlight. At that point in the race the road makes several sweeping curves, and I began running the tangents with Canada still thirty yards ahead and the other graybeard at my side. As I headed back to his side of the street I bumped into him. Surprised that he wasn't trying--as I was--to cut the distance we had to run, I stuck my arm out in front of him and pointed him in my direction. In the process, I glanced at him and noticed his disgruntlement. He obviously didn't like being directed where to run. That's tough, I thought. This was a race, and at that moment there were at least three people vying for first in our division. There'd be plenty of time for playing Mr. Nice Guy, later.

As we entered the park a thousand yards from the finish I looked ahead at Canada. He was running with a younger guy fifteen yards ahead, but well within my reach, and thirty yards beyond them was a group of five. I checked everyone in that group for another fifty year-old, but I couldn't see a gray hair in the pack. Good thing. I didn't want to risk an injury trying to sustain a strong surge necessary to catch that group. I could hear graybeard falling behind as I bore down on Canada, so I decided it was a two-man race. Yet I was still feeling edgy about the possibility of having overlooked someone.

A Strange Victory: The Honolulu Marathon finish line doubles as the finish for virtually every race ending in the Kapiolani Park area. The distance between the Diamond Head entrance to the park and the finish line is an agonizingly long stretch for many runners. But since I am often involved in a hotly contested race on the long straightaway, time goes quickly for me and I don't like to wait for the finish to catch a competitor with a lead on me at the entrance to the park. I prefer to use the tennis courts, two hundred yards from the finish, as my focal point for drawing even. If I'm with someone at that point, I'm confident my kick will prevail.

As I pulled up on Canada at the tennis courts, I could tell from his labored breathing he was running as hard as he could. I looked at the other guy and recognized him as Mike Chauvin, whom I'd often seen running the streets of Manoa and Kapiolani Park during the past fifteen years. Mike tried to stay with me as I surged ahead, but his race was over, too, and I knew I'd have an easy time of the last 150 meters. Glancing back over my shoulder I watched Mike and Canada until I was sure I had a commanding lead, and then I focused on the clock which was slowly ticking past 38:50 as I approached the finish line.

My time was 38:54--at least thirty seconds faster than I would have predicted for myself. I was elated with my performance. At the soft drink table there were the usual comments, questions and congratulations all around. But I left as soon as I could to stand at the finish line with Nancy and cheer my runners as they finished. Mine wasn't the only successful race, as several of my runners established personal records. It had turned out to be a beautiful morning in spite of the early downpour, and soon the guys were enjoying a pot luck meal compliments of the women in the training. They were returning the favor after having been treated to a post race feast by the guys after the women's 10-K the week before. I was sitting under an ironwood tree munching on a bagel and waiting for the awards ceremony when someone informed me that I had come in second in my age division.

Richard Senelly--a name I didn't recognize--had beat me by eleven seconds. He was one of those guys in the group ahead of Canada as we'd entered the park, I thought. A few minutes later, I met Richard. He had just turned fifty and didn't look a day over forty. He belonged to the Hawaiian Ultra Running Team and usually ran longer races, but he had run this one with his son, finishing first in the father and son division. He was obviously a nice guy and I was happy for him winning our age division, but I'd be on the lookout for him the next time I raced.

Meanwhile, I was taking my second place finish more as a reminder of my pre-race circumstances than a personal defeat. After all, I *had* been injured and the injury *had* disrupted my training for more than five weeks. Under the circumstances, I felt fortunate to have raced as well as I had. Nonetheless, I was certain my heart rate monitor would soon reveal some interesting information.

Thinking About the Race: As an analyzer, half the fun of racing for me was in figuring out what had worked. The first thing I checked was my pacing to see how close I had come to my pre-race goals.

My first 5-K was 19:30 and the second was six seconds faster, which was exactly how I'd wanted to run the race. My average mile pace was 6:16, but the uphill miles (one, four and five) were 6:32, 6:31 and 6:30, respectively, while the down hill miles (two, three and six) were 6:09, 6:01 and 5:57.

Despite the up and down nature of the course, my heart rate was as steady as it had been nine weeks earlier for the Pearl Harbor 10-K on a perfectly flat course. I had stayed as close as I could to my anaerobic threshold throughout both races. As a result, I was never in serious trouble from fatigue, as I certainly could have been had I gone out faster or forced the pace in the middle of the race. Thus, my pacing didn't seem to account for the sixty-eight second difference between Pearl Harbor and the faster Faerber 10-K.

My average heart rate was a little faster for Faerber (181 bpm versus 178 bpm), but I didn't think an additional 120 heart beats (out of a total of 7,222 during the Faerber 10-K) could account for a sixty-eight second difference in performance. Moreover, my perception of exertion for the two races didn't even follow suit with my heart rate averages. Until the last mile of the Faerber race, I was breathing audibly but not heavily. On the other hand, during the slower Pearl Harbor 10-K, I was breathing heavily and forcing my pace in the last 5-K as I struggled to catch Ron Peroff. I wondered whether my training could have accounted for these differences?

I ran the same number of miles the week immediately before both races (28), so I might have been equally well rested before both. But I had averaged 64 miles per week in the seven weeks before Pearl Harbor and only 47 miles per week in the seven weeks before Faerber. Furthermore, my weekly mileage had tapered off in the five weeks before Faerber, from 64 to 50, to 59, 43 and 28. By contrast, my weekly mileage hadn't dipped below 60 in the seventeen weeks before the Pearl Harbor race week. In addition, I did three hard workouts every week up to the week before Pearl Harbor, but I did a *total* of only two hard workouts in the previous seven weeks before Faerber.

There are two ways to view these differences in mileage and training effort. Either I should have been in better shape before the Pearl Harbor 10-K because my mileage was higher and my training was harder. Or I'd experienced a boost in workout energy before the Faerber 10-K because I was better rested. If I were better rested, I should have been more energetic. In fact, I was feeling ready or eager on 68.7% of my runs during the month before the Faerber race week. By contrast, I was feeling ready or eager on only 28.7% of my runs during the month before the Pearl Harbor race week.

Obviously, I was better rested for Faerber, but could this have accounted for the sixty-eight second difference in times? In an effort to determine the extent to which my capacity had increased by resting, I compared easy/lazy recovery runs at an average heart rate of 112 bpm going back to October 27. And I saw an amazing progression (see Figure 21.1). My times had dropped in a straight line from thirty-nine to thirty-six minutes for the four workouts between October 27 and February 24. Bucking this downward trend in times was the last performance in the series--the one for the March 3rd recovery run, during which I slowed to 38:07. Could my capacity have changed that much in a week?

Looking closer at my training diary, I discovered that, in the days between February 24 and March 3, I had done three novel workouts: a moderate/ready recovery run at a "fast" pace, a hard interval workout (my first in four weeks), and a sharp, moderate/eager interval workout. Thus, I may have been in shock from the combined effect of those new workouts, which would account for the relatively slow time for my March 3 recovery run.

The trend towards better times in my recovery runs was hardly incontrovertible evidence of having been "in better shape" for the Faerber race, but it did help to explain my ability to run a sixty-eight second personal record with less apparent effort than I had in the Pearl Harbor 10-K. Evidently, my body had restructured its metabolic systems in response to my base training in the fall, and perhaps in response to my subsequent intermittent sharpening. However, the main opportunity for this restructuring process was probably the rest I had given myself in the interim while I was injured.

Figure 21.1: Performance for Easy/Lazy Recovery Runs. Average Heart Rate Equaling 112 bpm.

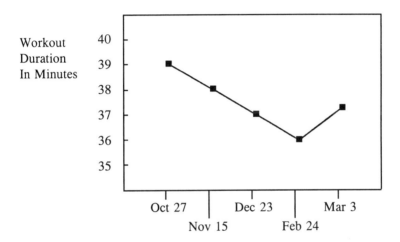

My times drop in this graph from 39 to 36 minutes for the four recovery runs between October 27 and February 24, indicating an adaptive trend. As indicated in the text, I may have been in shock for the March 3 workout, which explains why my time was slower than the two previous workouts shown in the graph.

Measuring Racing Proficiency: The sixty-eight second difference in my times was an objective measure of improvement, but there was also a *subjective* factor: my racing proficiency as measured on the following scale: unable, ineffective, passable, effective, and fully able.

I'd felt "effective" during the Pearl Harbor 10-K, meaning I was willing to assert myself competitively and I was near the top of my game. But I had also developed a side stitch in the second mile, and I was running low on energy and will power after the mid-point. Throughout the Faerber race, however, I'd felt fully able to run, always willing to exert an all-out effort, and completely on top of my game.

Proficiency

Fully Able: An aggressive willingness to exert an all-out effort. At the "top of one's game." Personal records possible. Feeling great energy and desire.
Effective: A quiet willingness to assert oneself in competition. Near the top of one's game, but personal records unlikely. Nonetheless, good race and training results possible.
Passable: A passive attitude towards high exertion. Little willingness to push beyond moderately hard efforts. Performances well off top racing potential.
Ineffective: Resistant to even moderate levels of exertion either because running energy is low or inflammation high.
Unable: Strong feeling of repulsion to all levels of effort other than easy jogging. Exhausted or severely injured.

The purpose of training is to reveal one's underlying performance potential. By repeating a workout, we expect to improve the ability it was meant to build. The better we get at using an ability, the greater our capacity for exertion and the stronger we begin to feel. I personally feel most proficient when I'm well-rested and I have a full complement of racing abilities. At that point in my training, I am usually able to run a best effort.

Being fully able is different from merely being eager. I had been eager to race during most of my races during the previous year--but I hadn't yet felt the kind of power and energy I experienced during the 1995 Faerber 10-K. I had to conclude, therefore, that the extended rest before Faerber had augmented my capacity and enabled me to run a faster time.

A Strange Victory in Perspective: After the race, Candy Smiley came up to me to comment on my performance. She knew that I'd been running seventy-mile weeks during the last quarter of 1994. Now she wondered whether a 38:54 was *worth* all that training. In other words, even she had expected a lot of my base training--evidently more than I had shown in the race.

I told Candy that my original expectations had been higher, too, and I explained how those expectations had led to my calf injury. Ironically, she could relate to my story because she had recently struggled through the same sort of problems with her own training. She even seemed to understand when I told her I was delighted with my performance, considering my self-imposed restriction to avoid an all-out effort.

Then I set the record straight about my base training. In fact, I wasn't at all disappointed with the training I had done in the fall. It is always nice to bring a training period to fruition with an outstanding race performance. But I had enjoyed my base training for itself. In my estimation, it had been my base training which had supplied the major impetus for the Faerber performance. Moreover, in spite of the injuries that forced me to rest during most of the sharpening period, I didn't think I had performed well in the Faerber race by accident. At a crucial moment, I had realized how I'd been destroying my chances for the great race I wanted desperately to run. At that point, I had taken control of my training.

I wasn't overlooking my serendipitous birthday encounter with Shakti Narayani, but rather I was acknowledging how my own choices had ultimately led to a very satisfying race experience. Furthermore, having performed well despite adversity, I had won a unique bonus. I'd learned to give myself the benefit of the doubt--unequivocally. Based on my training performances, I'd had no confidence coming into the race that I would perform well. With hindsight, I could hypothesize in a plausible manner to explain why I had been able to perform as well as I did. But from an emotional perspective, I had done little leading up to the race that led me to think I would be as strong as I was. Nothing, that is, except to train moderately and rest.

This was a valuable lesson. And although it seemed I'd learned it other times before, learning it again at this juncture enabled me to run the June 1995 Hard Rock 10-K several months later and to come in first in my age division with a slightly slower time and a harder effort, but with even less training in the ten weeks leading up to the race. If it had been a matter of confidence based on hard training, I never would have run that race either.

Chapter Twenty-One Synopsis:

- **The Main Issue:** How can I be at peak ability for a race?

■ **Concepts:**

1) Anaerobic threshold is the level of exertion above which you cannot run without breathing heavily. During a workout, my anaerobic threshold is about 88% of maximum heart rate, and during a race it's about 92% of maximum. Anaerobic threshold is a narrow range that overlaps the boundary between your threshold and ragged edge ranges of perceived exertion.

2) Tapering is the activity of cutting back on your training before a race so you are well rested and at a peak of energy. Proper tapering enables you to feel eager on race day.

3) A negative split is running the second half of a race faster than the first.

■ **Theoretical Tenets:**

1) The process of constant breakdown during heavy training never allows your body to rebuild itself to the point of full recovery and complete adaptation.

2) Cutting back to easy or moderate training before a race gives your body a chance to restructure itself in response to hard training.

3) Having no expectations for a race is conducive to a best effort because it takes effort to create and sustain expectations--effort best used on the race itself.

4) It's better to assume that you can perform well in a race than to assume the opposite. Negative thinking leads to poor performance expectations and despair. Better still to have no expectations, but to plan only to do your best.

5) Running at a heart rate just below your anaerobic threshold is more efficient than running above it. You can thus be faster for an anaerobic threshold race (such as the 10-K) when you run close to heavy breathing until near the finish.

6) You can maintain an ability for weeks or even months after having built it.

7) An effective mental context balances ambition with play, while focusing simultaneously on effort and energy.

■ **Relationships:**

1) The longer and harder you train, the longer you'll need to taper before a race.
2) The closer you are to being fully able in your training, the less tapering you'll need to achieve peak condition for a race.

■ **Principle:**   The purpose of training is to reveal your underlying performance potential, measured as unable, ineffective, passable, effective, and fully able.   By repeating a workout, we expect to improve the ability it was meant to build.

■ **Questions and Answers:**

1) Is there an optimum way of pacing a race?

   I believe that even pacing or slightly negative splits (second half faster than the first) are much more effective ways of pacing a race than running the first half significantly faster than the second. This is because your capacity grows during the first part of a race, especially when you are not pressing too hard. With an expanded capacity, you may be actually better able to run the second half of the race, despite having to increase your effort.

2) How much hard training do you need to maintain training effectiveness?

   Comparatively little. Once you have built an ability, it takes much less effort to maintain it. For example, if you were running a workout every week, you might get away with running it once a month. Or you might run a much shorter version at a specific level of exertion.

3) How can I be at peak ability for a race?

   The best way to peak may be to train easy, not hard. Easier training could give you more time to recover. And full recovery leads to full adaptation and maximum ability.

Remember, the adaptive process is cyclic. Every time a workout causes you to become fatigued, you have to recover your energy and reduce inflammation before you can do the workout again. If you never allow yourself to become fully recovered in your training--which is normal with hard/ready workouts--then your body never has a chance to become fully adapted. This is okay during base training, but it doesn't work before a goal race.

Chapter Twenty-Two
The Play Spirit in Running

In his jogging clinics during the 1960s, Bill Bowerman used to describe successful people as those who "enjoyed their activity." Bowerman enjoyed coaching. He played at it, puttering with shoes and experimenting with new ideas. So it was natural for him to develop runners by scheduling *fartlek* in their training.

As Bowerman described it, fartlek was a Swedish term meaning "speed play." The Swedes used fartlek workouts to augment their speed, much as we UO runners did with intervals. In the Oregon system, fartlek could also be steady-paced and slow. But the essential ingredient was play. Bowerman used to point at a distant peak and say, "Go play with that mountain!" In the ensuing weeks, his runners would slowly develop the stamina to encircle it or the power to high-step it to the top.

Bowerman's genius lay in recognizing how a training environment shaped an athlete's running experience. He could conjure an image of his runners doing fartlek on the rough forest paths around Eugene, and soon my buddies and I would be attacking the hills beyond Hendricks Park as though we were roller coasters. Even now I recall the fun we used to have, topping a rise and swooping down the other side, scattering fallen leaves behind us. A banked turn, and another! I remember laughing as we ran, and I can appreciate how fartlek really originated in the play areas of my childhood.

I once knew the fine art of frolic. I used to live in and for the moment, unburdened by ambition and self-importance. When I was a child, I could even relate to the way Ferdinand the Bull preferred to smell the flowers rather than hone his fighting skills. One day, as he roamed his pasture, Ferdinand was stung on his snout by a bee. In severe pain, he went on a rampage scattering his brethren, small trees and--as luck would have it--several bull buyers from Madrid. Impressed with his ferocious outburst, they paid his owner a handsome price and shipped Ferdinand off to the fights. But Ferdinand wasn't a crowd-pleaser. He sniffed the flowers that were lying around the ring and promptly found himself back in his pasture.

My other childhood hero--the one that more often drives my adult running--was Superman, the invincible warrior whose strength and will power could be counted on to gain the inevitable victory. In my early years of running, my mentor was Harold "Ky" Cole, the best distance runner in Hawaii and the closest person I knew to Superman. Ky had a "no pain, no gain" approach to training. On our six-mile training runs when I was a senior in high school, he used to take off at a five-minute pace, without a warmup, and attempt to get away from my line of vision before he had to slow down. I guess his competitive strategy was "out of sight, out of mind," and it worked on me because I would think only of how badly *I* was hurting and forget all about catching Ky.

Even in 1994, in the midst of a running comeback of his own, Ky would write me from his place of retirement in Kentucky, seeming to relish the pain he experienced in his training. Ky was ten years my senior and running faster 10-K times than I. Yet he'd also had so many knee injuries that, long ago, he'd had all his knee cartilage surgically removed. Personally I wasn't into pain, my history of running with it notwithstanding. Even if it meant taking a long lay-off from running, I'd always preferred to get rid of pain than endure it. I had taken three extended lay-offs in my career, but recently I'd come to the realization that I could no longer afford to disregard my health by backing off on training to the extent I had before.

The heart condition I described in chapter 14 made it imperative that I maintain a daily training regimen, perhaps until my dying day. And, in my opinion, the only thing that could prevent me from being faithful to my running was an excess of difficult training. I loved competitive running, but there was a limit to the amount of self abuse I could take before I had to take a vacation from it. Yet self-abuse and competitive success were not inextricably connected. I recall Bowerman cautioning his runners not to abuse themselves in their training, and he was right. In my experience, self abuse had never led to improved performances, though I knew how a certain frame of mind could create that illusion. The training process was inherently about breaking down, so it wasn't difficult to assume that more breakdown might be better than some theoretical optimum.

As I reflected on my comeback year, I could see how these habitual ways of thinking were still a part of me. Yet I could no longer countenance self-abuse. I stood for injury-free training and improved performance. And, though it was sometimes difficult in the moment to see how I could have one without at least being on the red-line with the other, nonetheless, injuries exposed my ordinary way of thinking for what it was.

The Ordinary Way of Thinking: Ordinarily, my body was merely the instrument that enabled me to achieve my racing goals. By this view, the harder I pushed myself the better my chances of winning. And the extent to which I could push my body was limited only by my superhero willingness to endure discomfort. Meanwhile, I resisted giving my physical presence its rightful place in the training process because I wanted it subservient to my will to win.

As long as I was injury-free and able to train, therefore, my body was an invisible, compliant partner, and my ambition was the driving force in my running. Sometimes--with nothing to balance my ambition psychologically--I would drive myself into injury, illness or exhaustion. Fortunately, however, extreme breakdown had a way of drawing attention to my body and its limitations. It also exposed the error in my ordinary way of thinking and presented me with the choice of giving credence to a more encompassing theory of progressive adaptation.

According to the theory, effective training was in harmony with discernible metabolic processes. The way to achieve great racing performances was to focus entirely on the way my body felt in response to training. This was very different from seeing my body as merely a vehicle for achieving my racing goals. Ultimately, of course, competitive running was about racing and winning. But that didn't necessarily mean winning at all cost. Running great races was essentially a function of using training effort to *play* with one's capacity for exertion. The play between effort and energy was absolutely inherent to the sport of competitive running.

Before I sat down at the computer to write this part of the book, I drew a master graph of my workout efforts and my workout energy during the eleven weeks leading up to the 1995 Johnny Faerber 10-K (see Figure 22.1). The traditional way to have viewed my training during that period would have been to count my miles or to analyze the pacing and exertion of my workouts, much as I did in the previous chapter. However, by drawing circles to represent my workouts and a continuous line to represent my workout energy from workout to workout, I could also see in graphic terms how my workouts had affected my metabolic engine.

For instance, during my first two weeks of training for Faerber, my workout energy fluctuated between sluggish and ready. For the most part, however, it was in the mid-range of the workout energy scale. I felt eager for none of the workouts in the two-week period, I was ready for four of them, lazy for nine, tired for seven, and sluggish for one. And from the graph I could see that the way my energy fluctuated from workout to workout was a reaction to the spacing of my three hard and eighteen easy workouts. Generally, my energy dropped initially after the hard workouts, and rose during the subsequent recovery periods, while I did the easy workouts.

The reader will recall from chapter six, that my theory postulates the idea of adaptive "effort/energy combinations," i.e., workouts which are hard enough to use one's ability at an adaptive level, yet easy enough to be in harmony with one's current recovery level. By that definition, all but one of my twenty-one workouts during those first two weeks were adaptive. During the next two weeks, however, I ran five non-adaptive workouts, i.e., my overall workout effort was too hard for the way I felt. During the same two weeks, I also did five *moderate* bike workouts in lieu of five *easy* recovery runs (see the dark circles in Figure 22.1). As a result of all this added effort, during weeks five and six, my median level of workout energy shifted from lazy--as it had been for the previous month--to tired (0 eager, 4 ready, 6 lazy, 9 tired, 1 sluggish).

Furthermore, the graph shows a probable cause-and-effect relationship between the previous two weeks of burdensome training and the next three weeks of injury. My usual weekly schedule included three hard workouts and about ten easy runs, which made a visual pattern of circles representing those training efforts. Adding the bike workouts changed the graphic pattern of workouts and recoveries. The most notable visual difference during the three weeks of injury was the color red I drew into the peak of each workout energy curve to signify my injuries. The color red represented pain and its position on the curve represented the way my injuries had restricted my training efforts. In this case, my injuries were such a limiting factor that the larger circles--representing hard workouts--disappeared from the graph during the period when I was injured.

In the midst of this period of injury, I decided to run a 20-K race (the February 5 circle on Figure 22.1). The race would be held at Barbers Point Naval Air Station located on the flat and open spaces of Oahu's arid western plain. I had been planning to do the race for months, and I couldn't resist the opportunity to test the half-marathon tempo ability I'd been building with mile intervals during my previous base-building period. The week before the 20-K race, I backed off on my training, carbo loaded, and gave myself an extra day off to heal the calf injury. Thus, I was shocked on Sunday morning by the *ineffective* way I felt before the race. I had little energy and little desire even to be there. Despite my mood of disgruntlement, I convinced myself that my energy would develop as I warmed up during the race itself.

At the start, I let all but the slowest runners take the lead, and eventually I began to warm up. By the fourth mile I was feeling ample energy, and I had picked up my pace enough to have caught several of the better runners in the 55-59 age group. I could also see, in the distance, the best in my age division coming back to me. But at that moment--on a severely cambered section of highway--my calf cramped up and I knew immediately that my race was over. Even though I didn't finish the race, I had learned what I wanted to know: I could be competitive at the half-marathon distance. Of course, this small boost in confidence was offset by another week of being injured and unable to take advantage of my soaring energy.

Needless to say, the Barbers Point 20-K hadn't been a great race. Yet given the way I'd been training recently, how could I have expected otherwise? In the past month I'd fallen into old mental habits, focusing compulsively on my racing goals to the exclusion of my physical self. In the process, I had overtrained and injured myself. Thus, I was having to pay for my imprudence by taking a prolonged rest.

The overtraining and injuries notwithstanding, my effort/energy graph provided me with a radically different way of viewing the training process. There--on paper--the focus was as much on my body's response to effort as it was on effort itself. This graphic way of presenting my effort and energy had pointed me clearly in the direction of a new mental context.

Putting on a New Way: Distance running is strenuous physical activity. Nonetheless, I could make it enjoyable or onerous, depending on how hard I ran. In my opinion, effective training needs to be occasionally violent. But intensity at the right moment can be exhilarating and highly adaptive. It's the relentless push of hard effort that destroys my mental attitude and makes my effort disagreeable.

In recent years, I had learned to measure my training attitudes, using the following scale as an indicator of my competitive direction. I

Figure 22.1: Eleven-Week Effort/Energy Record.

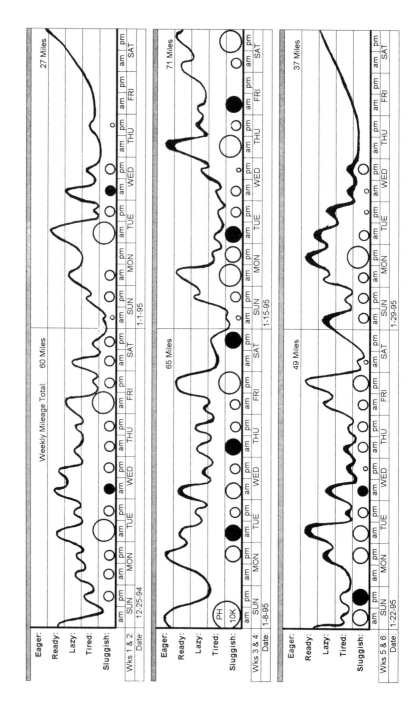

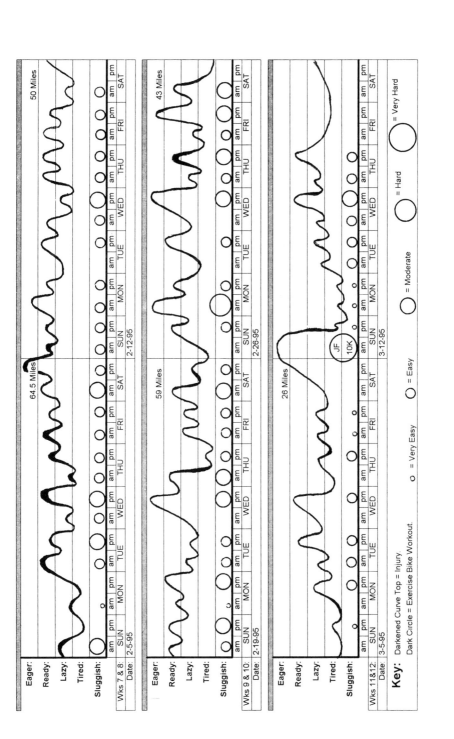

couldn't expect to enjoy my training all the time, but I knew I had to be at least satisfied by it, otherwise I wasn't on track to an outstanding race performance. And being burdened or oppressed by my running signaled abusive training and the possibility of imminent disaster.

Attitudes About Effort

Exhilarated: An uplifting feeling of supreme well being, including mild euphoria.

Enjoyed: Pleasurable, delightful or fun.

Satisfied: Okay; neither positive or negative.

Burdened: Feeling duty-bound to perform. No sense of pleasure. Wearisome.

Oppressed: Unpleasant, detestable drudgery.

Of course, most attitudes are transient. Sometimes only a sense of duty would get me out the door to find a satisfying experience in running. At other times my attitude would deteriorate with effort. An attitude can also linger or develop over a period of months. By late 1995, for instance, I was getting tired of being constantly tired. I wanted to eliminate times like those with a new way of thinking.

The only thing that seemed to help was to take a life-long perspective on my running. I had to ask myself who I had been as a runner, who I was currently, and who I aimed to be in the future, including the distant future. I had extensive experience in running: as a competitive runner, fitness jogger and coach. I was currently a program director working closely with several hundred athletes and two dozen assistant coaches every year. I had written two books on the subject of endurance training and I aimed to continue making a living from my work as a coach and author. Thus, I had a definite stake in who I was, and who I could become as a runner.

Furthermore, my personal integrity and the integrity of both my practical and my theoretical work was bound up in my present and future practices. I didn't want to be known as someone who'd had a great idea but couldn't apply it in his own life. Rather, I wanted to be an opening for others to see the possibility of training more effectively. Thus, instead of always trying for the hardest possible training efforts, it was incumbent on me to fine-tune them in harmony with my sense of running energy. It was also incumbent on me to see this activity as every bit as playful as running the trails with my undergraduate buddies at Oregon.

The Play Spirit in Perspective: Somewhere within me was the remnant of the child I used to be. It had been years since I had given the flower-sniffer free reign in my running. I had either been stuck in the utilitarian routine of jogging three times a week on the same course for basic fitness, or beating myself into the ground with arduous workouts on the track.

I hesitated to run the nearby mountain trails because I was afraid of getting injured. Yet I had been more or less continually injured during 1995. I had run four races in that time, winning my age division in three and placing second in the other. I had satisfied my ambition and kept intact my public persona. But who was I fooling? Certainly not the child who yearned for the fun he'd once enjoyed in running.

I knew what fartlek was from years before. According to Bowerman, "Competitive training was goal-oriented; fartlek was detached." Yet fartlek was far from worthless as a training tool. It could complement goal-oriented running by diverting the mind from the stopwatch, the measured distances, and the intense pace. In fact, under the Oregon system I had discovered that fartlek balanced my training by allowing the environment to suggest the running activity. Nothing could be too frivolous: like the time we kids chased a herd of cows home for an early milking. Nonetheless, I'd seen many runners--myself included--who had killed a part of themselves in the name of fartlek. Those telephone poles that measured the distance of our pick-ups were supposed to legitimatize the intensity of our effort. But the driving force was still ambition, and the effort was much too arduous for fun.

In the past, I had always designated certain times of year when the flower-sniffer or the superhero could be given their full reign. In my current comeback, however, I'd been constantly obsessed with training for some future race. It was as if Superman had a grip on me and wouldn't let go. In looking for a way to be released, I had told myself that the only way to maintain the freshness of my training was to experiment with it. I had read *Running Research News* so I could take advantage of theoretical advances to form and test my own hypotheses. I had viewed my body as a black box, the internal workings of which were incredibly complex and not well understood. I had jiggled and manipulated the box to learn how it worked. And as I'd measured my results, the process had become an intriguing, beguiling game.

Herein lay the undeniable attraction of our sport: the development of new knowledge generated in the spirit of play. In this sense, we are all scientists--testing ideas and experimenting with our subject of one. And yet, even though I told myself that I was playing with my training, I was only playing with effort, often at the expense of effort's counterpart, energy.

At the end of 1995, for instance, I added easy bike workouts to my schedule to build my quads, I backed off on yoga and avoided intervals to reduce the risk of injury, I ran only long slow distance to build my stamina, I lifted weights and did sit-ups to build my upper body, and I did heel raises to strengthen the attachments of my achilles tendons. And, all the while, the pain in my achilles persisted, my attitude deteriorated, and my enthusiasm began to flag.

I was coming to the conclusion that racing glory by itself didn't supply sufficient motivation for this sort of competitive training. Yes, racing can be exhilarating, and, for that reason, I'd heard people say they would love to end their life finishing a race. But racing by itself wouldn't sustain me. In fact, if I projected myself far enough ahead, I had to confront the absurdity of my striving.

It was difficult to see myself as a very old man running races only for the personal glory of winning or setting another age-group record. It wasn't even a new set of workouts that would make the difference in my training. I had to face the possibility that I was still running too hard, and recommit myself to running by feeling.

Chapter Twenty-Two Synopsis:

- **The Main Issue:** What is the play spirit in running? How can I take on the spirit of playful running? How can I achieve psychological balance in my training?

- **Concepts:**

    1) *Fartlek* is a Swedish term that refers to playful speed work. *Fartlek,* by its generic definition, is simply playful running.
    2) The play spirit in running takes delight in experimenting with all aspects of the game. For instance, it's an openness to using effort to play with your capacity for exertion. To do so effectively, you must be sensitive to your body's metabolic responses to effort.
    3) Sensitivity means feeling what's there and responding appro-

priately.

4) A hero is someone you want to emulate because of the scope of their awareness, the strength of their resolve, and the quality of their decisions. Early childhood heroes may influence us at an unconscious level, and thereby affect our decisions without our complete awareness.

5) The ordinary way of thinking about your training assumes there's no tomorrow. It's the superman mentality that says you can bust through pain and adversity to an inevitable victory. The ordinary way of thinking disregards the way your body feels in response to training.

6) A "no pain, no gain" approach to training is the belief that you cannot improve unless your exertion is uncomfortable. The "no pain, no gain" attitude says the harder I push myself, the better my chance of getting better.

7) A new way of thinking encompasses a theory of progressive adaptation. It focuses constantly on the way you feel in response to training. Moreover, it uses rest to respond appropriately to the first signs of overtraining.

8) You can measure overtraining by paying attention to the way you feel about the effort you exert: oppressed, burdened, satisfied, enjoyed, exhilarated.

■ Theoretical Tenets:

1) Intensity is only one of three training stimuli, along with frequency and duration. You can build five racing abilities, depending on how you structure the frequency, duration and intensity of your training. Thus, a "no pain, no gain" approach to training isn't the only way to build ability.

2) The play between effort and energy is absolutely inherent to the process of progressive adaptation.

3) It's okay to be satisfied and it may be rare to feel exhilarated. But if you are feeling burdened or oppressed, then you are overtraining.

■ Relationships:

1) The harder you train, the less likely you'll have fun doing it.

2)   The more you abuse yourself with running, the less likely
     you'll continue running at that level.
3)   Ultimately, your commitment to run by feeling is what keeps
     you in the game. You must balance your ambition with play.

■ **Questions and Answers:**

1)   How can I improve without having at least some intensity in
     my training?

     Intensity at the right moment can be exhilarating, highly
     adaptive, and very effective for race preparation. It's the
     relentless push of intense effort that drives your feelings down
     and makes your effort disagreeable.

2)   How can I achieve balance in my training?

     There is no such thing as perfect balance in this sport. Any
     ambitious runner who trains hard will at times approach the
     edge of overtraining.

     Thus, competitive running is like being on a gabled rooftop.
     It would be great to run along the peak, far from falling off
     the roof, and within striking distance of winning your next
     race. But the peaked surface is impossible to run on, so we
     run instead on the side of the roof, with gravity constantly
     pulling us toward the edge, which represents disaster.

     By this analogy, success is staying on the roof, while evening
     out the inevitable ups and downs so you remain as high on the
     roof and as close to achieving your goals as possible. In this
     sense, training is a constant feedback loop. If you slip a little,
     you must adjust a little to regain your position on the roof.

Ordering Books by Brian Clarke

Running by Feeling is destined to be a classic in the running literature. If you agree, please tell your friends about the book. Or you can use the order form below to purchase a copy for a friend who runs.

If you enjoyed reading *Running by Feeling* but need a way to apply its ideas to your personal running, *The Game of Running* is the book for you. This 65-page illustrated workbook accompanies Brian Clarke's in-class seminar on the training process, a course he has taught 35 times since 1979. The workbook comes with a training diary that you can use to log the effort and energy of your workouts, plus forms and questionnaires to help you analyze your training and racing.

- **ORDER FORM** -

❑ Please send *Running by Feeling* to:

        Name: _____

        Address: _____

        City/State/Zip: _____

❑ Please send *The Game of Running* to:

        Name: _____

        Address: _____

        City/State/Zip: _____

Running by Feeling $24.95
The Game of Running $18.95

Total (includes shipping and handling) .... $_____

Payment:

   ❑ Check to *Competitive Running Press, Inc.*
   ❑ Visa
   ❑ Master Card

Card # _____ Exp. _____ Signature: _____

Send order form to: *Competitive Running Press, Inc.,* 4133 Sierra Drive, Honolulu, HI 96816. Call or Fax (808) 737-4340, e-mail BrianCSRun@aol.com, or visit Clarke's website at http://members.aol.com/BrianCSRun.

Ordering Books by Brian Clarke

Running by Feeling is destined to be a classic in the running literature. If you agree, please tell your friends about the book. Or you can use the order form below to purchase a copy for a friend who runs.

If you enjoyed reading *Running by Feeling* but need a way to apply its ideas to your personal running, *The Game of Running* is the book for you. This 65-page illustrated workbook accompanies Brian Clarke's in-class seminar on the training process, a course he has taught 35 times since 1979. The workbook comes with a training diary that you can use to log the effort and energy of your workouts, plus forms and questionnaires to help you analyze your training and racing.

- **ORDER FORM** -

❑ Please send *Running by Feeling* to:

Name: _____

Address: _____

City/State/Zip: _____

❑ Please send *The Game of Running* to:

Name: _____

Address: _____

City/State/Zip: _____

Running by Feeling $24.95
The Game of Running $18.95

Total (includes shipping and handling) .... $_____

Payment:

❑ Check to *Competitive Running Press, Inc.*
❑ Visa
❑ Master Card

Card # _____ Exp. _____ Signature: _____

Send order form to: *Competitive Running Press, Inc.,* 4133 Sierra Drive, Honolulu, HI 96816. Call or Fax (808) 737-4340, e-mail BrianCSRun@aol.com, or visit Clarke's website at http://members.aol.com/BrianCSRun.

Ordering Books by Brian Clarke

Running by Feeling is destined to be a classic in the running literature. If you agree, please tell your friends about the book. Or you can use the order form below to purchase a copy for a friend who runs.

If you enjoyed reading *Running by Feeling* but need a way to apply its ideas to your personal running, *The Game of Running* is the book for you. This 65-page illustrated workbook accompanies Brian Clarke's in-class seminar on the training process, a course he has taught 35 times since 1979. The workbook comes with a training diary that you can use to log the effort and energy of your workouts, plus forms and questionnaires to help you analyze your training and racing.

- - - - - - - - - - - - - - - - - - - **ORDER FORM** -

❑ Please send *Running by Feeling* to:

        Name: _____

        Address: _____

        City/State/Zip: _____

❑ Please send *The Game of Running* to:

        Name: _____

        Address: _____

        City/State/Zip: _____

Running by Feeling $24.95
The Game of Running $18.95

Total (includes shipping and handling) .... $_____

Payment:

❑ Check to *Competitive Running Press, Inc.*
❑ Visa
❑ Master Card

Card # _____ Exp. _____ Signature: _____

Send order form to: *Competitive Running Press, Inc.,* 4133 Sierra Drive, Honolulu, HI 96816. Call or Fax (808) 737-4340, e-mail BrianCSRun@aol.com, or visit Clarke's website at http://members.aol.com/BrianCSRun.

Ordering Books by Brian Clarke

Running by Feeling is destined to be a classic in the running literature. If you agree, please tell your friends about the book. Or you can use the order form below to purchase a copy for a friend who runs.

If you enjoyed reading *Running by Feeling* but need a way to apply its ideas to your personal running, *The Game of Running* is the book for you. This 65-page illustrated workbook accompanies Brian Clarke's in-class seminar on the training process, a course he has taught 35 times since 1979. The workbook comes with a training diary that you can use to log the effort and energy of your workouts, plus forms and questionnaires to help you analyze your training and racing.

- **ORDER FORM** -

❑ Please send *Running by Feeling* to:

Name: _____

Address: _____

City/State/Zip: _____

❑ Please send *The Game of Running* to:

Name: _____

Address: _____

City/State/Zip: _____

Running by Feeling $24.95
The Game of Running $18.95

Total (includes shipping and handling) .... $_____

Payment:

❑ Check to *Competitive Running Press, Inc.*
❑ Visa
❑ Master Card

Card # _____ Exp. _____ Signature: _____

Send order form to: *Competitive Running Press, Inc.,* 4133 Sierra Drive, Honolulu, HI 96816. Call or Fax (808) 737-4340, e-mail BrianCSRun@aol.com, or visit Clarke's website at http://members.aol.com/BrianCSRun.

Ordering Books by Brian Clarke

Running by Feeling is destined to be a classic in the running literature. If you agree, please tell your friends about the book. Or you can use the order form below to purchase a copy for a friend who runs.

If you enjoyed reading *Running by Feeling* but need a way to apply its ideas to your personal running, *The Game of Running* is the book for you. This 65-page illustrated workbook accompanies Brian Clarke's in-class seminar on the training process, a course he has taught 35 times since 1979. The workbook comes with a training diary that you can use to log the effort and energy of your workouts, plus forms and questionnaires to help you analyze your training and racing.

- **ORDER FORM** -

❏ Please send *Running by Feeling* to:

Name: _____

Address: _____

City/State/Zip: _____

❏ Please send *The Game of Running* to:

Name: _____

Address: _____

City/State/Zip: _____

Running by Feeling $24.95
The Game of Running $18.95

Total (includes shipping and handling) .... $_____

Payment:

❏ Check to *Competitive Running Press, Inc.*
❏ Visa
❏ Master Card

Card # _____ Exp. _____ Signature: _____

Send order form to: *Competitive Running Press, Inc.*, 4133 Sierra Drive, Honolulu, HI 96816. Call or Fax (808) 737-4340, e-mail BrianCSRun@aol.com, or visit Clarke's website at http://members.aol.com/BrianCSRun.